The Future of Management: AI General Manager and Beyond

By: Mustafa Nejem

Preface

Management is traditionally considered as an art rather than a science. People use intuition and experience in their decision-making processes to enable prudent decision-making. However, objectivity is often a grey area in these decision-making processes and the managers struggle to defend their decisions if the tasks do not proceed as expected. The use of artificial intelligence (AI) has influenced every area of human endeavor and the management domain is no exception. We are already seeing robot recruiters and algorithm-based candidate selection processes.

In this book, I have argued that the future of management will be highly driven by AI technologies and we will also see algorithmic CEOs and peers. The organization of future will be a mix of human workers and robots. You might feel more comfortable reporting to a robot than a human. It is because the human decision-making is often influenced by biases and prejudices. There are complaints of favoritism and partially in every other organization. On the other hand, a robot CEO is highly objective and focused. It is available 24/7, never sleeps, and never gets ill. Despite the presence of an AI manager, there are still various tasks for which human presence will be needed in the organization.

Is an AI general manager answer to all these issues? Well, as I will explain throughout this book that there is no clear and precise answer yet. If humans have biases, then AI-based algorithms are also influenced by algorithms biases of the AI developers. But when a fully functional system is developed and the quality of training data is superior, it can be expected that the AI general managers will demonstrate far superior performance than humans.

AI based adoption in the organizations have also created a sense of job insecurity among the coworkers. If the robots can do most of the work effectively and without errors, why at all humans will be needed in the organizations? It is an ethical dilemma that I will also address in this book. When AI-based systems perform the conventional tasks of humans, they provide more opportunity to the coworkers to focus more on strategic and managerial level tasks. If recruitment and performance appraisal are carried out by algorithms, the HR managers will have the options to utilize the workforce in field visits, market analysis, and finding strategies of gaining a competitive advantage. The workers can also focus on sustainability issues and implementing green human resources strategies.

The main focus of this book is on highlighting how the managerial roles can be performed by an AI general manager. However, the title also indicates that the themes go even beyond the notion of algorithmic CEO. The book highlights how the overall organizational outlook can be optimized by using advanced tools and technologies based on AI.

I am hopeful and confident that this book will reveal tremendous tools and opportunities for using AI in the management domain. You will get the maximum benefit of this book by reading it throughout covering all chapters. In each chapter, I have introduced the concept of AI general manager from a different perspective, and the whole book reading will provide a holistic view to you regarding the use of robots and algorithms for developing a technology-driven organization.

[Name of the Author]

[Date]

Table of Contents

Chapter 1

Introduction

1. How AI Evolved in Management

The use of AI is influencing all aspects of a business entity. When there was a widespread adoption of AI tools and technologies in multinational organizations, the management professionals also thought that the AI concepts can be useful and significant in the managerial tasks as well because the emerging requirement of the management was to enable data-driven decision-making, and AI algorithms have the potential to process a huge amount of data quickly.

As highlighted in Figure 1, the use of AI in management is not a new phenomenon and some level of implementation was observed even as early as 1983. At that time, the database management tools such as oracle were used to process large amount of data and general intelligent reports and dashboard indicators.

Another landmark achievement was observed in 2016, when chatbots assistant were introduced. A chatbot assistant such as a WhatsApp chatbot remembers the solutions of the frequently asked questions by the clients. The queries are then responded by the chatbot in an automated manner without any intervention by the human. The beauty of this chatbot was that the support services became highly effective and were made available 24/7. Moreover, the accuracy of the responses was phenomenal because the responses are generated based on the processing of a large dataset.

The current era is characterized by the management solutions where the machine learning technologies are used for an effective project management. In fact, the project management was the first area where the significance of an AI general manager was acknowledged. The next era is of autonomous AI where the management functions will be performed autonomously by robots. It is this era where the focus of the book is, i.e. how a general manager, which is an AI robot, can be appointed that could perform all the management roles and the performance is far superior than a human manager.

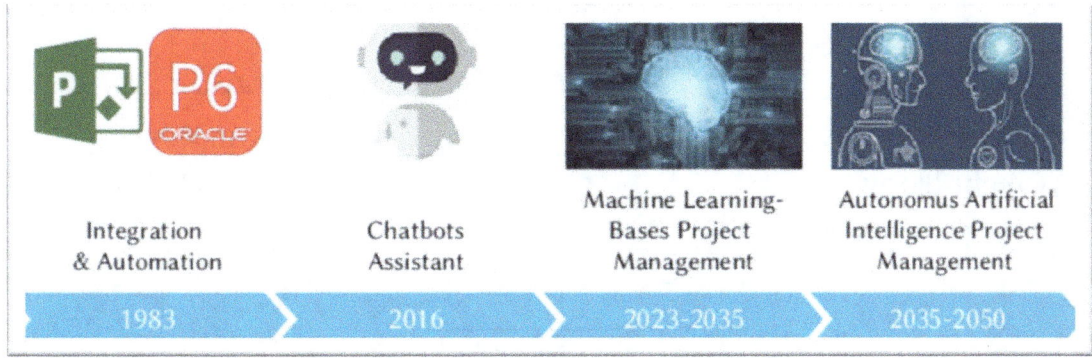

Figure 1: AI and Project Management[i]

1.1. AI General Manager

A blue-print of an AI-powered organization is displayed in Figure 2. There, you can see that the robots have taken control for almost all of the organization. They are performing routine tasks, management tasks, as well as surveillance tasks. The tasks are being executed in a robotic manner with an amazing level of accuracy. The queries will be responded promptly that will result in a happy customer and higher customer conversions.

Another aspect that you may appreciate in the current model is that the setup of a robotic organization is highly sophisticated and based on the state-of-the-art technologies. This is one area where the business entities will have to focus. They will need to review the requirements of their organizations and present a strong case to the senior management for implementing a robotic organization. In the absence of sufficient funds, it will be difficult to transform the organizational outlook.

Another aspect that you might also notice in the figure is that robots appear to be ready for responding to the events. It is possible in an AI-based organization when the AI general manager has all the required data available and the quality of data is extremely good. For example, if there is not required number of CVs received, the shortlisting and interviewing process will suffer despite the availability of robot recruiters.

Figure 2: AI-Powered Organization[ii]

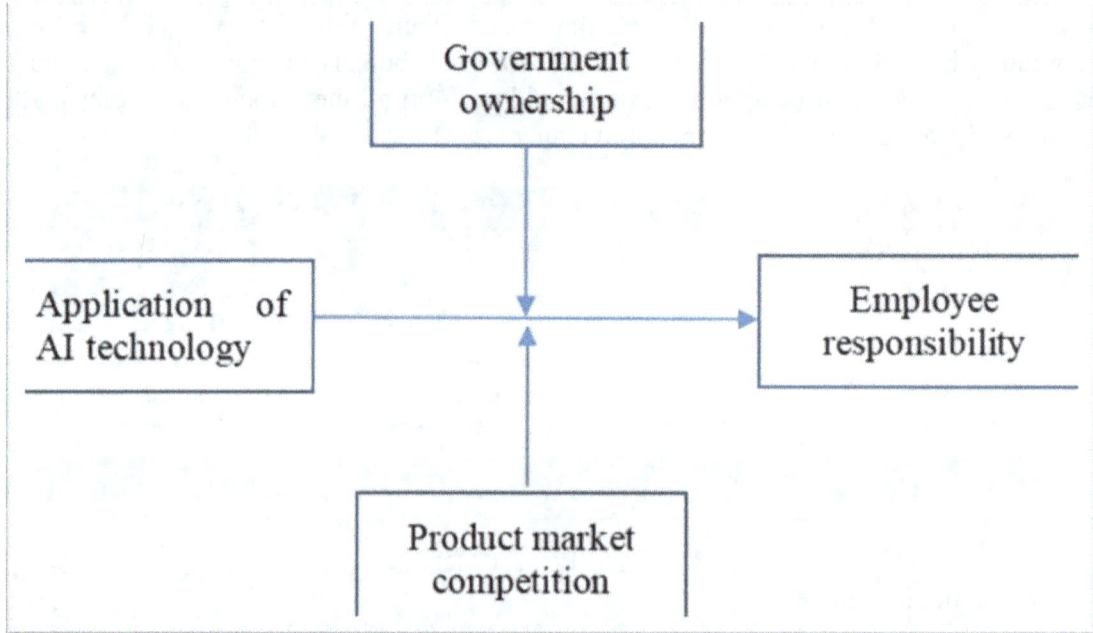

Figure 3: Dimensions of AI-Based Management

Figure 3 above highlights that the need for an AI general manager has emerged due to multiple factors. There is more and more government ownership and encouragement for implementing AI tools and technologies. The employees can also be held more responsible for their work by facilitating them with AI tools and technologies. The AI concepts have successfully been used in development the management solutions. The organizations also have a pressure from the competitors because if they become early adopters of AI, the organizations may lose their competitive advantage.

The first AI boss was developed by Hitachi Company as shown in Figure 4 below. It was introduced in 2015 that shows that the technology and management professionals were exploring the possibility of AI in management for quite long. They wanted more accuracy and objectivity in the decision-making process and provide more freedom of expression to the subordinates.

Figure 4: World's First AI Boss by Hitachi[iii]

1.2. Benefits of AI Management

As I highlighted in the preface of this book, there is a fear factor among employees that robots in the management domain will eat their jobs and they will become redundant. It is not going to be the case at least in the near future. As explained in Figure 5, there are some roles that can be performed efficiently by AI and there are also other roles that humans can perform even better than AI. It is these roles where the needs of humans will still be felt.

In the case of digital assistants, the training of these assistants will still be carried out by humans. The AI models will give specific and task-centered information. The generalization of this information and articulating the data to the organizational context will still be done by humans. The robots can code the knowledge into high-level and low-level processes. However, the handling of complex, exceptional tasks and social interactions will still be managed by humans. The analysis of AI-robots will be a quantitative analysis, however, qualitative analysis will still be carried out by humans. This qualitative analysis will indicate why a certain trend is developing and how the current roles and responsibilities of the management professionals can be modified.

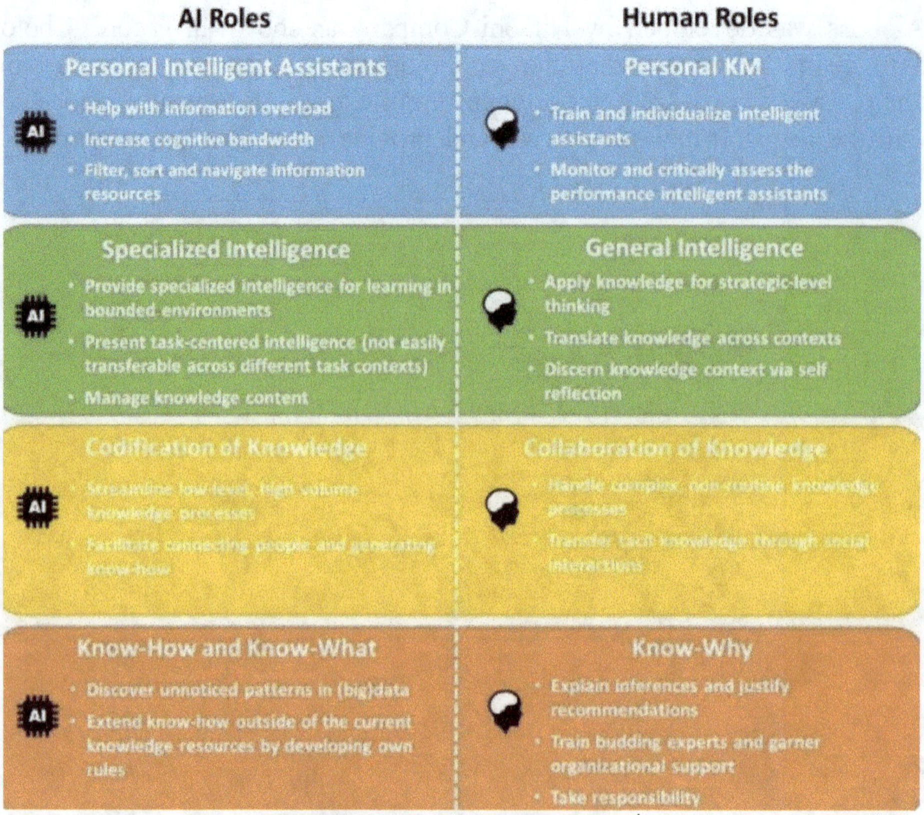

AI Roles	Human Roles
Personal Intelligent Assistants • Help with information overload • Increase cognitive bandwidth • Filter, sort and navigate information resources	**Personal KM** • Train and individualize intelligent assistants • Monitor and critically assess the performance intelligent assistants
Specialized Intelligence • Provide specialized intelligence for learning in bounded environments • Present task-centered intelligence (not easily transferable across different task contexts) • Manage knowledge content	**General Intelligence** • Apply knowledge for strategic-level thinking • Translate knowledge across contexts • Discern knowledge context via self reflection
Codification of Knowledge • Streamline low-level, high volume knowledge processes • Facilitate connecting people and generating know-how	**Collaboration of Knowledge** • Handle complex, non-routine knowledge processes • Transfer tacit knowledge through social interactions
Know-How and Know-What • Discover unnoticed patterns in (big)data • Extend know-how outside of the current knowledge resources by developing own rules	**Know-Why** • Explain inferences and justify recommendations • Train budding experts and garner organizational support • Take responsibility

Figure 5: AI vs Human Roles[iv]

A survey was recently conducted in which the managers were asked to respond what they think they would do better and which tasks can be performed more appropriately by the robots. Figure 6 below shows the tasks where the algorithmic CEO has an edge.

What can a robot do better than your manager?

Provide unbiased information	36%
Maintain work schedules	34%
Problem solve	29%
Manage a budget	26%
Answer confidential questions without causing fear of scrutiny	21%
Evaluate team performance	20%

Figure 6: Robot Advantage[v]

The above data makes it evident that the most important benefit of an algorithmic CEO is the provision of an unbiased information. The CEO never controls or filters the information. This advantage was endorsed by the maximum number of managers (36%). The algorithms are also highly efficient in maintaining work schedules. The performance of humans is influenced by external factors as well such as family issues or illnesses. However, the algorithmic workers are always available for the task execution as long as the required IT infrastructure is available and connected.

The algorithmic CEOs are also problem solvers and they can make an efficient utilization of the available budget. The algorithmic CEOs and workers will always be truthful because they do not have any fear of scrutiny or losing their jobs. The team performance can also be evaluated effectively by algorithmic CEOs.

The findings of this survey also indicated that it is not always the case that algorithms will outperform humans. There are also instances where human managers perform better than algorithms. These instances are shown in Figure 7 below.

One of these aspects is a better comprehension of the feelings. An algorithm will give a negative feedback to the employee without realizing the mental and emotional state of the employee. On the other hand, the humans will consider the environmental and contextual factors before issuing such remarks. The humans can also train other humans better than machines. An enabling work environment can also be ensured well by humans.

What can your manager do better than a robot?

Understanding my feelings	45%
Coach me	33%
Create (or promote) a work culture	29%
Evaluate team performance	26%
Problem solve	25%
Provide oversight/direction	24%

Figure 7: Human Advantage[vi]

Figure 8 highlights the benefits of AI in management by the mapping of AI technologies and the management support. The algorithmic managers are powered by machine learning technologies, neural networks, data mining, big data science, and business intelligence. All these AI-based concepts can provide immense support to the management. The benefits can be seen in the optimized decision-making and accurate decision-making. The benefit can also be observed in the improved functionality of the organization. The tasks such as recruitment, performance appraisal, wealth management, and supply chain management can all be automated.

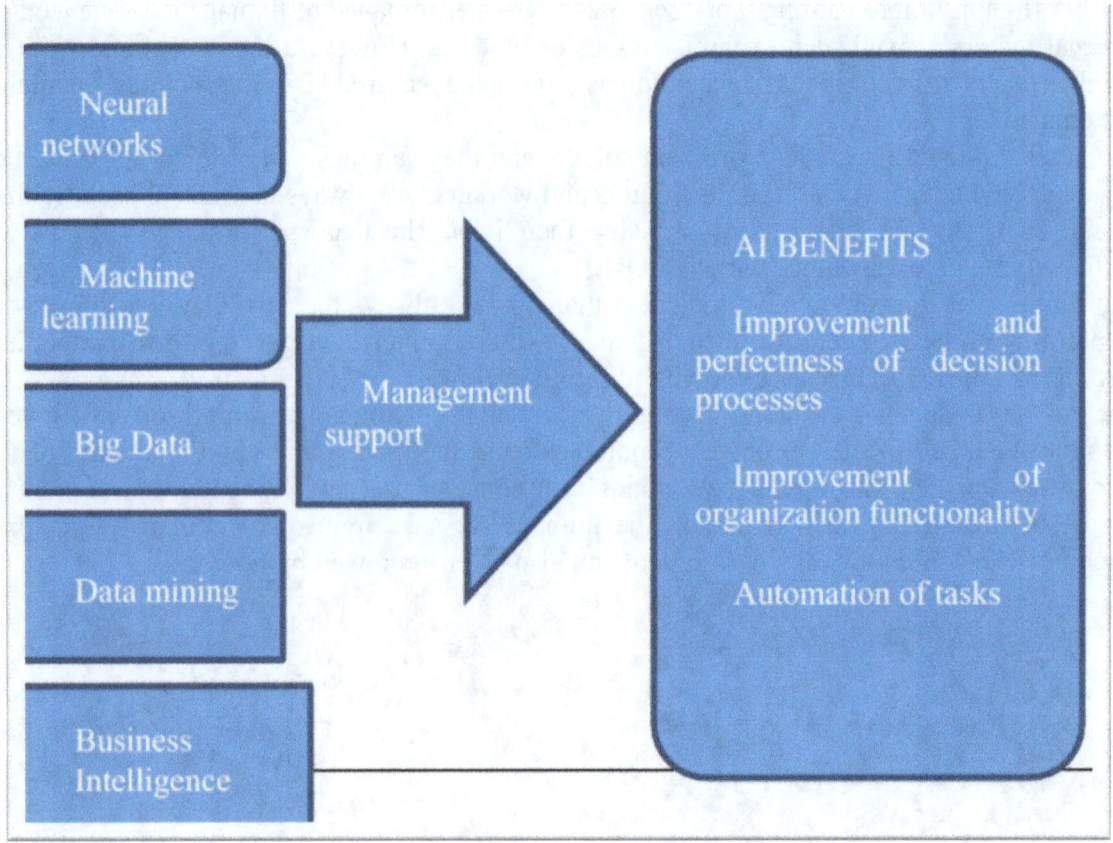

Figure 8: Management Support through AI Concepts[vii]

Another benefit of AI-based management is expressed in Figure 9. Robo-CEO is an algorithmic CEO that selects the most suitable candidate based on the available data. Unlike traditional CEO, the employee is most likely to move up the career ladder due to the objective decision-making of the algorithmic CEO.

Figure 9: Robo-CEO[viii]

1.3. Challenges of AI Management

Despite the promising outcomes of an AI general manager, there are still only a few successful case studies of an algorithmic CEO. This raises the question why organizations are reluctant to make the optimum utilization of the AI. Figure 10 below shows the findings of a survey where the managers have expressed their concerns and challenges in AI management.

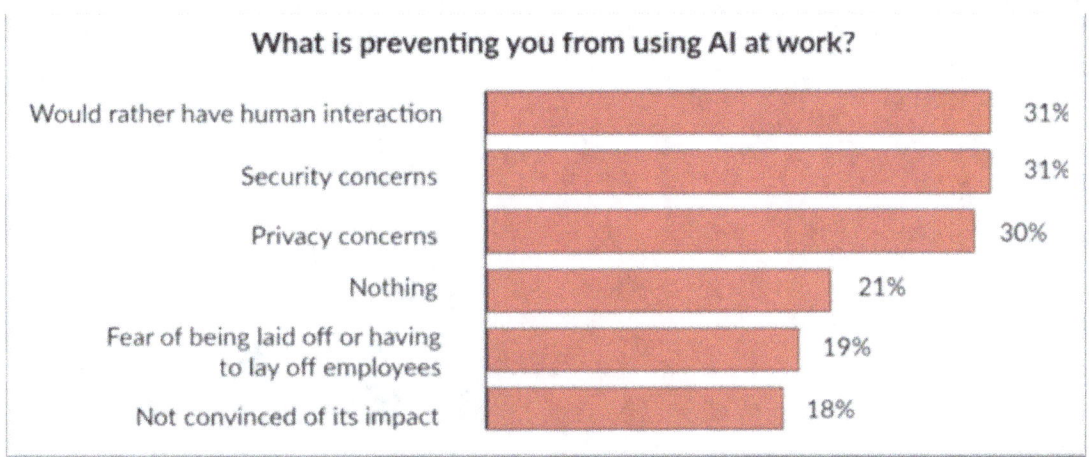

Figure 10: AI Fears and Concerns[ix]

The first challenge faced in AI based management is that employees are accustomed to interacting with other humans. They miss the human touch and socialization aspect in robotic environment. The environment becomes too mechanistic. The algorithmic CEOs assume that the receivers of their instructions are also robots and they will be able to follow each and every word of their instructions. The humans do not work that way and their rationality is always bounded by various constraints including the family constraints and technical constraints.

The second challenge is the issue of security and privacy of the data. There is so much connectivity of the devices for the efficient working of AI algorithms. The data exposure might be without consent or a data breach from a single device may aggravate to a massive data breach. The skill set of professionals regarding the maintenance of AI systems is limited. Therefore, hackers can exploit this opportunity and compromise the sanctity and integrity of the data.

Another challenge faced in the organizational setting is that as soon as the AI based implementation is announced, employees fear losing their jobs. The tasks for which they had established the timelines of two to three days can be done by robots in two to three hours. So, they anticipate that they will soon become redundant.

Another challenge highlighted in the survey is the lack of understanding of the potential impact of AI. If the management itself is not convinced that the AI based systems will transform the management landscape, then the AI based interventions will always be a distant dream.

Another key challenge in using AI boss is shown in Figure 11 below. The figure highlights that an algorithmic CEO may select a candidate for the job that is highly competitive. However, the candidate may not fit well to the current organizational setting. These aspects can best be judged by humans because it constitutes a dynamic reality and has an element of subjectivity.

Figure 11: Challenges in using AI Boss[x]

1.4. AI Management and Ethical Concerns

The AI-based management has raised concerns because of the intrusive nature of the AI algorithms. As I explained earlier, the AI algorithms process a large amount of data for making an efficient AI model. The development of the data model may access those data sets for which explicit information has not been provided. The quality of algorithms gets improved but the question arises whether legitimate means have been used for improving the efficiency of algorithms.

Figure 12 below shows that AI has invaded all aspects of the humanity. In the absence of a standard regulatory framework, the fate of the AI-based systems is left to the integrity of the AI developers. As I explained earlier, it usually creates an algorithmic bias.

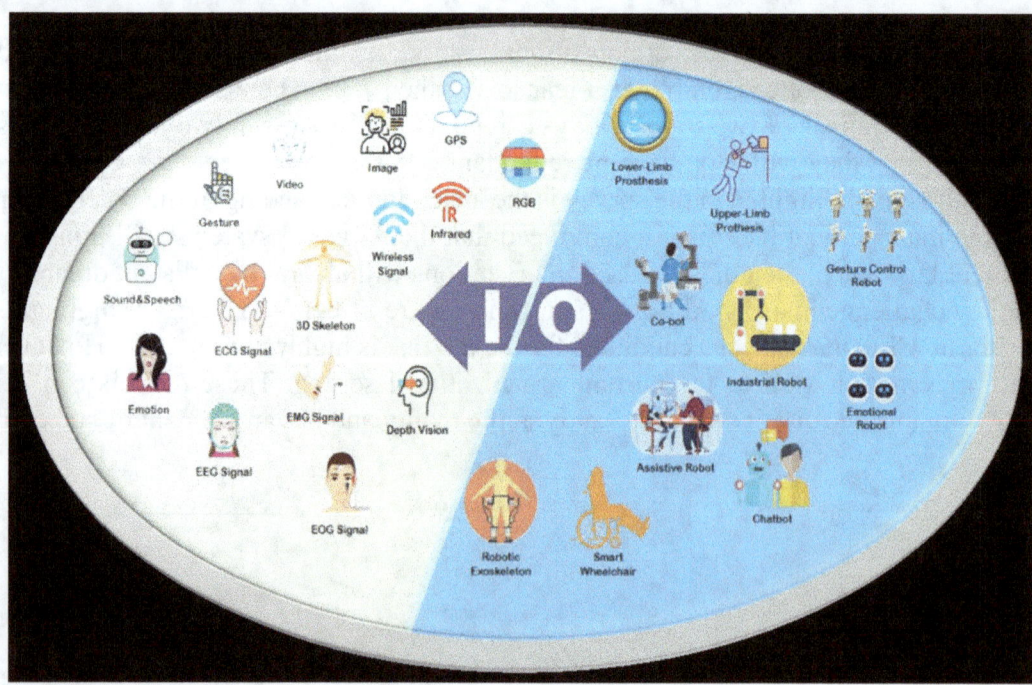

Figure 12: Advanced Technologies in Human Robot Intera

1.5. What this Book Covers

This book covers various topics and thematic areas related to the future of management with a specific focus on AI general manager and beyond. The first chapter introduces the concept of AI in management and the conceptual framework of an AI general manager.

The second chapter highlights different areas of interventions of AI robots. The third chapter is focused on AI and humans collaboration because AI-based implementation does not mean the elimination of human coworkers. They will work side by side and therefore, a comprehensive understanding of the interaction of both entities is crucial.

The fourth chapter highlights the learning mechanisms of AI. Different areas such as resource allocation, risk assessment, and project management have been explored. The fifth chapter introduces you to the CEO algorithm and how its impacts can be seen in different business aspects and HR functions.

The sixth chapter demystifies the robot boss by presenting different simulations. This chapter will give you a real feel as to how an AI general manager looks. The seventh chapter introduces you to several success stories where the algorithmic CEOs have been successful in the organizational context.

The eight chapter presents to you the complete management roadmap for implementing the CEO algorithm. Chapter nine concludes the book by presenting summary of the main points, key takeaways, and a glimpse to the new work environment where the organization will be a mix of human and algorithmic workers.

Through the coverage of these points, you will have observed that the book will not only tell you how AI has been successful in the management landscape by now but also how a powerful future of AI manager will soon become a reality. This book presents new and innovative ideas that will equip you to the latest knowledge in the field of AI for management. The managers always complain that they have too much to do in the company and the organizational working hours are not sufficient for them. However, we are now entering into a world where managers will have all the time just for strategic decision-making. Their day-to-day tasks will be handled by the AI general manager with remarkable efficiency and exemplary level of accuracy. The AI Boss

Chapter **2**

The AI Boss

2. AI Managing Humans as an Unbiased Boss

An algorithmic boss can be a real blessing for an organization if the implementation considers several key aspects and a formal strategy are developed for the transformation process. Figure 13 provides several recommendations in this regard. In the strategy phase, you will need to determine to what extent, the algorithmic management is needed in your organization. In the next step, you should develop a change management process. In this stage, you will have to train the existing staff for using algorithms instead of manual interventions. The management should still make the communication lines open because the change will be successful through an evolutionary process. Once the algorithmic management is in place, the management should constantly evaluate the management flow of the algorithms so that the algorithmic decision-making is not influenced by the algorithmic biases.

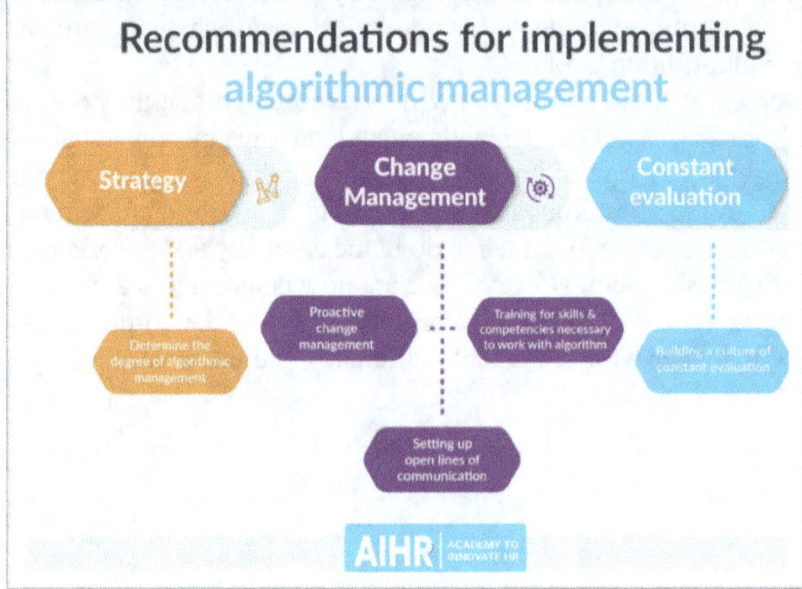

Figure 13: Algorithmic Management[xi]

Figure 14: AI Boss – Impartial and Focused[xii]

From the above AI boss, you will get a feel that the individual is very much focused on the work and there will be complete impartiality in the decision-making process. You may also discuss your concerns and issues with an open heart to an AI boss because there is no fear of retaliation and anger on the part of the boss. The boss is instructed to listen to the issues of the subordinates calmly and openly. The performance of the team will be measured strictly against the assigned objectives quarterly and annually.

Figure 15: Employees Happily Reporting to AI Boss[xiii]

Figure 15 highlights a key benefit of an algorithmic CEO that employees are reporting happily to them. They know that the behavior of the boss will be unbiased and the interaction will be limited to the assigned job responsibilities. There will be no favors and additional tasks asked by the boss. Moreover, the working day end within the working hour and there will be no stretched timings and late duties.

The future organizations are expected to be a nice blend of AI workers and human workers. It will also affect how the organograms will be presented and reported in different statutory reports. One such implementation is shown in Figure 16 below:

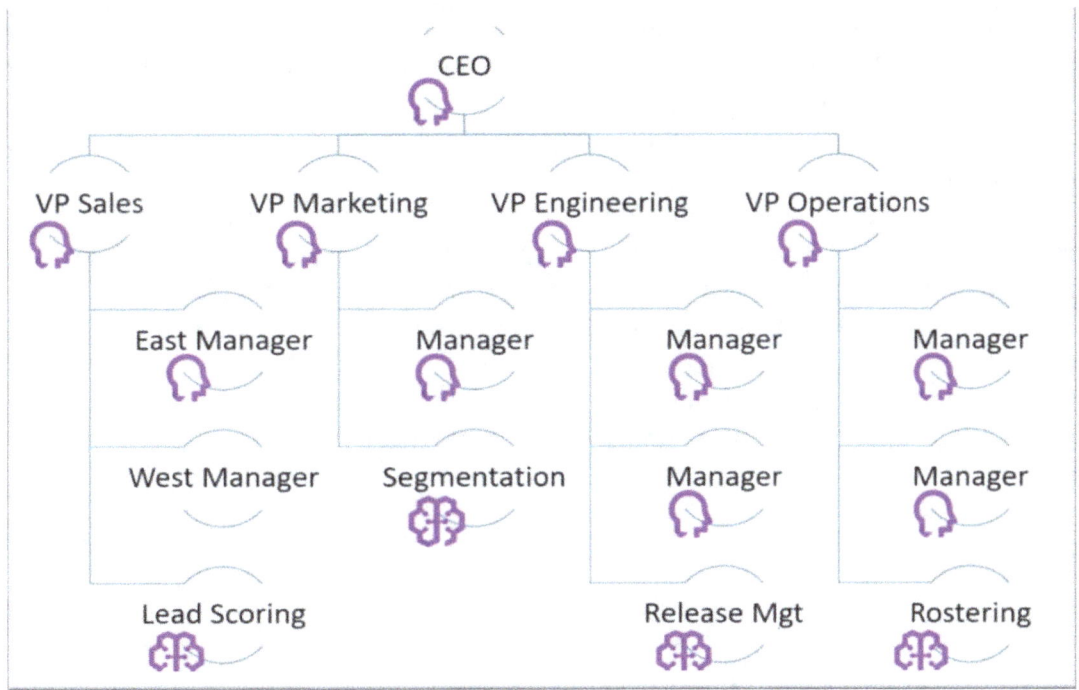

Figure 16: Organization Chart with Algorithmic CEO[xiv]

As highlighted in the figure above, in the sample organization, the CEO is an algorithmic CEO and all key leadership positions are occupied by robots. Humans have been assigned only to the operational work, and the technology-driven aspect of the organization has been endorsed at the level of the organization chart. AI bosses are not limited to the human resource function and they are also being used in other management and business functions. Figure 17 shows an implementation where the algorithmic managers have been used for an effective wealth management.

Figure 17: AI Boss in Wealth Management[xv]

2.1. Potential Biases in AI Algorithms

In order to understand the potential biases in AI algorithms, it is crucial to understand the complete lifecycle of AI algorithms. As shown in Figure 18, the lifecycle begins with the definition of a business problem. Then the relevant datasets are acquired and prepared in a consistent format. The next step is the development and training of an AI model. The quality of the AI model is continuously evaluated and refined based on new data and requirements. The system is deployed when the AI model has a sufficient level of maturity. Then machine learning operations are put into place.

From the lifecycle development, you will have noticed that the performance of AI-based systems significantly depend on two factors. The first is the quality and accuracy of the AI model. If the rules and feature extraction processes in AI algorithms are biased because the AI developer is convinced with a certain style of management, then the quality of the whole AI-based system will suffer. Another important factor is the quality of data. If the training examples in the dataset favor a certain segment of the population, then the AI model will learn wrong rules that will affect the algorithmic decision-making.

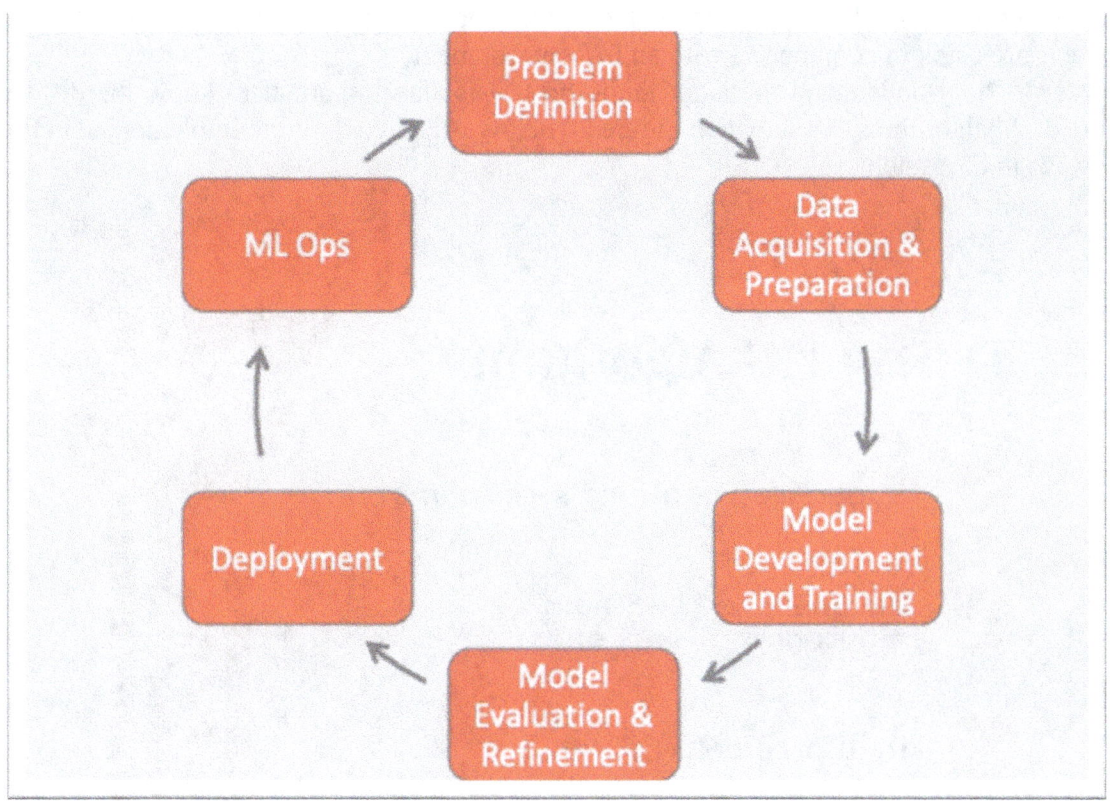

Figure 18: AI Lifecycle[xvi]

Due to these limitations of the AI algorithms, professionals working in AI always prefer narrow AI over general AI as shown in Figure 19 below:

Narrow AI	General AI
○ Application specific/ task limited	○ Perform general (human) intelligent action
○ Fixed domain models provided by programmers	○ Self-learns and reasons with its operating environment
○ Learns from thousands of labeled examples	○ Learns from few examples and/or from unstructured data
○ Reflexive tasks with no understanding	○ Full range of human cognitive abilities
○ Knowledge does not transfer to other domains or tasks	○ Leverages knowledge transfer to new domains and tasks
○ Today's AI	○ Future AI?

Figure 19: General vs. Narrow AI[xvii]

Figure above highlights the benefits of using narrow AI for management-based AI algorithms. This technology has a binding to a specific task. The technology is based on fixed-domain models. It might come as a limitation for some general managers because the general-AI has a self-learning process and the system developed in general-AI today will have a far optimized version in the next 6 months based on self-learning.

Another benefit of narrow AI is that the learning mechanism is based on a large number of examples and therefore, the concept development in the AI model is very strong. A limitation of narrow AI is that the system is reflexive instead of using cognitive abilities. In the above figure, the general AI has been designation as the future of the AI because the knowledge can be transferred to other domains. It is a highly significant feature particularly when the AI-based concepts are using in conjunction with an IoT environment.

In order to fully understand the algorithmic bias, it is also important to know the different nature of AI algorithms. As shown in Figure 20 below, AI algorithms are implemented in three key ways in the system.

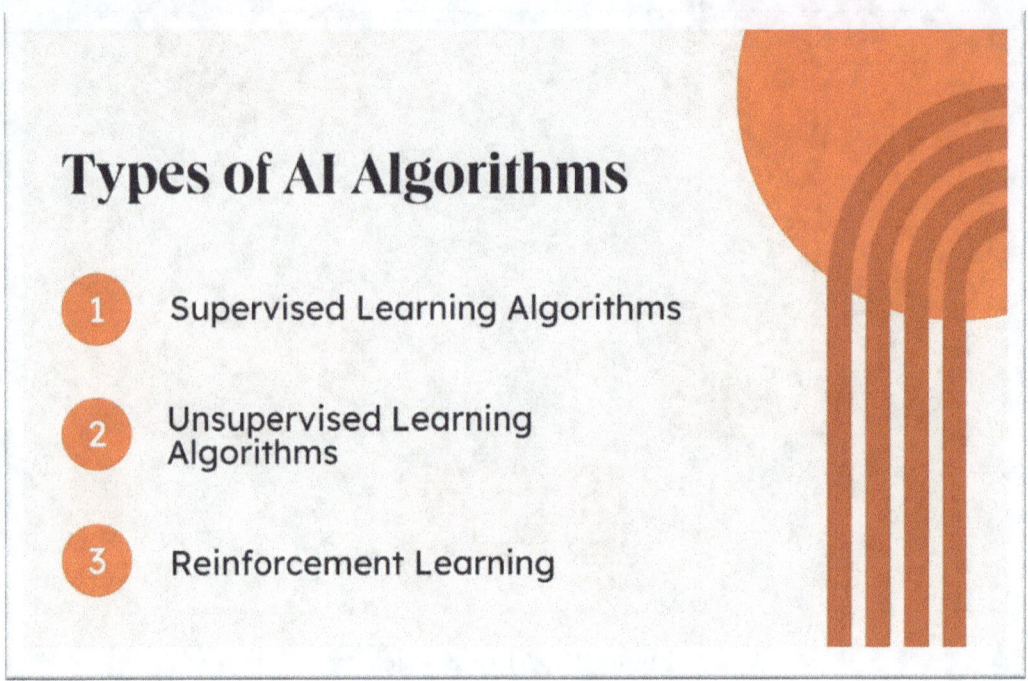

Figure 20: Nature of AI Algorithms[xviii]

The first form is supervised learning in which the self-learning system is not built into the model. The learning process is initiated at various time intervals and a trigger is generated in the system to initiate the learning process. The second form is unsupervised learning in which the algorithms enable learning as soon as they encounter new data points and interactions. The third form is reinforcement learning in which the learned data points are categorized into positive or negative reinforcers.

From these examples, it is easier to understand that the risk of algorithmic bias is higher in supervised learning because the learning process is at the discretion of the AI developer. Moreover, when negative reinforcers are identified in reinforcement learning, it is based on how the negativity is defined in the system by the AI developer that creates an algorithmic bias.

2.2. Algorithmic Bias versus Human Bias

Humans are generally more influenced by technology and they believe that the human biases will be overcome by the use of technology. However, the technology generates a new form of bias known as an algorithmic bias as shown in Figure 21 below. These biases can be found in the algorithms as well as how the data is acquired for the training of these algorithms. The figure shows a cycle, which is world, data, design, and use. If the AI developers are not the men of integrity, this cycle can become a vicious cycle.

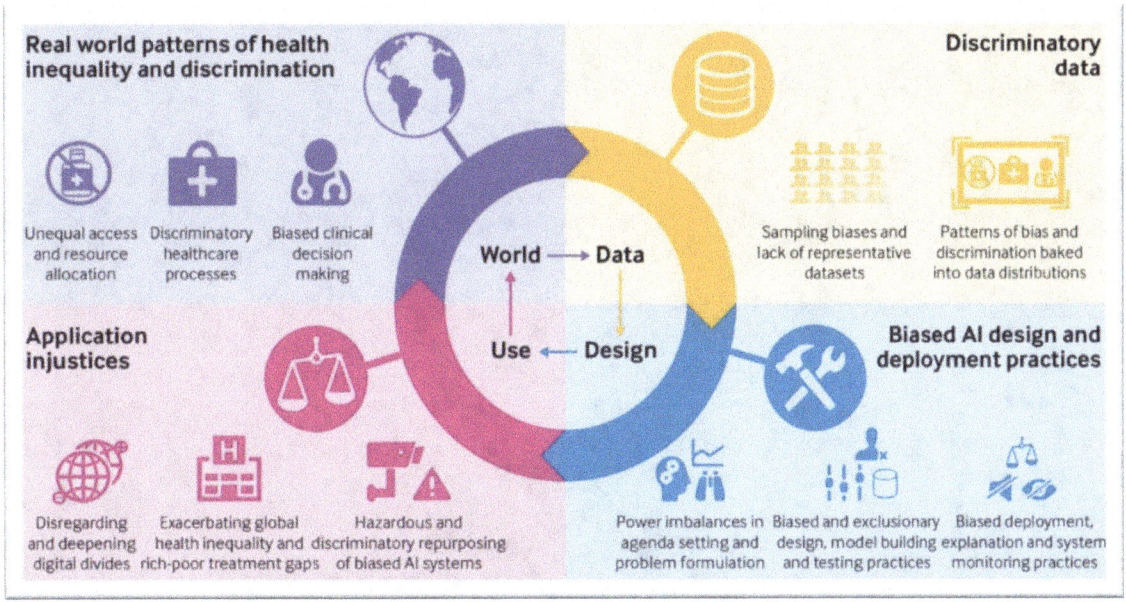

Figure 21: Algorithmic Biases[xix]

McKinsey recommends six strategies for overcoming algorithmic biases as shown in Figure 22. They can be addressed by having an awareness of the context, establishing key processes, fact-based communications, a good human-machine interaction, more investment in research, and more research in the AI field.

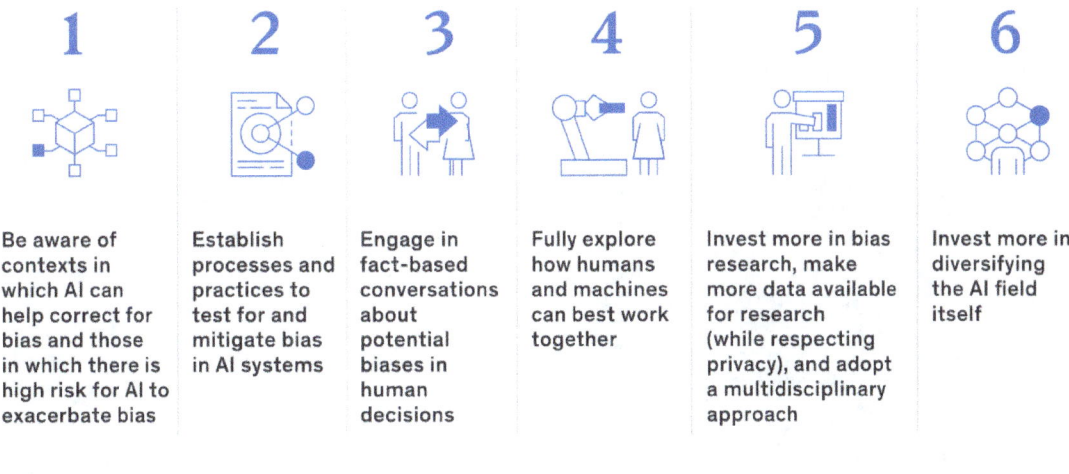

Figure 22: Overcoming Algorithmic Biases[xx]

2.3. AI Manager and the Recruitment Function

There is a successful implementation by a firm in which AI manager was used for talent acquisition and talent management. This talent acquisition manager is shown in Figure 23. This robot was given the responsibility of managing a $100 billion firm. The entire human resources of the company will be handled by the algorithmic CEO. The company aims to replace more and more humans with robots in key leadership positions.

Figure 23: AI Boss for Talent Acquisition Hired by a Firm[xxi]

Recruitment was one of the first HR functions where the algorithms were introduced in the form of a robot recruiter. The robots have been highly successful in conducting interviews and candidates express them comfortably in front of a robot. The responses are also processed efficiently by the robots and the same processing strategy is applied for all candidates. A robotic interviewee is shown in Figure 24 below:

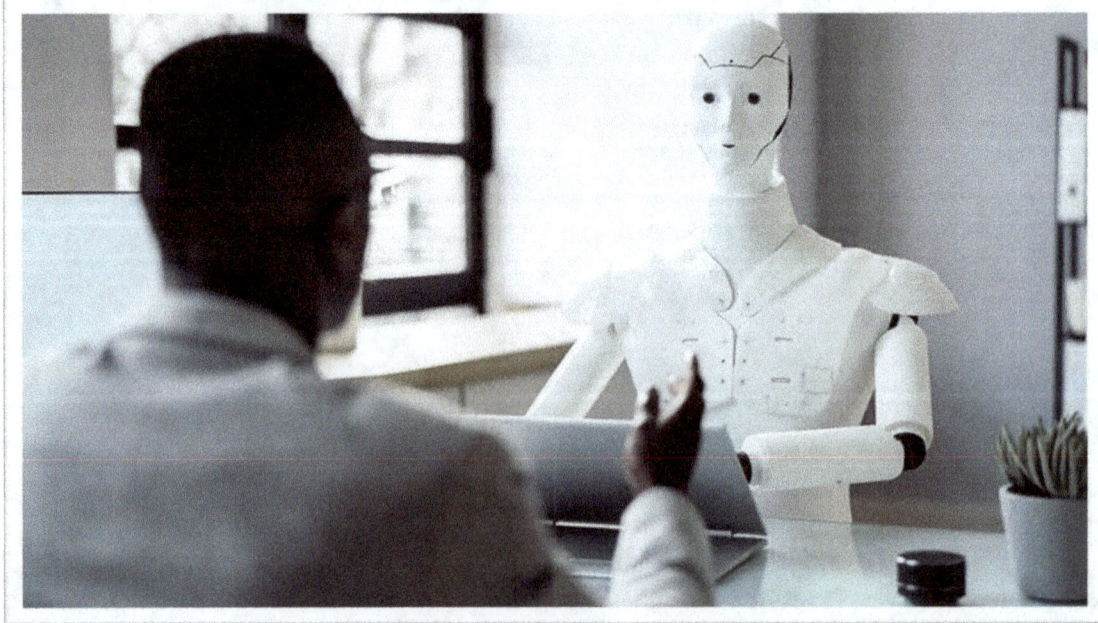

Figure 24: Robot Recruiter[xxii]

The function of a robot does not end at conducting an interview. The algorithms can also participate in the entire process of recruitment and selection. They can evaluate all the interview results and select the right and the most suitable candidate by matching the organizational requirements with the candidate skill sets as shown in Figure 25 below:

Figure 25: Robots Selecting the Right Candidate[xxiii]

With the growth of the automated screening process, the job candidates should also update their CVs so that the robots do not discard their resumes. The traditional CVs might not be considered worthy by the robots as shown in Figure 26 below:

Figure 26: Traditional CV not worthy in an Automated World[xxiv]

Therefore, the candidates will now have to ensure that their CVs and job applications include the keywords of the positions. The AI algorithms match the CVs with the internal dictionary and job descriptors. If the relevant keywords are not found then even the CV of a highly qualified individual might be overlooked.

2.4. AI Manager and Performance Evaluation

AI general manager can also conduct performance appraisal effectively. Employees always have reservations and complaints that their efforts are not compensated adequately and the appraisals are always biased to the likes of the supervisor. Due to this reason, the management literature also suggests 360 degree feedback in addition to the straight line method of appraisal. In an ideal scenario, the performance appraisal should begin with the Plan stage as shown in Figure 27 below. At this stage, the annual objectives of an employee should be set. The next stage is the Act stage where the employee applies the skill set to achieve those objectives. The third stage is the Track stage where the supervisor should periodically monitor the performance of the subordinate and provide feedback. The last stage is review where the performance of the employee should be evaluated, the achievements should be appreciated and the deficiencies should be highlighted. To overcome those deficiencies, the key learning opportunities should be identified for the employees.

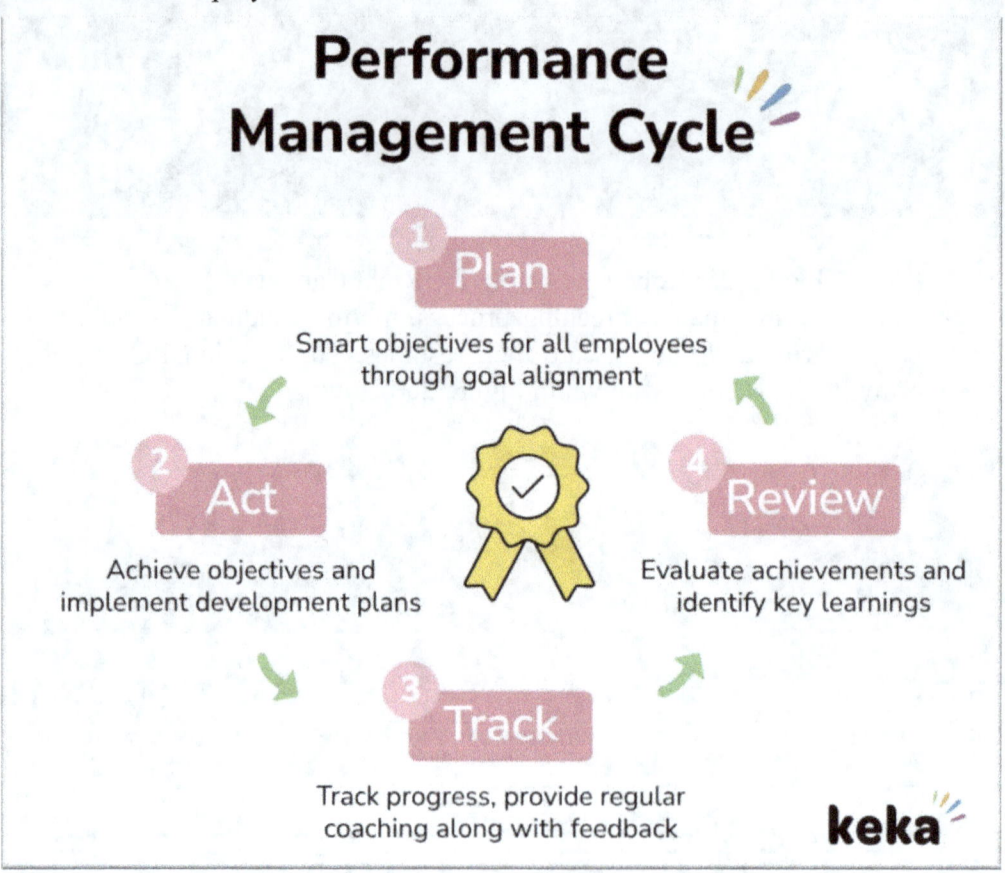

Figure 27: Performance Appraisal Life Cycle[xxv]

This appraisal cycle looks promising; however, in the real world environment, the supervisors are so busy in the regular tasks that they do not focus on the appraisal cycle. Moreover, due to the severe economic conditions, the employees are more worried regarding the survival of their jobs than the growth opportunities and performance appraisals.

Figure 28 below shows that an algorithmic CEO can optimize the appraisal systems by using strength-based appraisals. In this strategy, the performance ratings are based on the strengths and competencies of the employees. When there is a fairness and equity in the appraisal process, the motivation and morale of the workforce also improves and the employees are always motivated to improve their skill set.

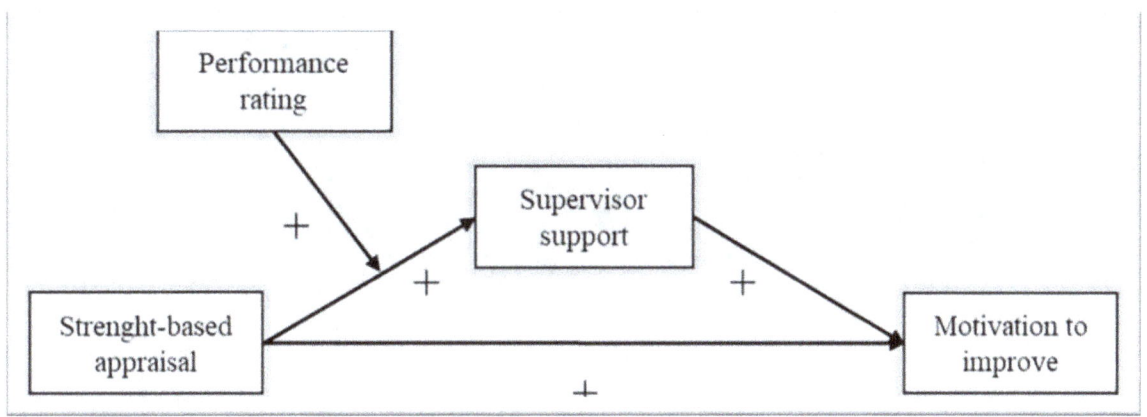

Figure 28: Appraisal based on Employees' Strengths[xxvi]

Performance appraisals are also a key source document for promoting the employees. As shown in Figure 29 below, the algorithmic performance appraisal evaluates each subordinate objectively and justly and only the most hardworking, competent, and devoted employee is selected for promotion and moving up the career ladder.

Figure 29: Algorithmic Performance Appraisal[xxvii]

2.5. AI Manager and Resource Allocation

The AI managers will make an impression in the organizations when their performances significantly outperform the human managers. Several successful implementations have been made in this regard so far. Figure 30 below shows an implementation of an algorithmic CEO that was tested in a Hong Kong based company. The boss is named Tang Yu and she is the CEO of mobile and gaming company. The model proved highly successful in the organization and there was a marked improvement in the speed of execution and the quality of work. The company where this model was successfully tested is NetDragon.

Figure 30: Successful AI CEO of a Hong Kong based Company[xxviii]

Chapter 3

AI and Humans
Collaboration

3. AI Perfect for Data-Driven Tasks

AI general manager will also need some tools for effective decision-making. The managerial aspect requires a high level of collaboration and effective business communication. There, AI humanoid CEO should be supported with various emerging and on-demand AI services. Some of the technologies that have gained a huge prominence in the AI world are shown in Figure 31 below. As highlighted in the figure, the chat services can be managed effectively by ChatGPT and Bard services. The document management systems and chatbots also assist in the effective management of the workspace by the AI manager.

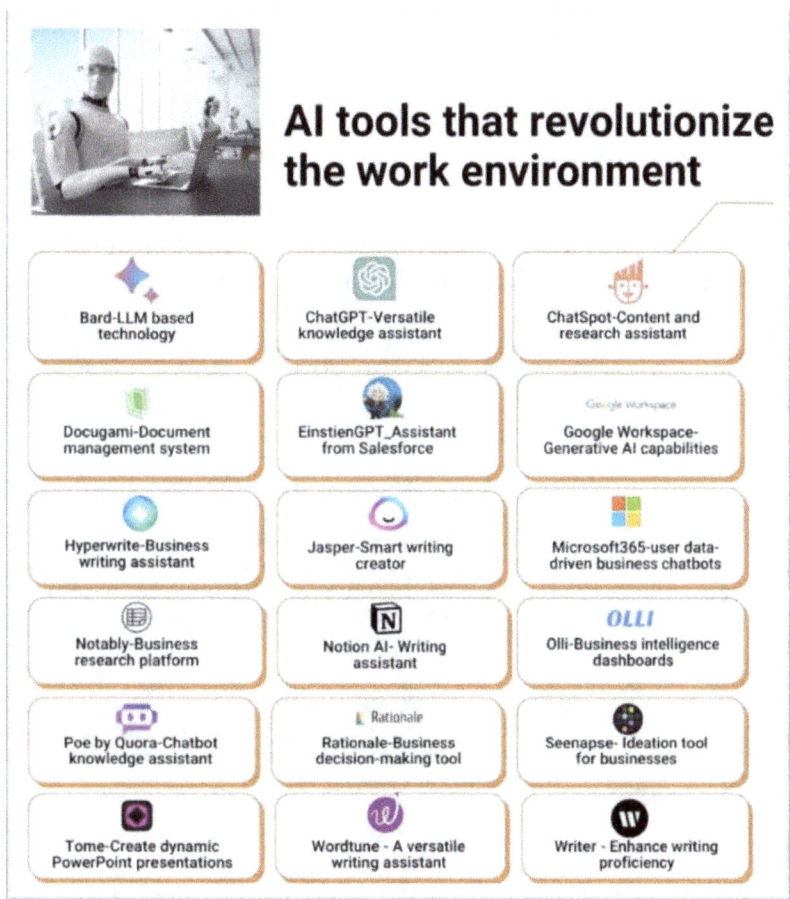

Figure 31: Technologies for Managing the Workspace[xxix]

In order to understand the significance of data-driven decision-making, it is crucial to know the evolutionary process of AI-based systems. As highlighted in Figure 32 below, the AI-based systems for data-driven decision-making were first presented as assisted intelligence systems. The key selling point of the systems at that time was that these systems can learn in an organized manner, whereas the humans do not take the learning process so seriously. In the next phase, it was realized that a good AI system is a product of human-machine interaction. It was argued that the quality of an AI system is influenced by the data model and if a good quality data is not provided by the humans, the algorithms cannot work effectively. Therefore, there was a gradual shift to augmented intelligence where machines facilitate humans and humans facilitate machines. The third phase or the current phase is regarded as autonomous intelligence. In this era, the nature of tasks changes very rapidly. Therefore, the decisions need to be taken by the AI manager in an automated manner based on data and predefined rules, policies, and procedures of the organization. The machines should have a mechanism of a continued learning. It means that the AI CEO that the subordinates are interacting with today will not have the same responses in the future because it is a machine. Based on a continued learning, the responses and the behavioral disposition of the algorithmic CEO will also change.

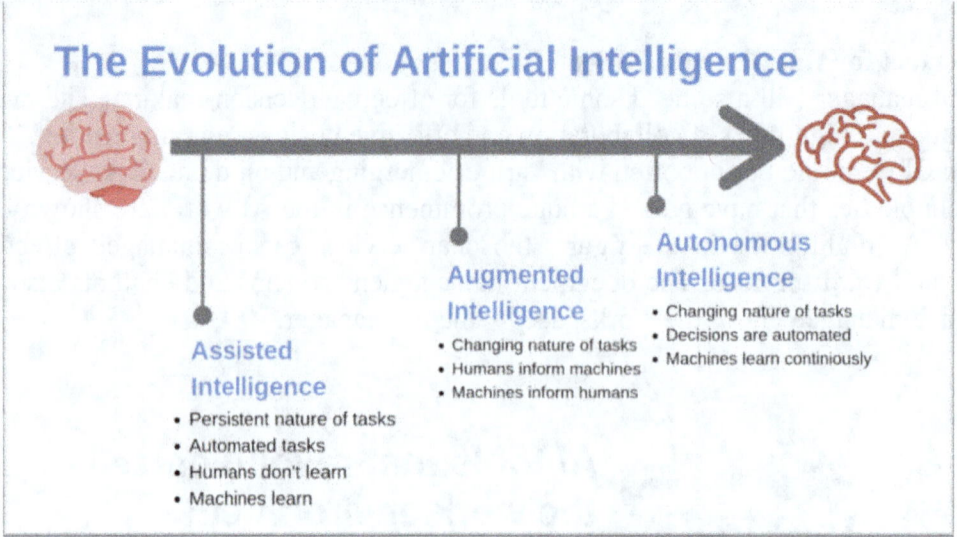

Figure 32: Evolution of the Data-Driven AI Algorithms[xxx]

The evolutionary process of AI-based systems is further elaborated in Figure 33 below:

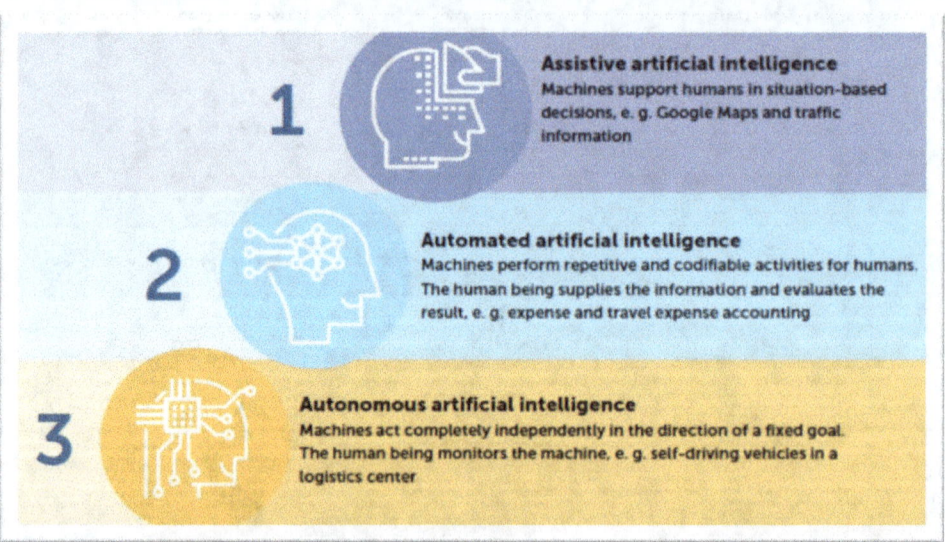

Figure 33: Evolutionary Process of AI-Based Algorithms[xxxi]

It is argued in the management literature that the data-based decision-making is possible only if the decisions of the managers are based on seven key pillars as shown in Figure 34 below. The first aspect is leadership. The decision-making process should provide leadership regarding the strategic directions of the organization. The second aspect is trust. The human managers as well as AI general manager can use the data only if it is trustworthy and is relied upon by all the stakeholders of the organization. If the quality of the data is very low, then the data-driven decision-making may prove to be counterproductive. The third aspect is the commitment level of the managers. They should keep their personal biases aside and follow the patterns and trends in data for effective decision-making. The other aspect is the use of metrics. An AI general manager should have the availability of all key metrics and dashboard indicators. These indicators should provide the real-time view of the organization. Another dimension is data literacy. It is a common argument against the AI algorithms that the users do not know how the algorithms arrived at a particular decision. An AI general manager should also consider this aspect and it should be able to explain the rationale of the decision-making to its human subordinates. Moreover, staff training and awareness are also essential in data-base approach to decision-making.

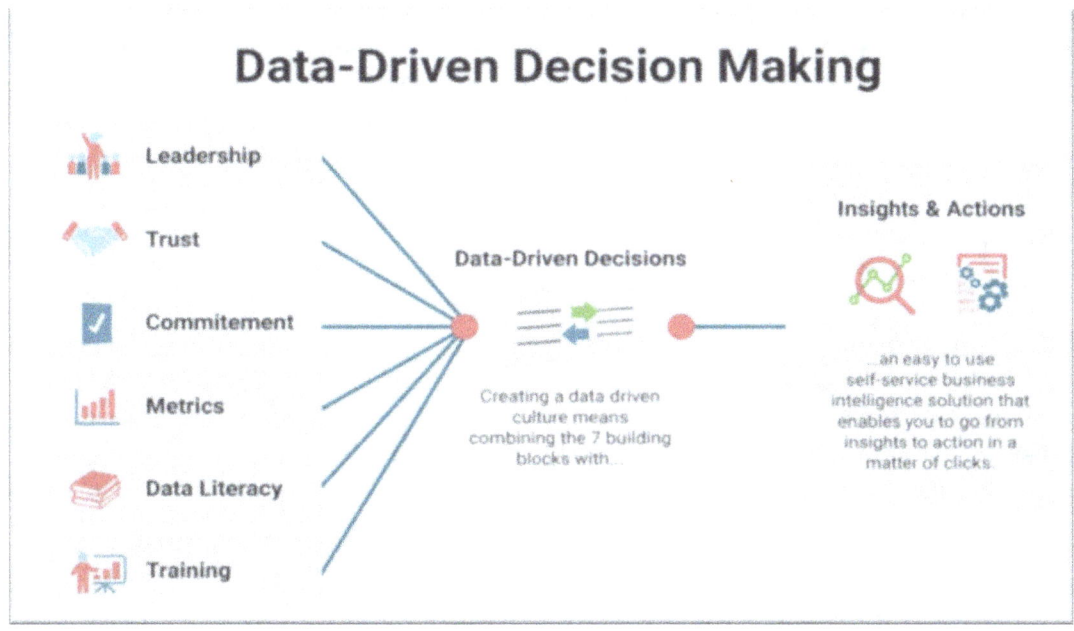

Figure 34: Seven Pillars to be considered by AI General Manager[xxxii]

3.2. Humans for Emotional Intelligence and Creative Tasks

As I explained earlier that the organization of future will be a mix of human workers and robots. You might feel more comfortable reporting to a robot than a human. It is because the human decision-making is often influenced by biases and prejudices. There are complaints of favoritism and partially in every other organization. On the other hand, a robot CEO is highly objective and focused. It is available 24/7, never sleeps, and never gets ill. Despite the presence of an AI manager, there are still various tasks for which human presence will be needed in the organization.

If humans have biases, then AI-based algorithms are also influenced by algorithms biases of the AI developers. When AI-based systems perform the conventional tasks of humans, they provide more opportunity to the coworkers to focus more on strategic and managerial level tasks. If recruitment and performance appraisal are carried out by algorithms, the HR managers will have the options to utilize the workforce in field visits, market analysis, and finding strategies of gaining a competitive advantage. The workers can also focus on sustainability issues and implementing green human resources strategies. Think of the tools such as ChatGPT and Google Bard. The job of the programmers is not gone. These tools can generate the code but the code still needs to be consolidated and deployed, which can only be done by a professional computer programmer. Therefore, an AI general manager will ease the task of the employees and make them more productive and useful in the organizational context.

As highlighted in Figure 5, there are some roles that can be performed efficiently by AI and there are also other roles that humans can perform even better than AI. It is these roles where the needs of humans will still be felt. In the case of digital assistants, the training of these assistants will still be carried out by humans. The analysis of AI-robots will be a quantitative analysis, however, qualitative analysis will still be carried out by humans. This qualitative analysis will indicate why a certain trend is developing and how the current roles and responsibilities of the management professionals can be modified.

As indicated in Figure 35, there are still some jobs where humans can demonstrate more impressive performance than AI robots. Humans are well-versed in critical thinking. For humans, everything is not just right and wrong. They also evaluate the grey areas and acknowledge the dynamic reality of the phenomenon. Humans can also become strategic thinkers through their visionary approach, whereas robots can only learn based on the available datasets. In creative jobs, humans can perform well. Drama and video scripts are being written by AI, but how about poetry. There will be only a few (if any) examples where a high-level creative, poetry work could be produced by a robot. The humans also show more empathy in the communication process and they may overlook the shortcomings of an employee based on the contextual, environmental, and personality factors. However, an AI general manager will be very objective in the communication. The good performances will be appreciated, but there will also be immediate and prompt feedback on the bad performance that may not be liked by those employees who are very sensitive and short-tempered.

Another aspect is the physical skills and the evaluation of the physical skills. An AI general manager might struggle in a factory setting where physical labor work is required. The robots could prove to be highly expensive in these tasks, and it might not be possible for them to evaluate the performance of the workers involved in the physical labor. Robots are being used in warehouses for the proper and efficient maintenance of the inventory. However, consider the construction sector. The robots will find it difficult to do the labor-intensive task in the construction sector. Therefore, physical skills is one area where humans still dominate the robots.

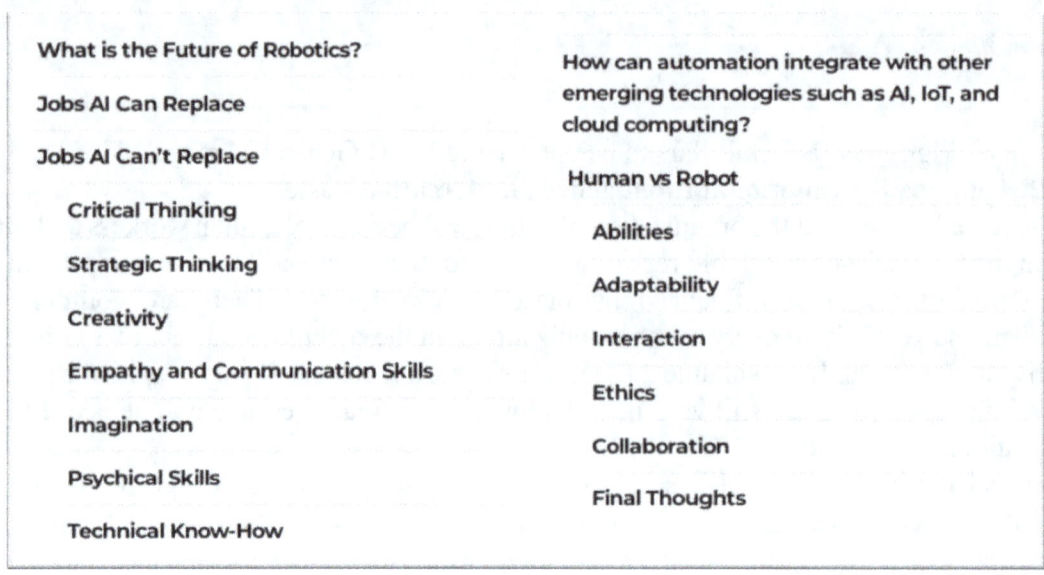

Figure 35: Jobs Humans can do better than AI[xxxiii]

The human brain and AI tools have their strengths and limitations as shown in Figure 36 below. A robotic organization can work well if it capitalizes on the strengths of both humans and AI and creates a hybrid model based on human-machine interaction.

Human Brain	Artificial Intelligence
Pattern recognition & matching	Linear and sequential processing
Creative	Linear & repetitive
Process information slowly	Process information fast
Good at coaching	Good at instruction
Finds meaning from information	Provides information/content
Good at innovation	Good at improvisation
Experiential learning	Rote learning
Focusses on the why & how	Focuses on the what & how
Thinker	Expert
Solve complex problems	Identifies problems
Limited memory	Unlimited memory
Emotion	Reason
People industries	Machine industries
Dynamic content	Set content

Figure 36: Human vs. AI: Strengths and Limitations[xxxiv]

3.3. Companies Successful in Hybrid Model

Figure 37: World's First AI Boss by Hitachi[xxxv]

The first AI boss was developed by Hitachi Company. It was introduced in 2015 that shows that the technology and management professionals were exploring the possibility of AI in management for quite long. They wanted more accuracy and objectivity in the decision-making process and provide more freedom of expression to the subordinates.

Figure 38: Robo-CEO[xxxvi]

Robo-CEO is an algorithmic CEO that selects the most suitable candidate based on the available data. Unlike traditional CEO, the employee is most likely to move up the career ladder due to the objective decision-making of the algorithmic CEO.

Figure 39: AI Boss in Wealth Management[xxxvii]

AI bosses are not limited to the human resource function and they are also being used in other management and business functions. Figure above shows an implementation where the algorithmic managers have been used for an effective wealth management.

Figure 40: AI Boss for Talent Acquisition Hired by a Firm[xxxviii]

There is a successful implementation by a firm in which AI manager was used for talent acquisition and talent management. This robot was given the responsibility of managing a $100 billion firm. The entire human resources of the company will be handled by the algorithmic CEO. The company aims to replace more and more humans with robots in key leadership positions.

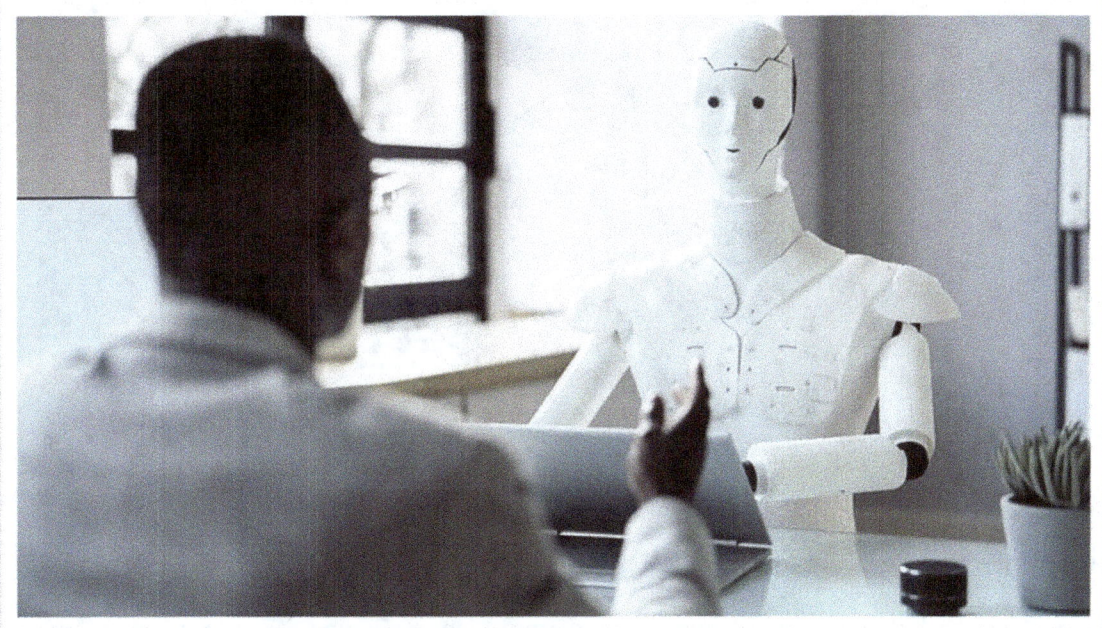

Figure 41: Robot Recruiter[xxxix]

Recruitment was one of the first HR functions where the algorithms were introduced in the form of a robot recruiter. The robots have been highly successful in conducting interviews and candidates express them comfortably in front of a robot. The responses are also processed efficiently by the robots and the same processing strategy is applied for all candidates.

Figure 42: Robots Selecting the Right Candidate[xl]

With the growth of the automated screening process, the job candidates should also update their CVs so that the robots do not discard their resumes. The traditional CVs might not be considered worthy by the robots.

Figure 43: Algorithmic Performance Appraisal[xli]

Performance appraisals are also a key source document for promoting the employees. The algorithmic performance appraisal evaluates each subordinate objectively and justly and only the most hardworking, competent, and devoted employee is selected for promotion and moving up the career ladder.

Figure 44: Successful AI CEO of a Hong Kong based Company[xlii]

Figure above shows an implementation of an algorithmic CEO that was tested in a Hong Kong based company. The boss is named Tang Yu and she is the CEO of mobile and gaming company. The model proved highly successful in the organization and there was a marked improvement in the speed of execution and the quality of work. The company where this model was successfully tested is NetDragon.

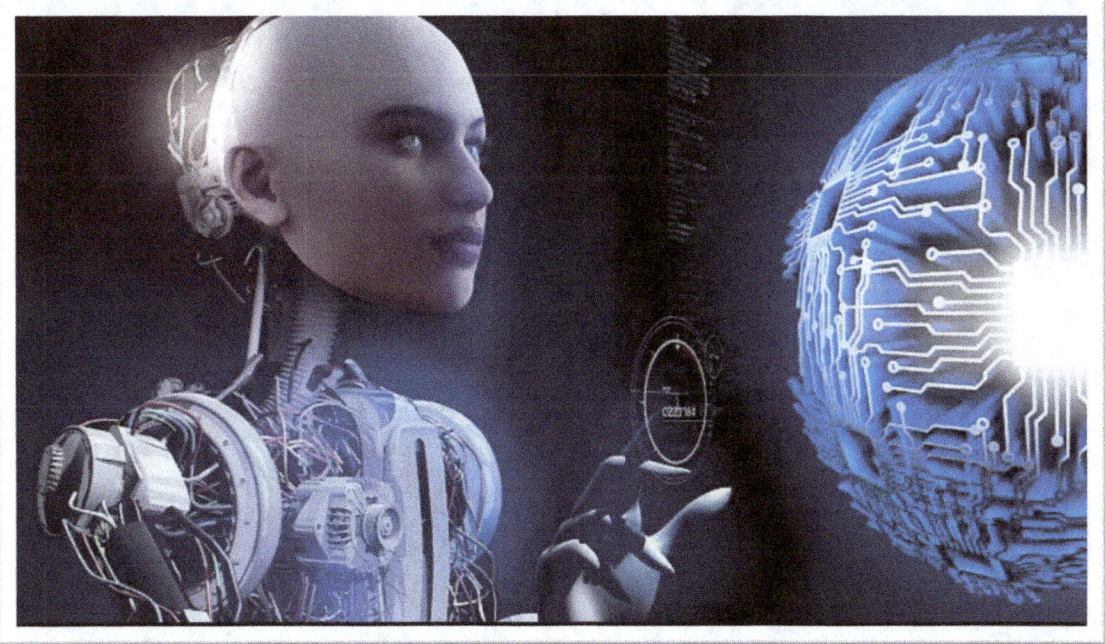

Figure 45: Robot CEO Tang Yu[xliii]

In the current context, a robot CEO was appointed by a Chinese firm NetDragon. The robot CEO was appointed with the intent that the process flow of the business entity will be streamlined and the speed of task execution will improve substantially.

Figure 46: CEO Mika[xliv]

Mika became the CEO of a Drinks Company. She promised the availability of 24/7 for their subordinates and told them that there would not be any layoffs in the company. She performs the tasks of identifying the potential customers and the artists for the new and innovative designs of the bottles.

Figure 47: Archax Robot CEO by Tsubame Industries[xlv]

The above robot was developed by a Japanese company and this robot is planned to be deployed for managing the manufacturing operations in Japan. It has been developed by Ryo Yoshida, who himself is a CEO of a Japanese company.

Figure 48: Robots' Press Conference[xlvi]

In a landmark event at telecommunication conference, there was also a press talk of robots. The robots emphasized in this press conference that humans should not fear losing their jobs due to robots. Moreover, they do not have any plans to rebel against humans.

3.4. Challenges in Human-AI Collaboration

As I highlighted earlier that the use of AI is influencing all aspects of a business entity. The multinational companies are fearful that if they do not embrace AI, they may lose their competitive advantage. However, the limited knowledge of the AI algorithms makes them hesitant in embracing AI at a mass scale. When there was a widespread adoption of AI tools and technologies in multinational organizations, the management professionals also thought that the AI concepts can be useful and significant in the managerial tasks as well because the emerging requirement of the management was to enable data-driven decision-making, and AI algorithms have the potential to process a huge amount of data quickly. However, the business entities are also not in favor that they do things where the decision-making is quick but they do not have any clue how a particular course of action was selected.

A landmark achievement was observed in 2016, when chatbots assistant were introduced. A chatbot assistant such as a WhatsApp chatbot remembers the solutions of the frequently asked questions by the clients. The queries are then responded by the chatbot in an automated manner without any intervention by the human. The beauty of this chatbot was that the support services became highly effective and were made available 24/7. Moreover, the accuracy of the responses was phenomenal because the responses are generated based on the processing of a large dataset. However, the users of the technology are also much aware of the potential and limitations of the technology. They know that they are talking to a chatbot that might give them general purpose answer but may not answer their specific queries and concerns. Even at the level of call centers, if the caller has the option of using automated menu options or calling to an operator, many callers would prefer calling to an operator because it provides a human touch and a personalized interaction. The beauty of human interaction is one area where the robots will never be able to beat the humans. It is a human nature that the people treat everyone differently. People develop a perception regarding the personality preferences of an individual and respond to their queries accordingly. On the other hand, a chatbot assistant will treat all human equally. The difference in responses based on the information and assistance needs of the individual is still beyond the capabilities of a chatbot. Some of the plagiarism checking websites such as turnitin can also detect if a given piece of text was written by a human or a chatbot. This capability makes it evident that the behavioral styles of a machine and a human are entirely different and a machine can never write with a human touch.

The use of AI in management is not a new phenomenon and some level of implementation was observed even as early as 1983. At that time, the database management tools such as oracle were used to process large amount of data and general intelligent reports and dashboard indicators. But the AI of today has found much more usage of the technology and this book takes one next step to highlight the benefits of an algorithmic CEO.

The current era is characterized by the management solutions where the machine learning technologies are used for an effective project management. In fact, the project management was the first area where the significance of an AI general manager was acknowledged. The next era is of autonomous AI where the management functions will be performed autonomously by robots. It is this era where the focus of the book is, i.e. how a general manager, which is an AI robot, can be appointed that could perform all the management roles and the performance is far superior to a human manager. The book argues that there is a huge significance of appointing an algorithmic CEO. However, it should be a hybrid model and the intent of the business managers should not be to replace humans.

In an AI-powered organization, you might see that the robots have taken control for almost all of the organization. They are performing routine tasks, management tasks, as well as surveillance tasks. The tasks are being executed in a robotic manner with an amazing level of accuracy. The queries will be responded promptly that will result in a happy customer and higher customer conversions. This task efficiency should be an ultimate goal of the organization and the human interface should still be used in conjunction with the robotic environment.

Another aspect that you may appreciate in the current model is that the setup of a robotic organization is highly sophisticated and based on the state-of-the-art technologies. This is one area where the business entities will have to focus. They will need to review the requirements of their organizations and present a strong case to the senior management for implementing a robotic organization. In the absence of sufficient funds, it will be difficult to transform the organizational outlook. As highlighted in Figure 49 below, the development of a robot CEO or an industrial CEO should not only be seen in the context of the development cost but also in the context of the running cost or the operation cost. The running cost involves the power consumption cost, downtime cost, and maintenance cost.

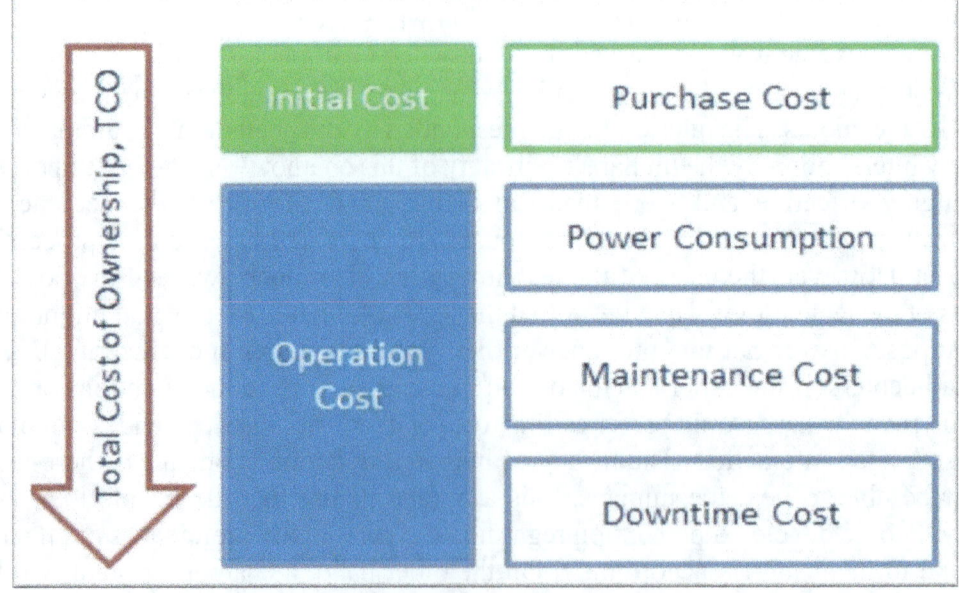

Figure 49: Cost Heads for Algorithmic CEO[xlvii]

Another aspect that you might also notice is that robots appear to be ready for responding to the events. It is possible in an AI-based organization when the AI general manager has all the required data available and the quality of data is extremely good. For example, if there is not required number of CVs received, the shortlisting and interviewing process will suffer despite the availability of robot recruiters. It is a major challenge in the AI-based systems that the algorithms are data-driven. If the supplied data is of poor quality, no AI algorithm can give you good quality results. Figure 50 below highlights how a successful data model can be developed in an AI-based system.

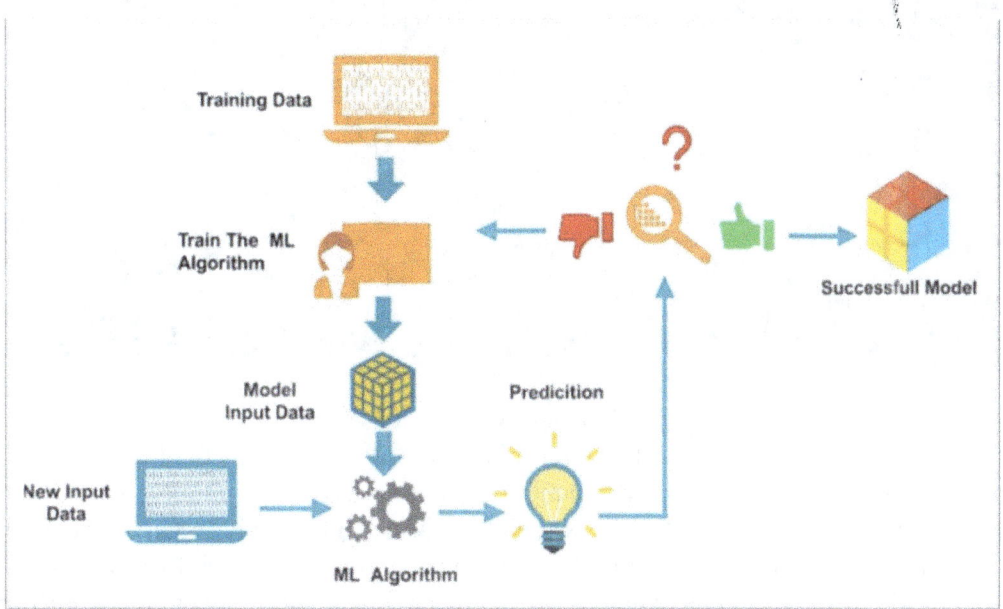

Figure 50: Development of an AI Data Model[xlviii]

The above figure highlights that the quality of a successful AI model is driven by both the training data and the new input data. If all the efforts are aimed at developing a successful algorithm, the required results may still not be achieved due to the poor quality of the data.

The need for an AI general manager has emerged due to multiple factors. There is more and more government ownership and encouragement for implementing AI tools and technologies. The employees can also be held more responsible for their work by facilitating them with AI tools and technologies. The AI concepts have successfully been used in developing the management solutions. The organizations also have a pressure from the competitors because if they become early adopters of AI, the organizations may lose their competitive advantage. The first AI boss was developed by Hitachi Company. It was introduced in 2015 that shows that the technology and management professionals were exploring the possibility of AI in management for quite long. They wanted more accuracy and objectivity in the decision-making process and provide more freedom of expression to the subordinates. In the current context, a robot CEO was appointed by a Chinese firm NetDragon as shown in Figure 51 below:

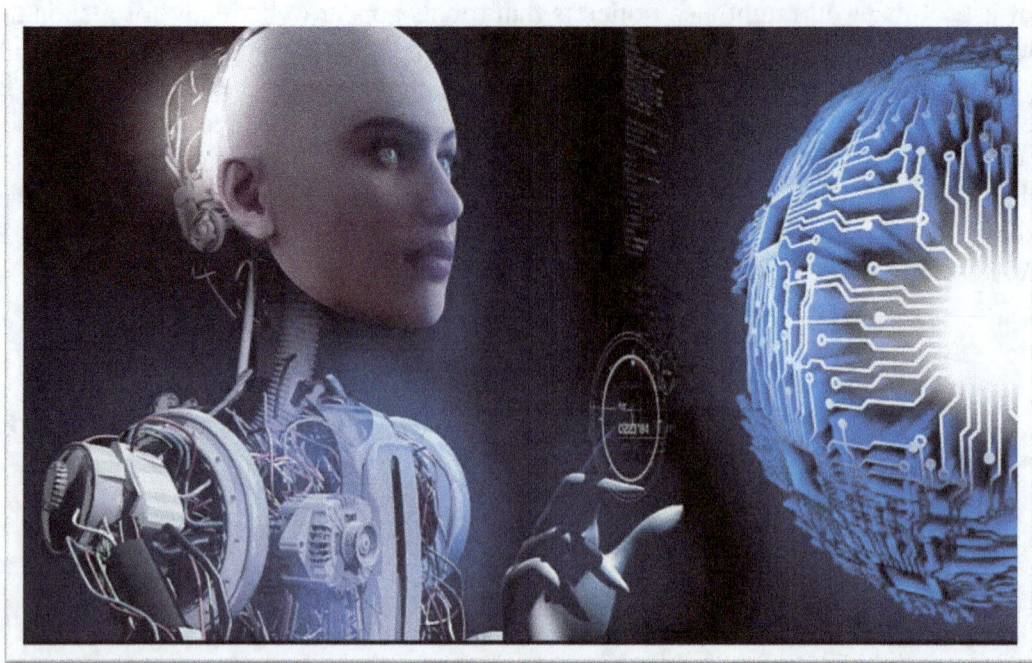

Figure 51: Robot CEO Tang Yu[xlix]

The robot CEO was appointed with the intent that the process flow of the business entity will be streamlined and the speed of task execution will improve substantially. However, at the implementation level, various challenges were also observed by the company. The employees tended to be always connected in the metaverse and the physical activity during the working hours reduced significantly. There was a reduced level of socialization because the CEO always got connected through Zoom calls. With this implementation, it emerged that the robot CEOs may increase the anxiety levels and depersonalization effect.

There is also a fear factor among employees that robots in the management domain will eat their jobs and they will become redundant. It is not going to be the case at least in the near future. As explained earlier, there are some roles that can be performed efficiently by AI and there are also other roles that humans can perform even better than AI. It is these roles where the needs of humans will still be felt. In this era, it is crucial for the professionals to know about the AI tools and technologies that itself will be a good skill and it will also enable them to do the smartly rather than hardly.

In the case of digital assistants, the training of these assistants will still be carried out by humans. The AI models will give specific and task-centered information. The generalization of this information and articulating the data to the organizational context will still be done by humans. The robots can code the knowledge into high-level and low-level processes. However, the handling of complex, exceptional tasks and social interactions will still be managed by humans. The analysis of AI-robots will be a quantitative analysis, however, qualitative analysis will still be carried out by humans. This qualitative analysis will indicate why a certain trend is developing and how the current roles and responsibilities of the management professionals can be modified.

A survey was recently conducted in which the managers were asked to respond what they think they would do better and which tasks can be performed more appropriately by the robots. From the survey, it emerged that the most important benefit of an algorithmic CEO is the provision of an unbiased information. The CEO never controls or filters the information. This advantage was endorsed by the maximum number of managers (36%). The algorithms are also highly efficient in maintaining work schedules. The performance of humans is influenced by external factors as well such as family issues or illnesses. However, the algorithmic workers are always available for the task execution as long as the required IT infrastructure is available and connected.

The algorithmic CEOs are also problem solvers and they can make an efficient utilization of the available budget. The algorithmic CEOs and workers will always be truthful because they do not have any fear of scrutiny or losing their jobs. The team performance can also be evaluated effectively by algorithmic CEOs. The findings of this survey also indicated that it is not always the case that algorithms will outperform humans. There are also instances where human managers perform better than algorithms.

One of these aspects is a better comprehension of the feelings. An algorithm will give a negative feedback to the employee without realizing the mental and emotional state of the employee. On the other hand, the humans will consider the environmental and contextual factors before issuing such remarks. The humans can also train other humans better than machines. An enabling work environment can also be ensured well by humans.

AI benefits in management by the mapping of AI technologies and the management support. The algorithmic managers are powered by machine learning technologies, neural networks, data mining, big data science, and business intelligence. All these AI-based concepts can provide immense support to the management. The benefits can be seen in the optimized decision-making and accurate decision-making. The benefit can also be observed in the improved functionality of the organization. The tasks such as recruitment, performance appraisal, wealth management, and supply chain management can all be automated. It should be noted that various individual components make up an AI robot and the unique, mechanistic blend of these components improve the processing capabilities of an AI manager as shown in Figure 52 below:

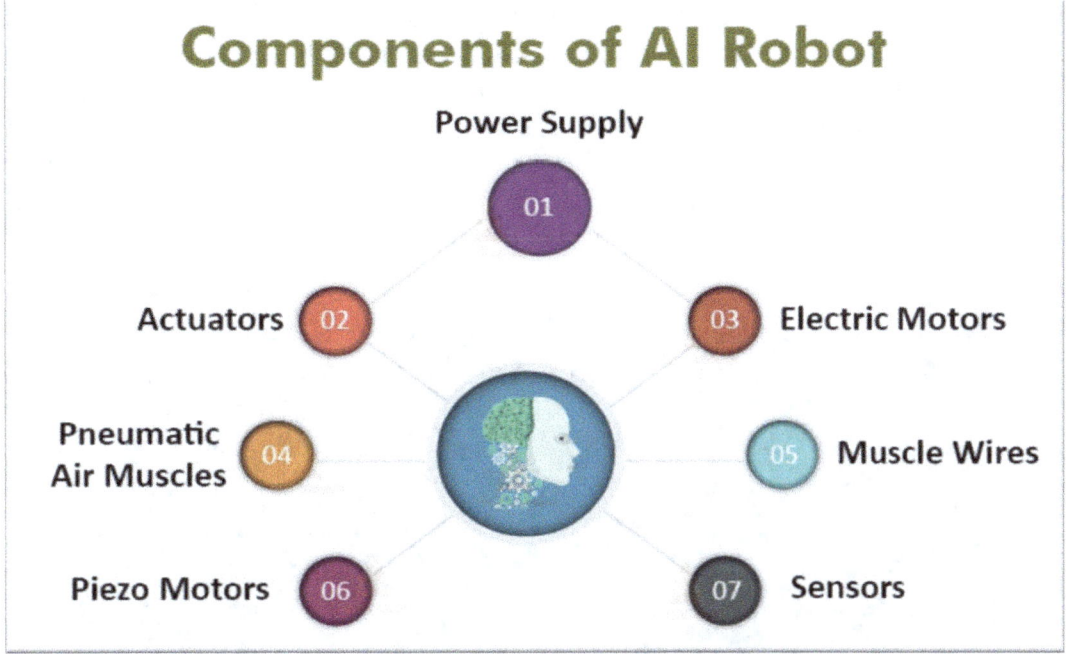

Figure 52: Components of Robot CEO[1]

Robo-CEO is an algorithmic CEO that selects the most suitable candidate based on the available data. Unlike traditional CEO, the employee is most likely to move up the career ladder due to the objective decision-making of the algorithmic CEO. The higher level of automation in robots may also cause serious issues in an automated workplace. In a recent incident, a robot in the famous Tesla Company launched an attack on the human engineer of the company as shown in Figure 53 below. Tesla later explained that it was due to a violent malfunction of the robot. It was a critical case because the unintended action of the robot could have harmed the lives of the employees.

Figure 53: Attack on Tesla Workers by Robots[li]

Due to these incidents, despite the promising outcomes of an AI general manager, there are still only a few successful case studies of an algorithmic CEO. This raises the question why organizations are reluctant to make the optimum utilization of the AI. The first challenge faced in AI based management is that employees are accustomed to interacting with other humans. They miss the human touch and socialization aspect in robotic environment. The environment becomes too mechanistic. The algorithmic CEOs assume that the receivers of their instructions are also robots and they will be able to follow each and every word of their instructions. The humans do not work that way and their rationality is always bounded by various constraints including the family constraints and technical constraints.

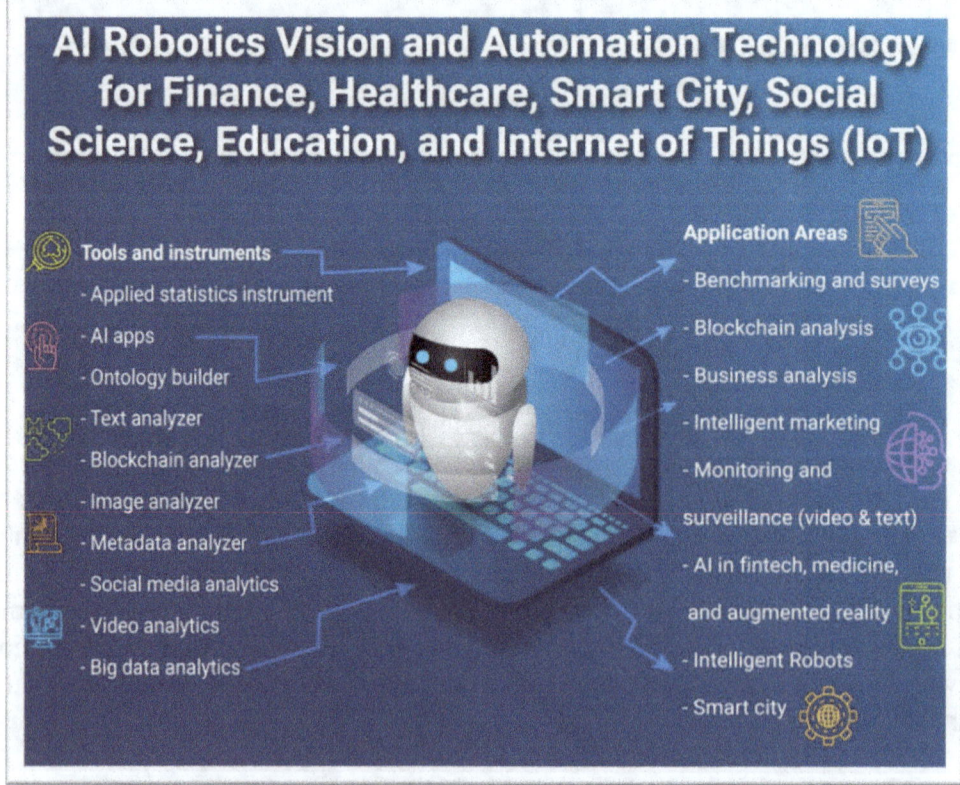

Figure 54: Applications of AI in Different Domains[lii]

The second challenge is the issue of security and privacy of the data. As shown in Figure 54, there are so many applications of AI in the organizational context and there is so much connectivity of the devices for the efficient working of AI algorithms. The data exposure might be without consent or a data breach from a single device may aggravate to a massive data breach. The skill set of professionals regarding the maintenance of AI systems is limited. Therefore, hackers can exploit this opportunity and compromise the sanctity and integrity of the data.

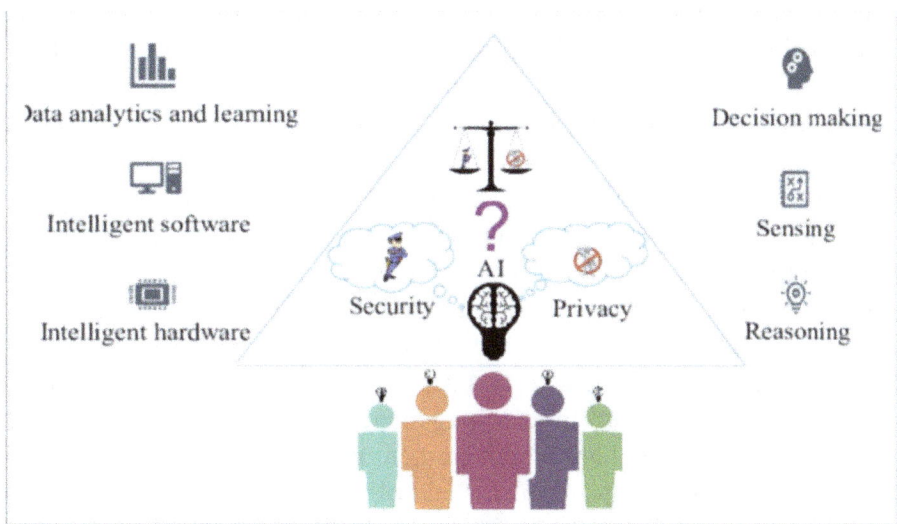

Figure 55: Security and Privacy Concerns[liii]

Figure 55 highlights that when the organizations opt for AI-based systems, they have to make a tradeoff between data exposure and intelligent decision-making. The benefits are experienced in the form of good decision-making, sensing, and sound reasoning. However, the organizations may lose their control over data in a highly interconnected environment.

Another challenge faced in the organizational setting is that as soon as the AI based implementation is announced, employees fear losing their jobs. The tasks for which they had established the timelines of two to three days can be done by robots in two to three hours. So, they anticipate that they will soon become redundant. Another challenge highlighted in the survey is the lack of understanding of the potential impact of AI. If the management itself is not convinced that the AI based systems will transform the management landscape, then the AI based interventions will always be a distant dream.

Another key challenge is that an algorithmic CEO may select a candidate for the job that is highly competitive. However, the candidate may not fit well to the current organizational setting. These aspects can best be judged by humans because it constitutes a dynamic reality and has an element of subjectivity.

Figure 56: Humanoid Robot NAO[liv]

Figure 56 shows the CEO robot NAO that was introduced in 2018 in Germany. It was claimed that these robots will operate in a human-like way and the human jobs will be replaced significantly. However, most of the times, the robot was seen watching and observing the employees and the employees felt that they have lost their freedom at work. In an article by vox, it was mentioned that an employee in Bangladesh complained that the robot CEO monitors him so closely that a picture of him is taken after every ten minutes to confirm that the employee is sitting at his computer.[lv]

The AI-based management has raised concerns because of the intrusive nature of the AI algorithms. As I explained earlier, the AI algorithms process a large amount of data for making an efficient AI model. The development of the data model may access those data sets for which explicit information has not been provided. The quality of algorithms gets improved but the question arises whether legitimate means have been used for improving the efficiency of algorithms. AI has invaded all aspects of the humanity. In the absence of a standard regulatory framework, the fate of the AI-based systems is left to the integrity of the AI developers. As I explained earlier, it usually creates an algorithmic bias.

An algorithmic boss can be a real blessing for an organization if the implementation considers several key aspects and a formal strategy are developed for the transformation process. Several recommendations have been presented in this regard. In the strategy phase, you will need to determine to what extent, the algorithmic management is needed in your organization. In the next step, you should develop a change management process. In this stage, you will have to train the existing staff for using algorithms instead of manual interventions. The management should still make the communication lines open because the change will be successful through an evolutionary process. Once the algorithmic management is in place, the management should constantly evaluate the management flow of the algorithms so that the algorithmic decision-making is not influenced by the algorithmic biases.

From the above AI boss, you will get a feel that the individual is very much focused on the work and there will be complete impartiality in the decision-making process. You may also discuss your concerns and issues with an open heart to an AI boss because there is no fear of retaliation and anger on the part of the boss. The boss is instructed to listen to the issues of the subordinates calmly and openly. The performance of the team will be measured strictly against the assigned objectives quarterly and annually.

A key benefit of an algorithmic CEO that employees are reporting happily to them. They know that the behavior of the boss will be unbiased and the interaction will be limited to the assigned job responsibilities. There will be no favors and additional tasks asked by the boss. Moreover, the working day end within the working hour and there will be no stretched timings and late duties. However, a low-performer will also be reprimanded by the robot CEO and there will be no sympathy towards his low performance. It is this area where the employees might not like an AI general manager that is totally oblivion to their feelings.

The future organizations are expected to be a nice blend of AI workers and human workers. It will also affect how the organograms will be presented and reported in different statutory reports. It might be the case that the CEO is an algorithmic CEO and all key leadership positions are occupied by robots. Humans have been assigned only to the operational work, and the technology-driven aspect of the organization has been endorsed at the level of the organization chart. In order to understand the potential biases in AI algorithms, it is crucial to understand the complete lifecycle of AI algorithms. The lifecycle begins with the definition of a business problem. Then the relevant datasets are acquired and prepared in a consistent format. The next step is the development and training of an AI model. The quality of the AI model is continuously evaluated and refined based on new data and requirements. The system is deployed when the AI model has a sufficient level of maturity. Then machine learning operations are put into place.

Figure 57: CEO of a Drinks Company[lvi]

Figure 57 shows the robot CEO of Drinks Company in Poland that was experimented in November 2023. The CEO performed efficiently the tasks of project management, marketing, sales, and strategic management. From the lifecycle development, you will have noticed that the performance of AI-based systems significantly depend on two factors. The first is the quality and accuracy of the AI model. If the rules and feature extraction processes in AI algorithms are biased because the AI developer is convinced with a certain style of management, then the quality of the whole AI-based system will suffer. Another important factor is the quality of data. If the training examples in the dataset favor a certain segment of the population, then the AI model will learn wrong rules that will affect the algorithmic decision-making. Due to these limitations of the AI algorithms, professionals working in AI always prefer narrow AI over general AI.

There are benefits of using narrow AI for management-based AI algorithms. This technology has a binding to a specific task. The technology is based on fixed-domain models. It might come as a limitation for some general managers because the general-AI has a self-learning process and the system developed in general-AI today will have a far optimized version in the next 6 months based on self-learning. Another benefit of narrow AI is that the learning mechanism is based on a large number of examples and therefore, the concept development in the AI model is very strong. A limitation of narrow AI is that the system is reflexive instead of using cognitive abilities. In the above figure, the general AI has been designation as the future of the AI because the knowledge can be transferred to other domains. It is a highly significant feature particularly when the AI-based concepts are using in conjunction with an IoT environment.

In order to fully understand the algorithmic bias, it is also important to know the different nature of AI algorithms. The first form is supervised learning in which the self-learning system is not built into the model. The learning process is initiated at various time intervals and a trigger is generated in the system to initiate the learning process. The second form is unsupervised learning in which the algorithms enable learning as soon as they encounter new data points and interactions. The third form is reinforcement learning in which the learned data points are categorized into positive or negative reinforcers.

From these examples, it is easier to understand that the risk of algorithmic bias is higher in supervised learning because the learning process is at the discretion of the AI developer. Moreover, when negative reinforcers are identified in reinforcement learning, it is based on how the negativity is defined in the system by the AI developer that creates an algorithmic bias. There is a successful implementation by a firm in which AI manager was used for talent acquisition and talent management. This talent acquisition manager is shown in Figure 23. This robot was given the responsibility of managing a $100 billion firm. The entire human resources of the company will be handled by the algorithmic CEO. The company aims to replace more and more humans with robots in key leadership positions.

Recruitment was one of the first HR functions where the algorithms were introduced in the form of a robot recruiter. The robots have been highly successful in conducting interviews and candidates express them comfortably in front of a robot. The responses are also processed efficiently by the robots and the same processing strategy is applied for all candidates. The function of a robot does not end at conducting an interview. The algorithms can also participate in the entire process of recruitment and selection. They can evaluate all the interview results and select the right and the most suitable candidate by matching the organizational requirements with the candidate skill sets.

AI general manager can also conduct performance appraisal effectively. Employees always have reservations and complaints that their efforts are not compensated adequately and the appraisals are always biased to the likes of the supervisor. Due to this reason, the management literature also suggests 360 degree feedback in addition to the straight line method of appraisal. As shown in Figure 58 below, there are numerous benefits of performance appraisals when conducted by robots. The risks of human errors are eliminated. The projects and training assessments are data-driven. A better level of employee engagement can be expected. However, the performance reviews by the robots gather too much information from the connected devices that the employees may find intrusive.

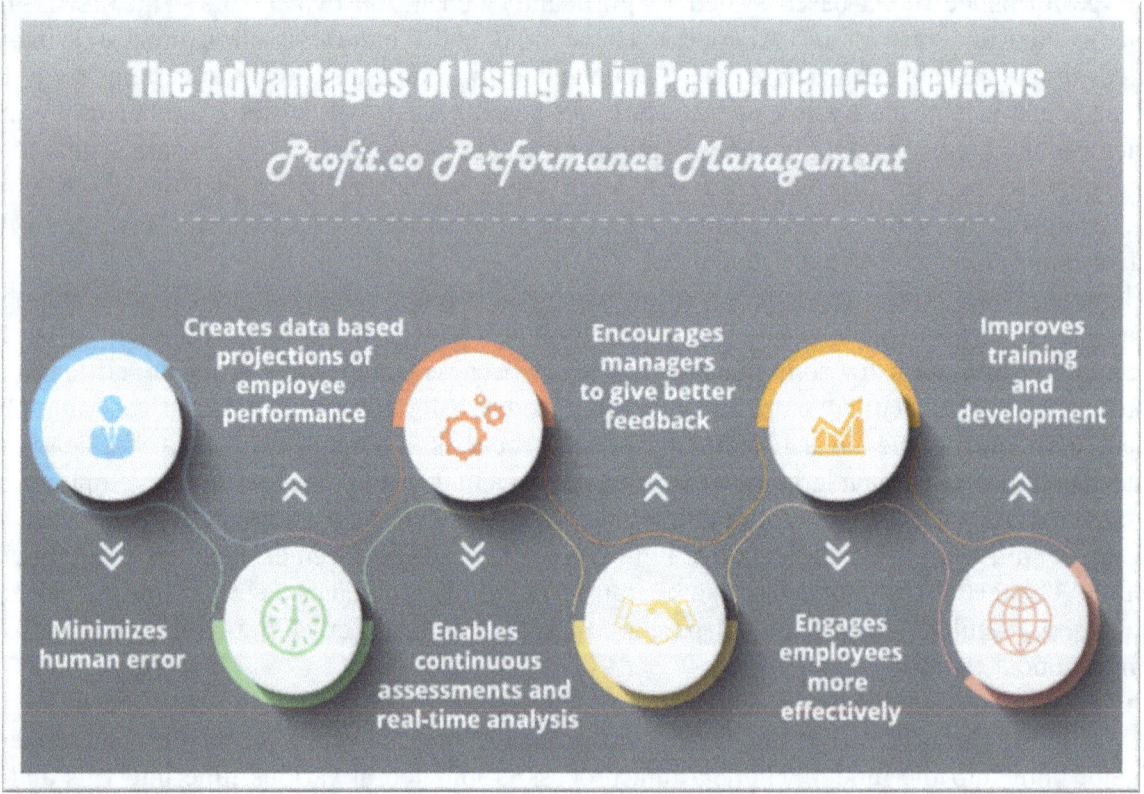

Figure 58: Performance Appraisals by Robots[lvii]

In an ideal scenario, the performance appraisal should begin with the Plan stage. At this stage, the annual objectives of an employee should be set. The next stage is the Act stage where the employee applies the skill set to achieve those objectives. The third stage is the Track stage where the supervisor should periodically monitor the performance of the subordinate and provide feedback. The last stage is review where the performance of the employee should be evaluated, the achievements should be appreciated and the deficiencies should be highlighted. To overcome those deficiencies, the key learning opportunities should be identified for the employees.

This appraisal cycle looks promising; however, in the real world environment, the supervisors are so busy in the regular tasks that they do not focus on the appraisal cycle. Moreover, due to the severe economic conditions, the employees are more worried regarding the survival of their jobs than the growth opportunities and performance appraisals.

An algorithmic CEO can optimize the appraisal systems by using strength-based appraisals. In this strategy, the performance ratings are based on the strengths and competencies of the employees. When there is a fairness and equity in the appraisal process, the motivation and morale of the workforce also improves and the employees are always motivated to improve their skill set.

Performance appraisals are also a key source document for promoting the employees. The algorithmic performance appraisal evaluates each subordinate objectively and justly and only the most hardworking, competent, and devoted employee is selected for promotion and moving up the career ladder. The AI managers will make an impression in the organizations when their performances significantly outperform the human managers. Several successful implementations have been made in this regard so far.

Chapter 4

AI for an Efficient Learning Mechanism in Management

AI algorithms can prove to be an effective general manager because of their abilities of enabling a process of continued learning. For the humans, the management has to ask them to go for continued professional development. Moreover, some managers do not have the required aptitude for the leadership positions, and they are successful in securing the positions based on the tenure of their employment. All these aspects can be addressed effectively by an AI general manager because it does not require an aptitude and interest for learning. The algorithms will learn in an automated, mechanistic style. In this chapter, I will highlight how the AI learning can benefit in executing the management process successfully and what its specific benefits are in the context of resource allocation, project management, and risk assessment. At the end of the chapter, I have also highlighted the drawback of machine learning in management to give you both perspectives and theoretical frameworks.

To fully understand the potential of AI learning in resource allocation, project management, and risk assessment, it is crucial to gain a basic understanding of how the learning process works in the AI-based systems. As shown in Figure 59, active learning in AI is a function of Label, Enrich, Train, and Query processes. First, a given sample or a resource will be assigned a label by the system. It facilitates in identifying the sample and assigning it to a class or a category. The training dataset is enriched by the inclusion of the newly labelled sample because the system sees it as an opportunity of learning and strengthening the system protocols. In the Train phase, the AI model receives the training based on the available dataset. This dataset includes the past, historical data as well as the newly added samples. The query process can also be used by the learning function to view and select different samples available in the dataset. This simple example shows the power of AI-based algorithms that they are always ready for the new learning. As soon as they receive the newly added samples, they trigger the training phase and train the AI model based on the current and new data.

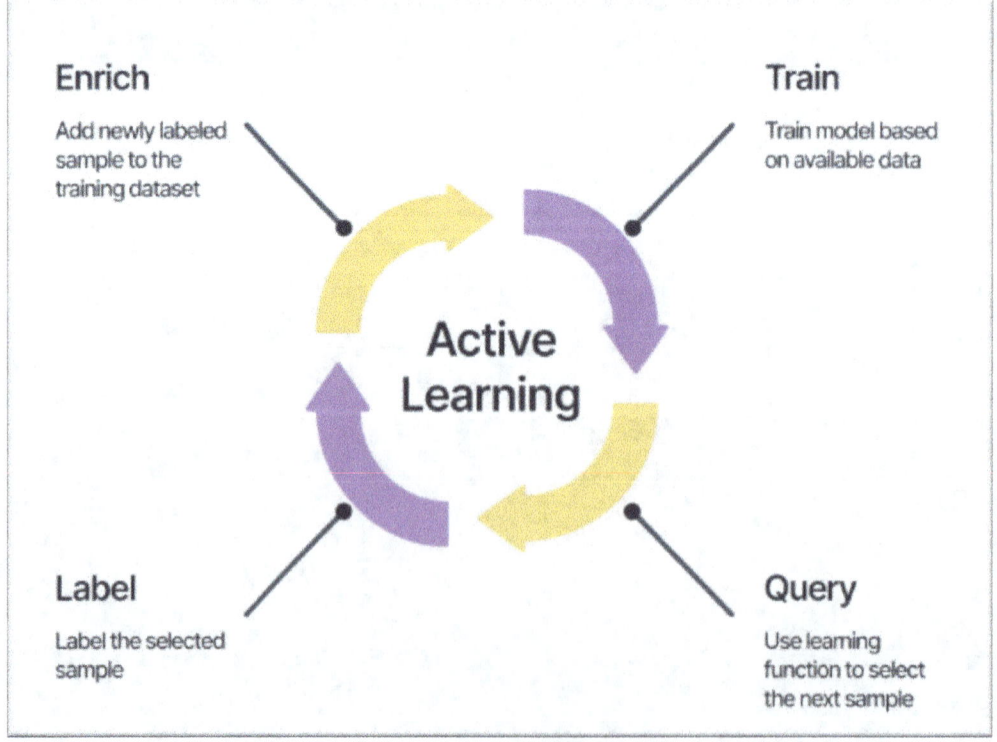

Figure 59: Learning Process in AI-based Systems[lviii]

As I explained earlier, the algorithmic managers are powered by machine learning technologies, neural networks, data mining, big data science, and business intelligence. All these AI-based concepts can provide immense support to the management. The benefits can be seen in the optimized decision-making and accurate decision-making. The benefit can also be observed in the improved functionality of the organization. The tasks such as recruitment, performance appraisal, wealth management, and supply chain management can all be automated.

I had also highlighted that the learning process can be effective if there are no algorithmic biases in the AI-based systems. The key factor in AI systems is the quality of data. If the training examples in the dataset favor a certain segment of the population, then the AI model will learn wrong rules that will affect the algorithmic decision-making. Due to these limitations of the AI algorithms, professionals working in AI always prefer narrow AI over general AI.

While considering the benefits of AI learning in resource allocation, project management, and risk management, another key area of consideration is the distinction between supervised and unsupervised learning. The first form is supervised learning in which the self-learning system is not built into the model. The learning process is initiated at various time intervals and a trigger is generated in the system to initiate the learning process. The second form is unsupervised learning in which the algorithms enable learning as soon as they encounter new data points and interactions. The third form is reinforcement learning in which the learned data points are categorized into positive or negative reinforcers. It is easier to understand that the risk of algorithmic bias is higher in supervised learning because the learning process is at the discretion of the AI developer. Moreover, when negative reinforcers are identified in reinforcement learning, it is based on how the negativity is defined in the system by the AI developer that creates an algorithmic bias.

4. Benefits of AI Learning in Resource Allocation

The resource allocation based on AI learning is executed in a highly sophisticated manner. Considering this aspect, the AI developers recommend that various parameters should be reviewed by the technology team before implementing resource allocation. In a study, these considerations have been considered into three key categories of task, approach, and computing paradigm as shown in Figure 60 below. The first area of consideration is that how many resource allocation strategies will be input into the system and how the power consumption can be optimized during the algorithmic decision-making. The efficient power management is always crucial in AI-based software because the AI models process huge datasets that might consume energy beyond the available resources of the organization. The second factor is the AI approach in which the technology team should select from the available machine learning techniques and deep learning techniques. The third factor is the computing paradigm. Ideally, the resource allocation should be processed in the cloud computing environment because various nodes and parameters will be processed that will require extensive storage space and the computing power. Other options may also be considered such as the IoT environment, edge computing, or mobile edge computing.

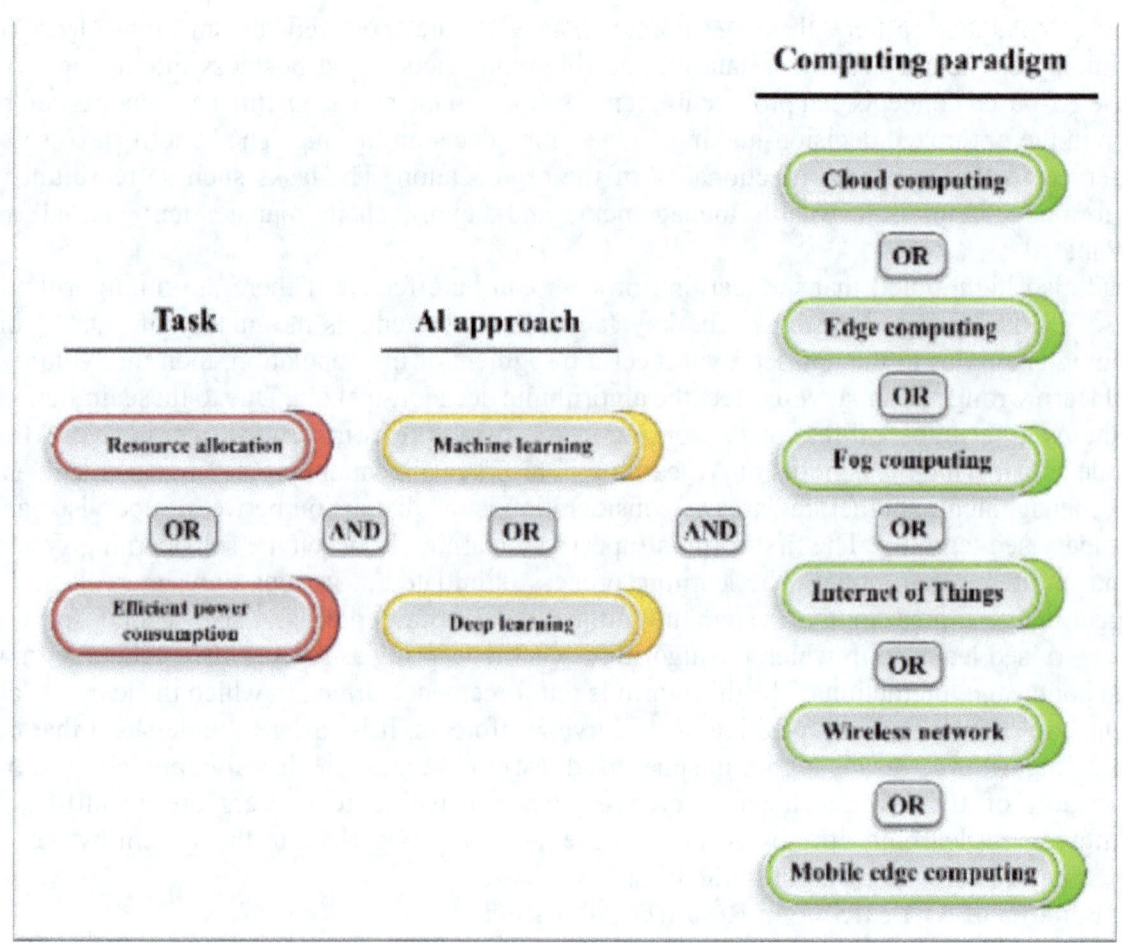

Figure 60: Critical Considerations in AI-based Resource Allocation[lix]

As highlighted in Figure 61, the AI-based resource allocation can offer various advantages to the senior management. These benefits are further optimized when the CEO or the general manager of the company is an AI robot and not a human. It is because the resource allocation management software based on AI concepts assume that the user of these tools will also be well versed in executing the different functions and interfaces of the software. In the case of an AI CEO, this intelligence is built into the CEO algorithms that increases the benefits of an AI-based resource allocation.

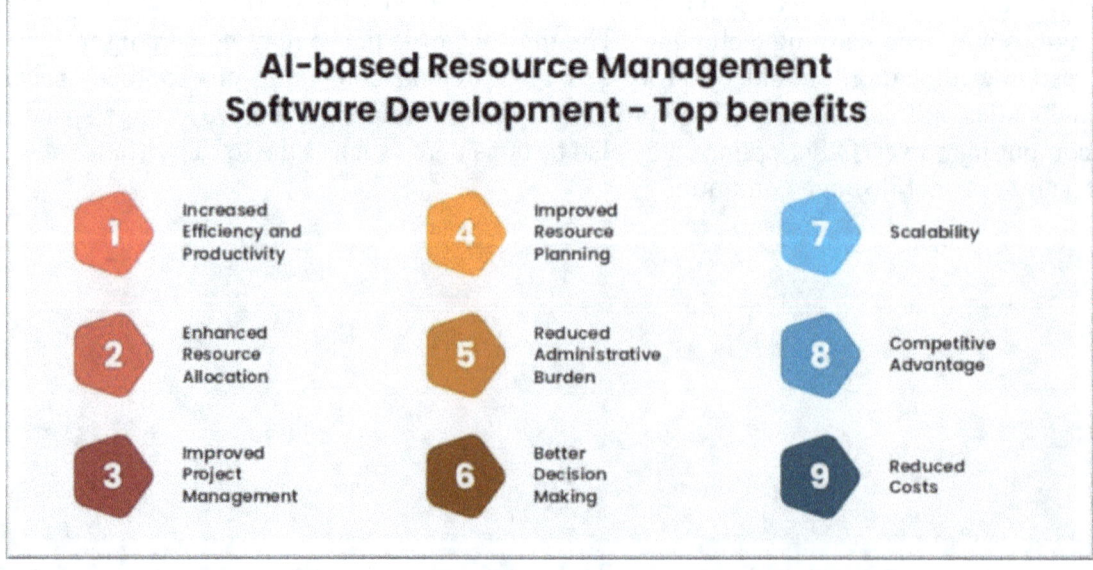

Figure 61: Advantages of AI-based Resource Allocation[lx]

As indicated in the figure above, when the resource allocation takes advantage of the AI concepts, the efficiency and productivity of the workforce increases because the system learns from the mistakes and makes continuous adaptations to the resource allocation process. The resource planning is also optimized because it is based on the predefined rules and criteria and alternate plans and strategies are also made part of the algorithmic process. The burden of the administration is reduced significantly because the resource allocation is accomplished automatically and everyone is aware of their roles and possible tasks that might be assigned in the near future. The organizations can also reduce costs and gain a competitive advantage through AI-based resource allocation.

Figure 62: Options and Features in Resource Allocation Software[lxi]

Figure 62 mentions the features and options that are offered by different AI vendors in the resource allocation software. As can be seen in the very first entry, the resource allocation becomes entirely automated in the AI-based software. The predictive management is also a well-known feature of the AI where the issues and problems in the existing strategies are tracked by the system proactively and alternate strategies are recommended. The dashboard indicators also show the real-time availability of all available resources. There are also options for time tracking and project management. The resources needed for future projects and future years can also be forecasted by the system and then the algorithmic CEO can initiate the hiring process for meeting the higher demand of resources in the future. The resources may also be needed in the form of financial resources and material resources. In those cases, the procurement department may be intimated for acquiring the materials and funding agencies may be contacted for receiving the required funds for the future projects.

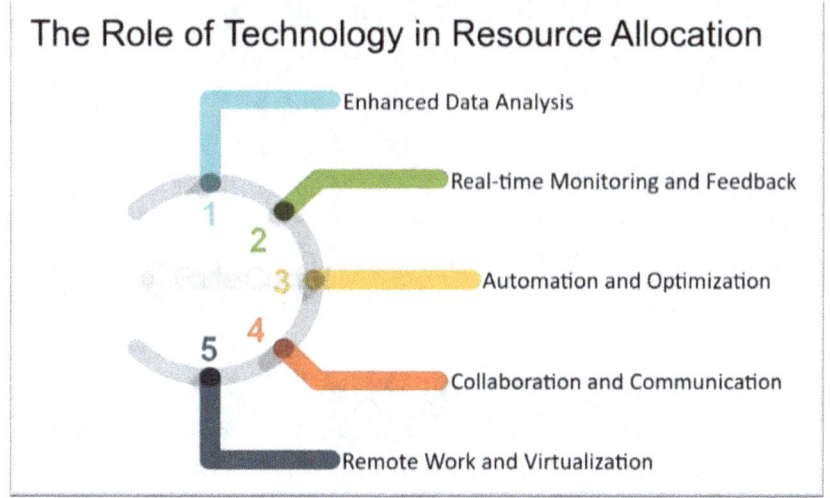

Figure 63: Resource Allocation from the Technology Perspective[lxii]

Figure 63 highlights the benefits of resource allocation from the technology paradigm. When the organizations opt for AI-based resource allocation in management, the quality of data analysis improves significantly. The entered data is not only used for reporting and descriptive statistics, but inferences are also drawn and future state of the organization is also predicted based on the current data. In this way, if there are loopholes in any strategy, they can be rectified well before their occurrence. The real-time monitoring of the resource allocation is also possible because the resource allocation is carried out by the systems and all the decision-making steps are recorded and reported by the system. The collaboration process is also improved significantly and the resource allocation can also cover remote workers through the use of virtualization hardware, software, and systems.

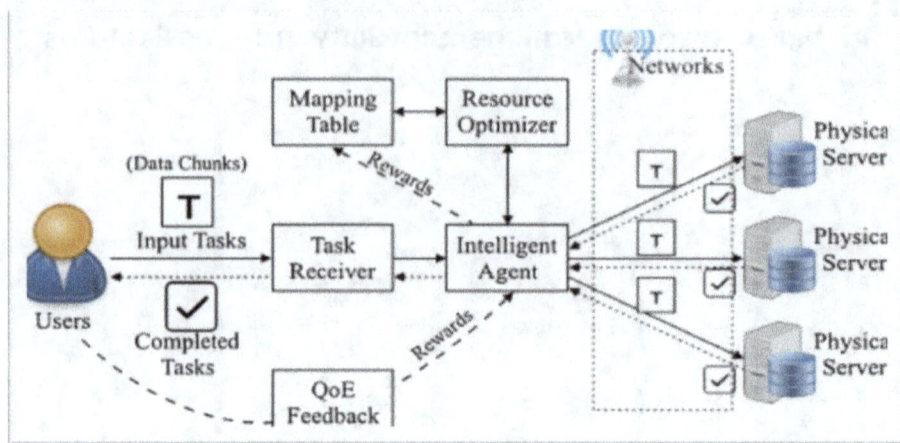

Figure 64: Resource Allocation with Reinforcement Learning[lxiii]

Figure 64 shows a model of AI resource allocation software in which reinforcement learning has been used. The learning mechanism ensures that the quality of experience is at an optimum level when the output is sent to the end users. Between the users and the physical servers, there is a whole system of network topologies and AI-based systems. When the tasks are received by the task receiver, the intelligent agent is used for generating rewards and assigning resources. This information is stored in the mapping table. The intelligent agent also receives the feedback from the end users regarding the quality of experience and then the improvements are made by reinforcement learning. This whole AI-based resource allocation system not only ensures an efficient allocation of resources but also learns from the feedback of the users and make improvements in the resource allocation tasks for the future scenarios.

Cognitive Projects by Type

We studied 152 cognitive technology projects and found that they fell into three categories.

Technology projects

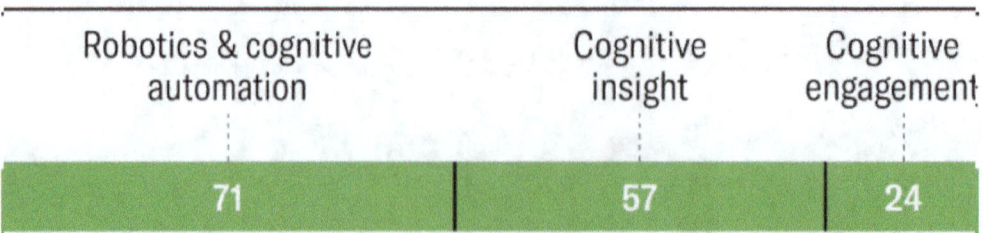

Figure 65: Cognitive Insights in Resource Allocation[lxiv]

Figure 65 shows the results of a study in which 152 cognitive projects were studied. As is evident from the figure, robotics and automation is also being used extensively in cognitive projects and it significantly increases the power of resource allocation, AI-based software. Currently, general managers spend significant time in identifying the best fit for a project or a management task. Even during the course of the project, they might find out that they erred in the decision-making and did not find the right person for the right job. These limitations in the decision-making has a lot to do with the cognitive potential of a leader. However, an AI-based general manager can improve the cognitive potential of an AI CEO due to objective decision making and using the cognitive thinking facilities of the latest AI-based software. As a result, the managers can always be confident that they have the best team available and each employee has been assigned the tasks based on the person-organization fit. The assigned person possesses all the capabilities and skills for executing the assigned task.

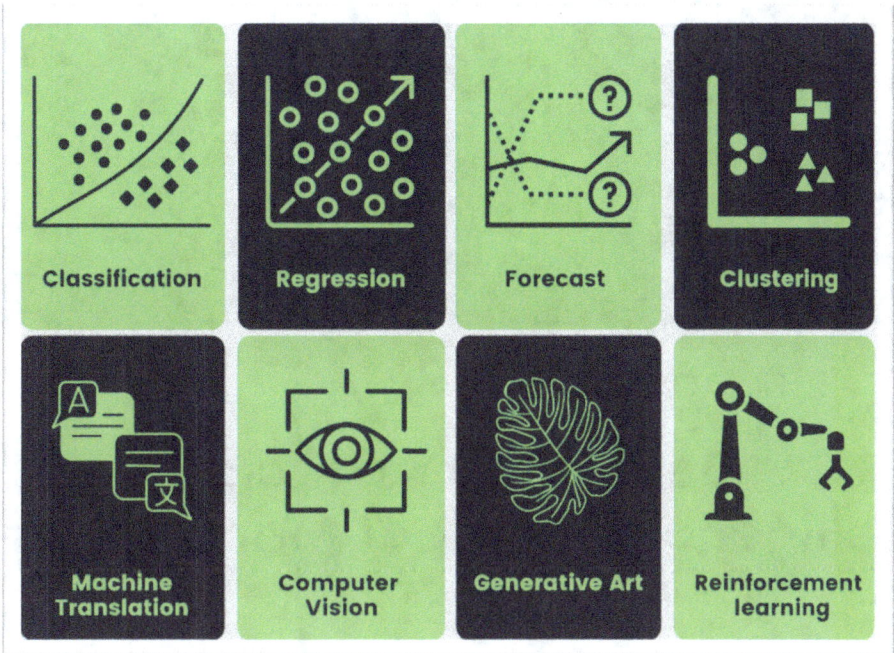

Figure 66: AI Tools and Technologies in Resource Allocation[lxv]

Figure 66 shows the tools and technologies that can be used in AI-based resource allocation. The data points are classified by the algorithms for feature extraction. The regression analysis indicate the contribution of each resources in the accomplishment of overall organizational objectives. The forecasting models predict the future demand of resources based on the objectives and goals set by the organization. The clustering mechanism uses the features and highlights groups and patterns in the data. The process of machine translation codifies the strategies for algorithmic decision-making. The computer vision technology may also be used for identifying and recommending the resources. The generative AI can be used in the process of collaboration and communication. The reinforcement learning makes it possible that the system improves over time based on the bottlenecks emerged in the current strategies of resource allocation.

4.1. Benefits of AI Learning in Project Management

AI learning provides huge benefits in project management. As I highlighted earlier, the project management was the first area in the management domain where the significance of AI was acknowledged. The current era is characterized by the management solutions where the machine learning technologies are used for an effective project management. In fact, the project management was the first area where the significance of an AI general manager was acknowledged. The next era is of autonomous AI where the management functions will be performed autonomously by robots. It is this era where the focus of the book is, i.e. how a general manager, which is an AI robot, can be appointed that could perform all the management roles and the performance is far superior to a human manager.

Figure 67 highlights that a successful AI learning in project management should result in task automation, efficient resource allocation, advanced predictive analytics, and effective natural language processing.

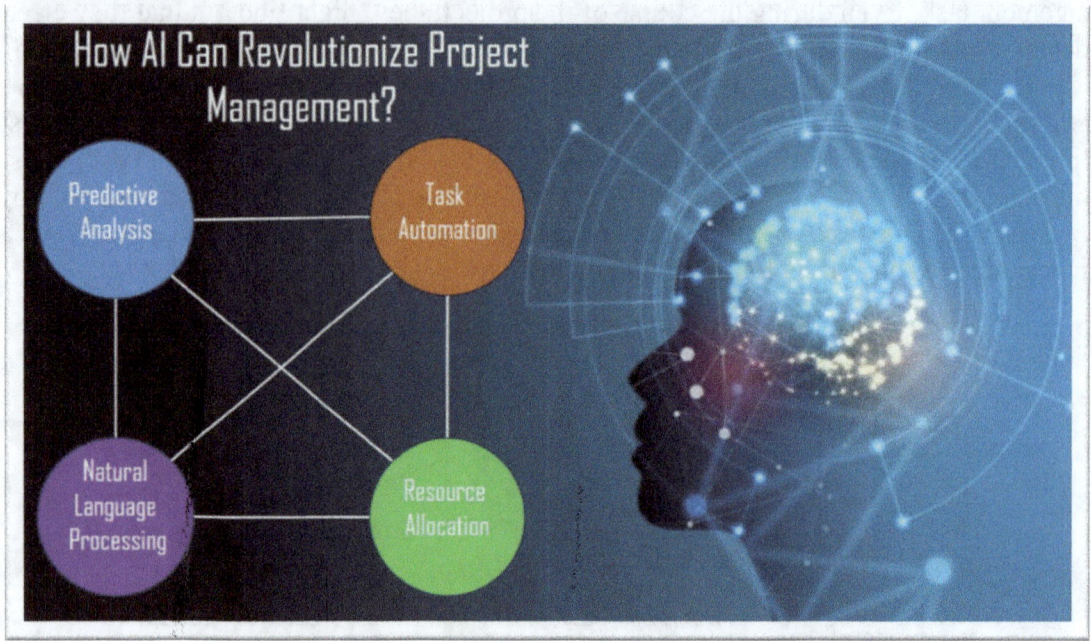

Figure 67: Benefits in Project Management Domain[lxvi]

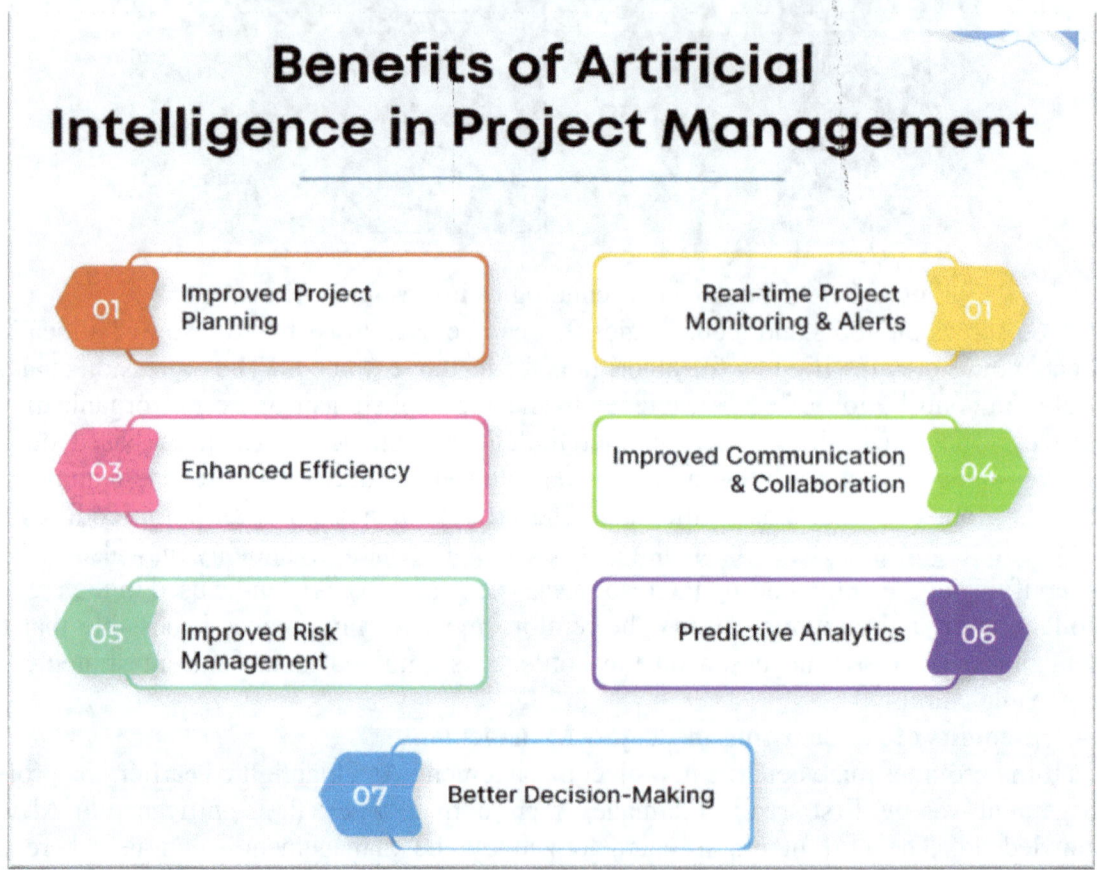

Figure 68: Advantages of AI Learning in Project Management[lxvii]

Figure 68 shows some of the benefits of AI in project management. The project planning is improved significantly because the project managers can take advantage of the recommendations and data-based suggestions provided by the AI algorithms. The project monitoring also becomes easier because AI keeps track of all the project tasks and provides alerts on those tasks where the deadlines might be missed. Hence, the project managers can focus on those tasks that require their immediate attention and leave the monitoring of those tasks where there is a good report given by the AI systems. In this way, an enhanced efficiency of the project managers can be ensured. The predictive analytics feature provides an edge to the AI-based software to the conventional project management software. The AI-based software also predict and simulate the future state of the project and alert the project managers if there are any complications and issues in achieving the desired outcomes. A marked improvement in the overall decision-making process can be observed by implementing AI in project management.

It is imperative to understand how the AI models develop a predictive model for an efficient project management. The complete flow of the machine learning algorithms is depicted in Figure 69 below. With the help of the training set, the algorithms perform both supervised and unsupervised learning. The new data is also continuously added in the training data. Features are then extracted from the training set. Then the machine learning algorithms work on the developed AI model and the annotated data. Ultimately, the grouping of objects is accomplished and predictive models are developed. These predictive models inform the project managers regarding the future state of the project. The project managers can review these scenarios and compare them with the desired scenarios. In the case of discrepancies, the strategies can be modified and updated by the project managers.

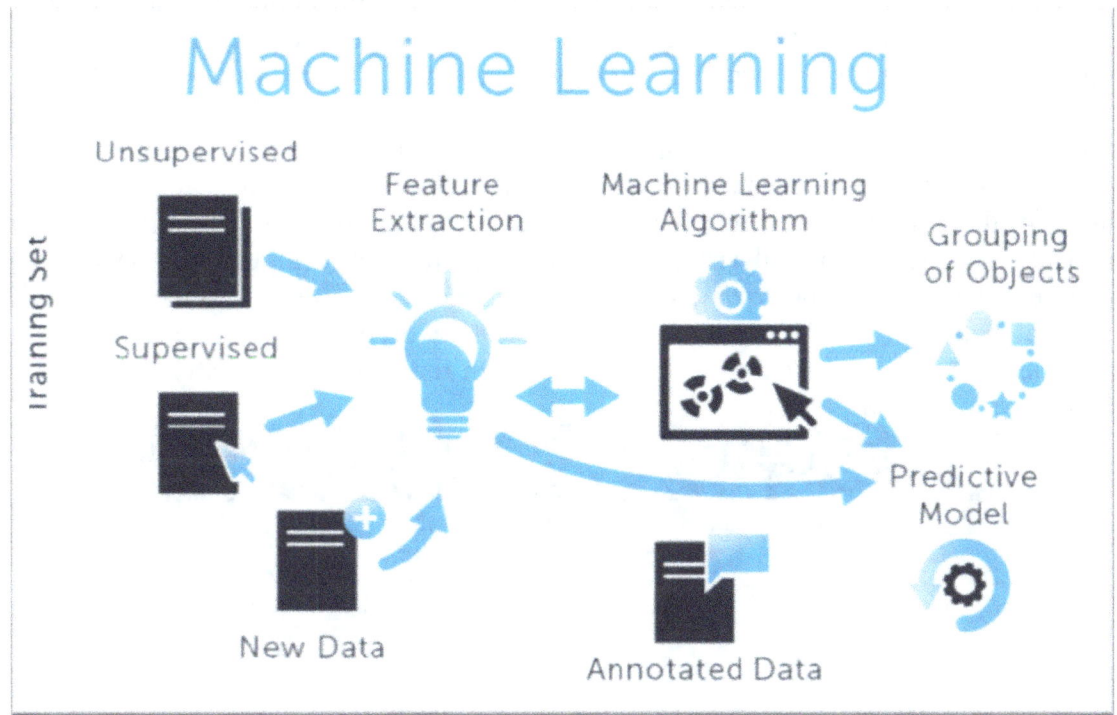

Figure 69: Predictive Analytics in Project Management[lxviii]

Advantages of AI in project management have also been endorsed by the Project Management Institute as shown in Figure 70 below. According to PMI, automation and optimization can be achieved by AI learning. Risk management strategies can also be improved by the use of AI tools. The data-driven insights improve the process of decision-making by the project managers. The algorithms also streamline the process of resource scheduling and resource allocation.

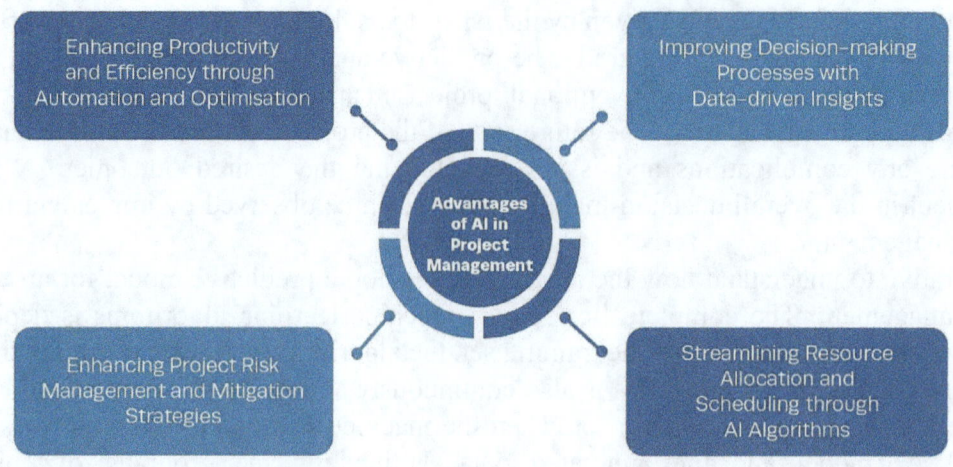

Figure 70: AI Learning Endorsement by PMI[lxix]

It should be noted that at the technical level, different AI types provide varied level of benefits to the project managers. Therefore, the technology team in the organizations should build understanding of all the AI types that they are anticipating for the implementation. Figure 71 below shows the relevance of each AI type in the project management paradigm. The machine learning algorithms are more beneficial in project analytics and risk assessment. The deep learning algorithms can be utilized for the optimization of task scheduling. The supervised learning should be used for project costing and budgeting. The unsupervised learning should be utilized for team creating and team management. The reinforcement learning is a good strategy for the resource allocation tasks. The natural language processing algorithms should be utilized for the sentiment analysis of the team performance. The computer vision technology should be used for the summarization of the educational videos related to the project. The adversarial networks should be utilized for the testing of projects in a safe and secure environment. The expert systems will be needed when risk management is to be carried out based on historical data.

AI Type	Definition	Example in Project Management
Machine Learning (ML)	Algorithms learn from data without explicit coding	Predictive project analytics for risk assessment
Deep Learning	Specialized ML using deep neural networks	Optimized task scheduling
Supervised Learning	Trained on labeled data to make predictions	Cost estimation for project budgeting
Unsupervised Learning	Learns patterns from unlabeled data	Creating teams of people based on common characteristics or communication preferences
Reinforcement Learning	Learns from environmental feedback to achieve a goal	Dynamic resource allocation based on changing priorities
Natural Language Processing (NLP)	Interprets and generates human language	Sentiment analysis for team feedback
Computer Vision	Interprets visual information (images, videos)	Summarizes meetings and educational videos.
Generative Adversarial Networks (GANs)	Generate synthetic data similar to real data	Synthetic data generation for safe project testing
Expert Systems	Mimics human expert decision-making	Risk management decision support using historical data

Figure 71: Relevance of each AI Type[lxx]

From an AI boss, you will get a feel that the individual is very much focused on the work and there will be complete impartiality in the decision-making process. You may also discuss your concerns and issues with an open heart to an AI boss because there is no fear of retaliation and anger on the part of the boss. The boss is instructed to listen to the issues of the subordinates calmly and openly. The performance of the team will be measured strictly against the assigned objectives quarterly and annually.

In the project management paradigm, there are several key processes and the AI systems should be able to optimize all these processes. As shown in Figure 72, a typical project will involve the estimation of tasks and resources. Then the costing and resource scheduling should be done. The project manager also needs to do sequencing and collating of data. They also identify risks and trends in the projects. The AI-based systems should assist in all these areas. Good AI-based systems offer automated scheduling, optimization of all tasks, predictive analytics features, and machine learning algorithms for all AI types.

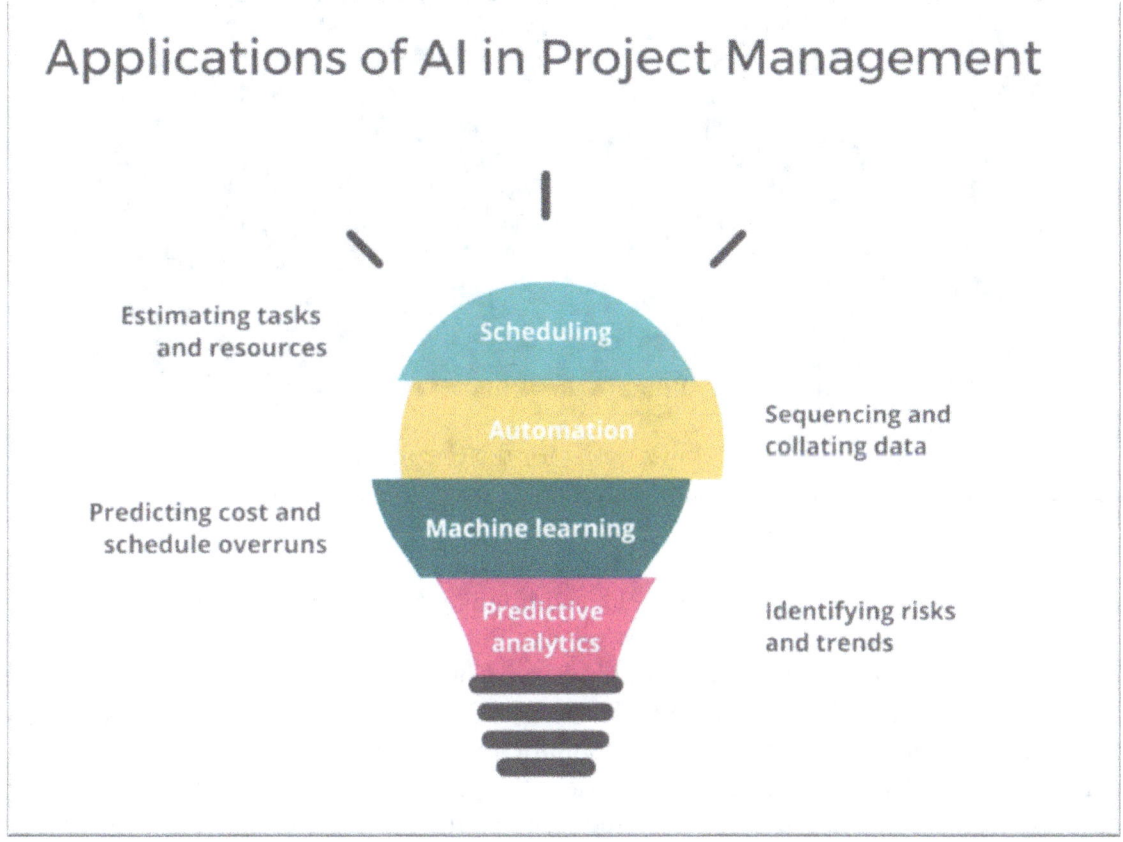

Figure 72: Project Management Tasks and AI[lxxi]

This book highlights the role of AI general manager and beyond. Therefore, the benefits of AI-based project management should also be viewed as to how AI can assist general managers if it is not possible to appoint an AI general manager altogether. Figure 73 highlights the benefits that can be gained in those cases. The training and development of the employees will be based on the analysis of their learning habits by the AI software. The resource allocation will be optimized due to which it will be easier to release the employees from the operational tasks and depute them to the project activities. The project team will be able not only to track the progress of the project but also predict the future activities of the project. The budgeting and scheduling tasks will all be automated. The complex, employee-based analytics will be handled smoothly by the AI software. Therefore, AI algorithms will sever as a virtual assistant of the project manager in cases where it is not possible to appoint an AI project manager.

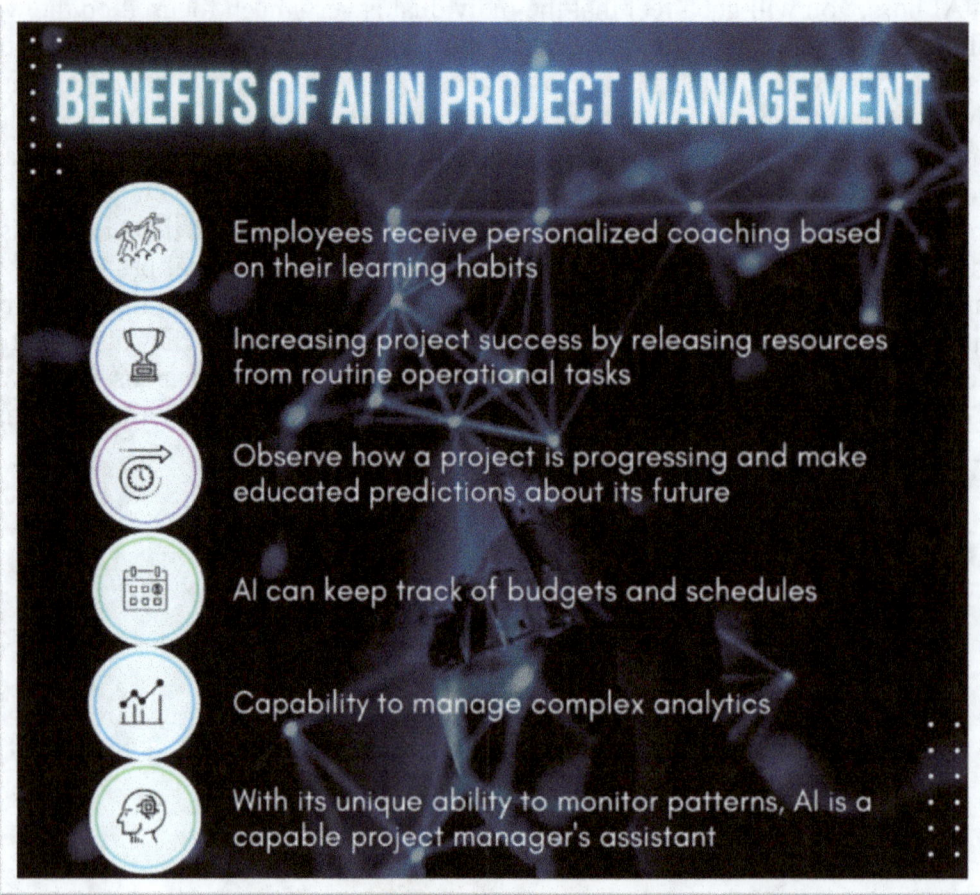

BENEFITS OF AI IN PROJECT MANAGEMENT

Employees receive personalized coaching based on their learning habits

Increasing project success by releasing resources from routine operational tasks

Observe how a project is progressing and make educated predictions about its future

AI can keep track of budgets and schedules

Capability to manage complex analytics

With its unique ability to monitor patterns, AI is a capable project manager's assistant

Figure 73: AI Benefits for the Employees[lxxii]

AI general manager can also conduct performance appraisal effectively. Employees always have reservations and complaints that their efforts are not compensated adequately and the appraisals are always biased to the likes of the supervisor. Due to this reason, the management literature also suggests 360 degree feedback in addition to the straight line method of appraisal. In an ideal scenario, the performance appraisal should begin with the Plan stage. At this stage, the annual objectives of an employee should be set. The next stage is the Act stage where the employee applies the skill set to achieve those objectives. The third stage is the Track stage where the supervisor should periodically monitor the performance of the subordinate and provide feedback. The last stage is review where the performance of the employee should be evaluated, the achievements should be appreciated and the deficiencies should be highlighted. To overcome those deficiencies, the key learning opportunities should be identified for the employees.

This appraisal cycle looks promising; however, in the real world environment, the supervisors are so busy in the regular tasks that they do not focus on the appraisal cycle. Moreover, due to the severe economic conditions, the employees are more worried regarding the survival of their jobs than the growth opportunities and performance appraisals.

An algorithmic CEO can optimize the appraisal systems by using strength-based appraisals. In this strategy, the performance ratings are based on the strengths and competencies of the employees. When there is a fairness and equity in the appraisal process, the motivation and morale of the workforce also improves and the employees are always motivated to improve their skill set.

Performance appraisals are also a key source document for promoting the employees. The algorithmic performance appraisal evaluates each subordinate objectively and justly and only the most hardworking, competent, and devoted employee is selected for promotion and moving up the career ladder.

4.2. Benefits of AI Learning in Risk Assessment

Risk assessment has become a highly crucial activity for the general managers because the projects in the organizations incur significant costs. In the competitive world, the costs should be justified and risk mitigation strategies should also be developed by the management to keep the organization sustainable.

As highlighted in Figure 74, the risk assessment activities usually begin with the identification of risks in the internal and external environment. Then the risks are analyzed and their severity level are ascertained. In the final stage, strategies are developed for the management of these risks. A good AI-based system automates all these three processes of risk management. The net outcomes is the development of more relevant and efficient risk management strategies.

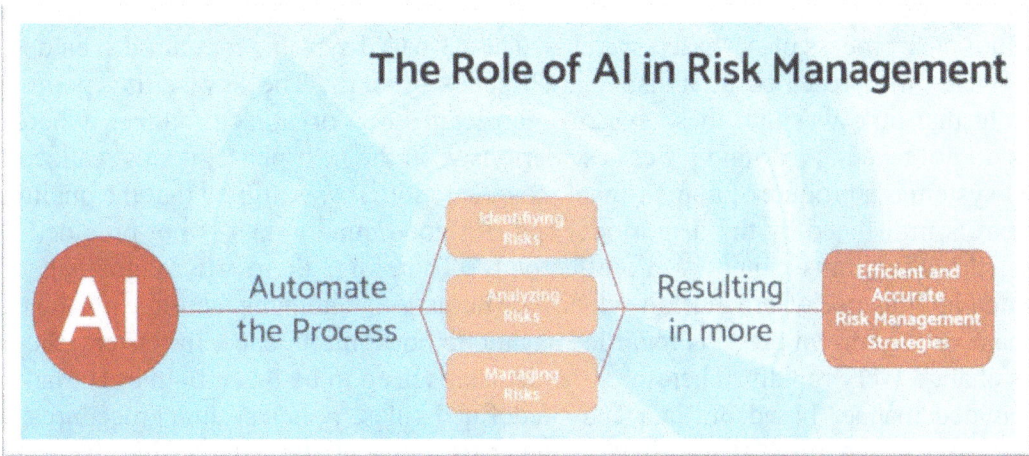

Figure 74: AI Based Risk Assessment[lxxiii]

Figure 75 shows an example of risk assessment using AI tools and how it can be successfully used for the assessment of underwriting. The accuracy level is improved because AI algorithms analyze huge datasets. The efficient AI algorithms process big data speedily and generate meaningful results. The systems provide the details of the most profitable market segments. The fraudulent claims are quickly identified based on the historical data. The system also offers personalized recommendations to the customers based on their needs. The overall cost of operation is reduced due to accuracy and protecting fraudulent claims.

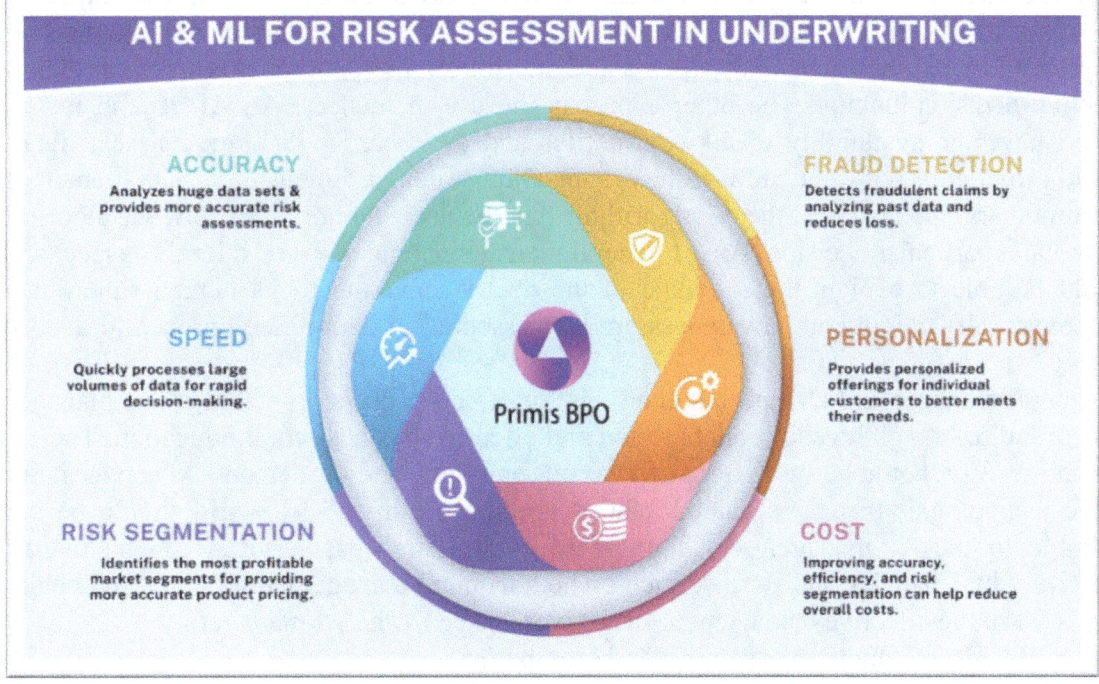

Figure 75: An Example AI Risk Assessment in Underwriting[lxxiv]

The algorithmic CEOs are also problem solvers and they can make an efficient utilization of the available budget. The algorithmic CEOs and workers will always be truthful because they do not have any fear of scrutiny or losing their jobs. The team performance can also be evaluated effectively by algorithmic CEOs.

AI general manager will also need some tools for effective decision-making. The managerial aspect requires a high level of collaboration and effective business communication. There, AI humanoid CEO should be supported with various emerging and on-demand AI services. Some of the technologies have gained a huge prominence in the AI world. The chat services can be managed effectively by ChatGPT and Bard services. The document management systems and chatbots also assist in the effective management of the workspace by the AI manager.

In order to understand the significance of data-driven decision-making, it is crucial to know the evolutionary process of AI-based systems. The AI-based systems for data-driven decision-making were first presented as assisted intelligence systems. The key selling point of the systems at that time was that these systems can learn in an organized manner, whereas the humans do not take the learning process so seriously. In the next phase, it was realized that a good AI system is a product of human-machine interaction. It was argued that the quality of an AI system is influenced by the data model and if a good quality data is not provided by the humans, the algorithms cannot work effectively. Therefore, there was a gradual shift to augmented intelligence where machines facilitate humans and humans facilitate machines. The third phase or the current phase is regarded as autonomous intelligence. In this era, the nature of tasks changes very rapidly. Therefore, the decisions need to be taken by the AI manager in an automated manner based on data and predefined rules, policies, and procedures of the organization. The machines should have a mechanism of a continued learning. It means that the AI CEO that the subordinates are interacting with today will not have the same responses in the future because it is a machine. Based on a continued learning, the responses and the behavioral disposition of the algorithmic CEO will also change.

It is argued in the management literature that the data-based decision-making is possible only if the decisions of the managers are based on seven key pillars. The first aspect is leadership. The decision-making process should provide leadership regarding the strategic directions of the organization. The second aspect is trust. The human managers as well as AI general manager can use the data only if it is trustworthy and is relied upon by all the stakeholders of the organization. If the quality of the data is very low, then the data-driven decision-making may prove to be counterproductive. The third aspect is the commitment level of the managers. They should keep their personal biases aside and follow the patterns and trends in data for effective decision-making. The other aspect is the use of metrics. An AI general manager should have the availability of all key metrics and dashboard indicators. These indicators should provide the real-time view of the organization. Another dimension is data literacy. It is a common argument against the AI algorithms that the users do not know how the algorithms arrived at a particular decision. An AI general manager should also consider this aspect and it should be able to explain the rationale of the decision-making to its human subordinates. Moreover, staff training and awareness are also essential in data-base approach to decision-making.

AI general manager will also need some tools for effective decision-making. The managerial aspect requires a high level of collaboration and effective business communication. There, AI humanoid CEO should be supported with various emerging and on-demand AI services. Some of the technologies that have gained a huge prominence in the AI world should be made available to the AI manager. As highlighted earlier, the chat services can be managed effectively by ChatGPT and Bard services. The document management systems and chatbots also assist in the effective management of the workspace by the AI manager.

4.3. Pitfalls of Machine Learning in Management

In the above sections, I have highlighted various benefits of AI learning for resource allocation, project management, and risk management. However, similar to other technological advancements, the use of machine learning in management may also be associated with various issues and problems. I am highlighting these issues so that you are more aware about all that AI has to offer and the associated pitfalls. I would still urge you to go for an AI general manager because in the overall analysis, the benefits still significantly outweigh the pitfalls.

As highlighted in Figure 76 below, the first drawback of using machine learning is the acquisition of data. The quality of AI data model is reliant on the quality of training data, and in many cases, acquiring the data may become a cumbersome activity. There may also be issues regarding the legitimate rights of accessing and using those datasets. If the dataset is limited, then AI algorithms will not give you the desired results because their key strength lies in big data processing and providing meaningful results based on the comprehensive analysis of data. The second drawback is the time and resources needed for AI implementation. Although the automation and quick processing will be achieved by using AI algorithms, these benefits will only be seen in the long run. In the short run, more time will be consumed in implementing the systems and training the workforce. In some organizations, there is a high employee turnover rate that further increases the time to learn.

The third drawback is to interpret the results produced by the AI algorithms. The algorithms process huge datasets before providing recommendations. A human general manager may find it difficult to know the rationale behind a specific recommendation. If the things do not go as expected, the human manager may struggle in justifying their moves.

The fourth drawback is the risk of error in the absence of data. There is no doubt that AI algorithms will provide accurate results when the relevant data is available. However, when the relevant data is not available, there is a general tendency of the algorithms to produce the results based on whatever is available to them. You might have observed it while using ChatGPT or Google Bard. If these chatbots do not have the relevant data, they still respond you with irrelevant and inaccurate results. It can become a serious limitation in the organizational context when the processes will have automated and there will be a huge reliance on the AI based systems.

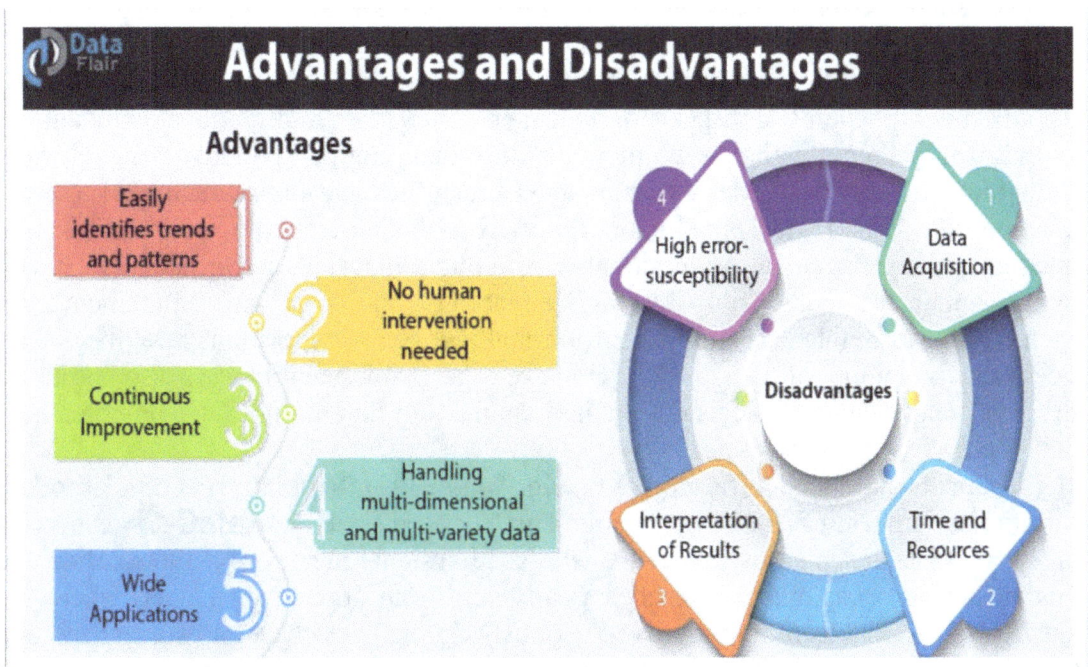

Figure 76: Drawback of using Machine Learning[lxxv]

Figure 77 highlights some more issues with machine learning in management. The organizations may face cost overruns because appointment an AI general manager and automating all tasks require a complete overhaul of the current IT infrastructure. The training of the remaining human workforce will also incur a significant cost. There is also limited capabilities of AI developers available in the IT industry that are particularly proficient in AI based implementations. There is also a great potential of misuse of the technology because as I mentioned earlier, the AI-based systems also suffer with the algorithmic bias. Moreover, the end users can manipulate the system by benefitting from the limited expertise of the senior management in using AI-based systems.

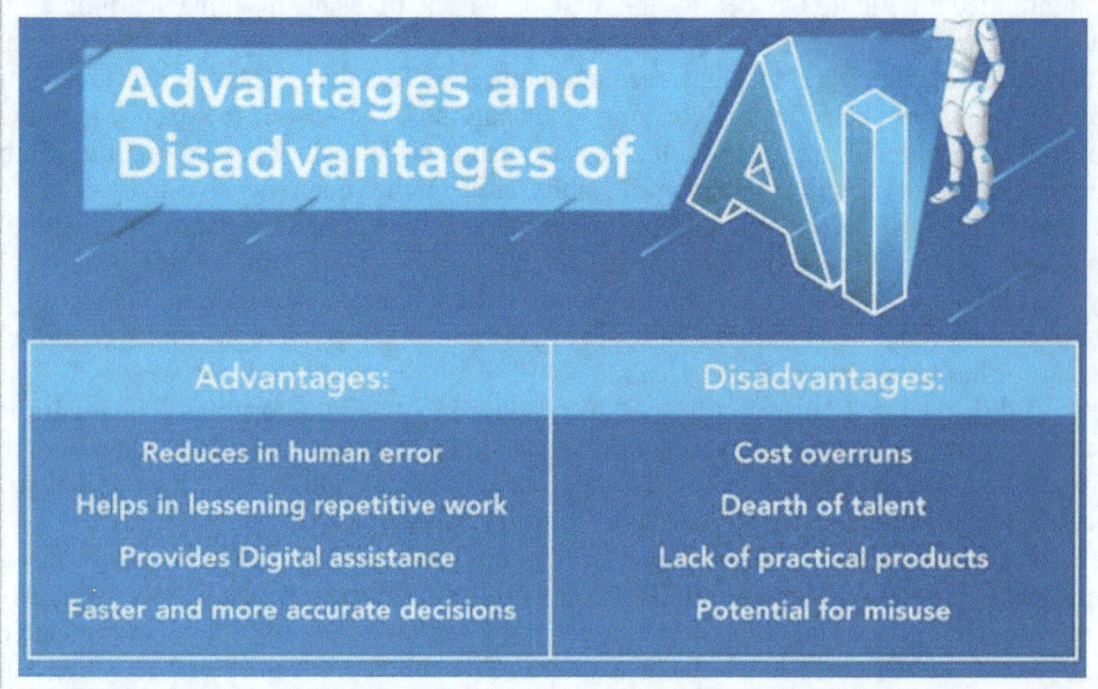

Figure 77: Disadvantages of Machine Learning[lxxvi]

The setup of a robotic organization is highly sophisticated and based on the state-of-the-art technologies. This is one area where the business entities will have to focus. They will need to review the requirements of their organizations and present a strong case to the senior management for implementing a robotic organization. In the absence of sufficient funds, it will be difficult to transform the organizational outlook.

The use of AI is influencing all aspects of a business entity. The multinational companies are fearful that if they do not embrace AI, they may lose their competitive advantage. However, the limited knowledge of the AI algorithms makes them hesitant in embracing AI at a mass scale. When there was a widespread adoption of AI tools and technologies in multinational organizations, the management professionals also thought that the AI concepts can be useful and significant in the managerial tasks as well because the emerging requirement of the management was to enable data-driven decision-making, and AI algorithms have the potential to process a huge amount of data quickly. However, the business entities are also not in favor that they do things where the decision-making is quick but they do not have any clue how a particular course of action was selected.

In order to understand the significance of data-driven decision-making, it is crucial to know the evolutionary process of AI-based systems. The AI-based systems for data-driven decision-making were first presented as assisted intelligence systems. The key selling point of the systems at that time was that these systems can learn in an organized manner, whereas the humans do not take the learning process so seriously. In the next phase, it was realized that a good AI system is a product of human-machine interaction. It was argued that the quality of an AI system is influenced by the data model and if a good quality data is not provided by the humans, the algorithms cannot work effectively. Therefore, there was a gradual shift to augmented intelligence where machines facilitate humans and humans facilitate machines. The third phase or the current phase is regarded as autonomous intelligence. In this era, the nature of tasks changes very rapidly. Therefore, the decisions need to be taken by the AI manager in an automated manner based on data and predefined rules, policies, and procedures of the organization. The machines should have a mechanism of a continued learning. It means that the AI CEO that the subordinates are interacting with today will not have the same responses in the future because it is a machine. Based on a continued learning, the responses and the behavioral disposition of the algorithmic CEO will also change.

There is a fear factor among employees that robots in the management domain will eat their jobs and they will become redundant. It is not going to be the case at least in the near future. There are some roles that can be performed efficiently by AI and there are also other roles that humans can perform even better than AI. It is these roles where the needs of humans will still be felt.

In the case of digital assistants, the training of these assistants will still be carried out by humans. The AI models will give specific and task-centered information. The generalization of this information and articulating the data to the organizational context will still be done by humans. The robots can code the knowledge into high-level and low-level processes. However, the handling of complex, exceptional tasks and social interactions will still be managed by humans. The analysis of AI-robots will be a quantitative analysis, however, qualitative analysis will still be carried out by humans. This qualitative analysis will indicate why a certain trend is developing and how the current roles and responsibilities of the management professionals can be modified.

It is not always the case that algorithms will outperform humans. There are also instances where human managers perform better than algorithms. One of these aspects is a better comprehension of the feelings. An algorithm will give a negative feedback to the employee without realizing the mental and emotional state of the employee. On the other hand, the humans will consider the environmental and contextual factors before issuing such remarks. The humans can also train other humans better than machines. An enabling work environment can also be ensured well by humans.

A key challenge in machine learning in management is the issue of security and privacy of the data. There is so much connectivity of the devices for the efficient working of AI algorithms. The data exposure might be without consent or a data breach from a single device may aggravate to a massive data breach. The skill set of professionals regarding the maintenance of AI systems is limited. Therefore, hackers can exploit this opportunity and compromise the sanctity and integrity of the data.

A challenge faced in AI based management is that employees are accustomed to interacting with other humans. They miss the human touch and socialization aspect in robotic environment. The environment becomes too mechanistic. The algorithmic CEOs assume that the receivers of their instructions are also robots and they will be able to follow each and every word of their instructions. The humans do not work that way and their rationality is always bounded by various constraints including the family constraints and technical constraints.

Another challenge is the lack of understanding of the potential impact of AI. If the management itself is not convinced that the AI based systems will transform the management landscape, then the AI based interventions will always be a distant dream.

Another challenge faced in the organizational setting is that as soon as the AI based implementation is announced, employees fear losing their jobs. The tasks for which they had established the timelines of two to three days can be done by robots in two to three hours. So, they anticipate that they will soon become redundant.

Another key challenge is that an algorithmic CEO may select a candidate for the job that is highly competitive. However, the candidate may not fit well to the current organizational setting. These aspects can best be judged by humans because it constitutes a dynamic reality and has an element of subjectivity.

The AI-based management has also raised ethical concerns because of the intrusive nature of the AI algorithms. The AI algorithms process a large amount of data for making an efficient AI model. The development of the data model may access those data sets for which explicit information has not been provided. The quality of algorithms gets improved but the question arises whether legitimate means have been used for improving the efficiency of algorithms. It is argued that AI has invaded all aspects of the humanity. In the absence of a standard regulatory framework, the fate of the AI-based systems is left to the integrity of the AI developers. As I explained earlier, it usually creates an algorithmic bias.

An algorithmic boss can be a real blessing for an organization if the implementation considers several key aspects and a formal strategy are developed for the transformation process. In the strategy phase, you will need to determine to what extent, the algorithmic management is needed in your organization. In the next step, you should develop a change management process. In this stage, you will have to train the existing staff for using algorithms instead of manual interventions. The management should still make the communication lines open because the change will be successful through an evolutionary process. Once the algorithmic management is in place, the management should constantly evaluate the management flow of the algorithms so that the algorithmic decision-making is not influenced by the algorithmic biases.

Chapter 5

The CEO Algorithm
AI becoming the Executive Branch

In order to gain a good understanding of the CEO algorithm and making AI the executive branch of the organization, let's first evaluate how the organizations have so far implemented humanoid robo CEOs.

The first AI boss was developed by Hitachi Company. It was introduced in 2015 that shows that the technology and management professionals were exploring the possibility of AI in management for quite long. They wanted more accuracy and objectivity in the decision-making process and provide more freedom of expression to the subordinates.

Robo-CEO is an algorithmic CEO that selects the most suitable candidate based on the available data. Unlike traditional CEO, the employee is most likely to move up the career ladder due to the objective decision-making of the algorithmic CEO.

AI bosses are not limited to the human resource function and they are also being used in other management and business functions. There is also an implementation where the algorithmic managers have been used for an effective wealth management.

There is a successful implementation by a firm in which AI manager was used for talent acquisition and talent management. This robot was given the responsibility of managing a $100 billion firm. The entire human resources of the company will be handled by the algorithmic CEO. The company aims to replace more and more humans with robots in key leadership positions.

Recruitment was one of the first HR functions where the algorithms were introduced in the form of a robot recruiter. The robots have been highly successful in conducting interviews and candidates express them comfortably in front of a robot. The responses are also processed efficiently by the robots and the same processing strategy is applied for all candidates.

With the growth of the automated screening process, the job candidates should also update their CVs so that the robots do not discard their resumes. The traditional CVs might not be considered worthy by the robots.

Performance appraisals are also a key source document for promoting the employees. The algorithmic performance appraisal evaluates each subordinate objectively and justly and only the most hardworking, competent, and devoted employee is selected for promotion and moving up the career ladder.

There is also an implementation of an algorithmic CEO that was tested in a Hong Kong based company. The boss is named Tang Yu and she is the CEO of mobile and gaming company. The model proved highly successful in the organization and there was a marked improvement in the speed of execution and the quality of work. The company where this model was successfully tested is NetDragon.

In the current context, a robot CEO was appointed by a Chinese firm NetDragon. The robot CEO was appointed with the intent that the process flow of the business entity will be streamlined and the speed of task execution will improve substantially.

Mika became the CEO of a Drinks Company. She promised the availability of 24/7 for their subordinates and told them that there would not be any layoffs in the company. She performs the tasks of identifying the potential customers and the artists for the new and innovative designs of the bottles.

A robot was developed by a Japanese company and this robot is planned to be deployed for managing the manufacturing operations in Japan. It has been developed by Ryo Yoshida, who himself is a CEO of a Japanese company.

In a landmark event at telecommunication conference, there was also a press talk of robots.

The robots emphasized in this press conference that humans should not fear losing their jobs due to robots. Moreover, they do not have any plans to rebel against humans.

All these success stories indicate that AI has a significant role in improve the managerial aspects of an organization. AI systems can become a CEO of the organization. In the other cases, the robots can assist the general managers and make them more productive and working smartly.

A landmark achievement was observed in 2016, when chatbots assistant were introduced. A chatbot assistant such as a WhatsApp chatbot remembers the solutions of the frequently asked questions by the clients. The queries are then responded by the chatbot in an automated manner without any intervention by the human. The beauty of this chatbot was that the support services became highly effective and were made available 24/7. Moreover, the accuracy of the responses was phenomenal because the responses are generated based on the processing of a large dataset. However, the users of the technology are also much aware of the potential and limitations of the technology. They know that they are talking to a chatbot that might give them general purpose answer but may not answer their specific queries and concerns. Even at the level of call centers, if the caller has the option of using automated menu options or calling to an operator, many callers would prefer calling to an operator because it provides a human touch and a personalized interaction. The beauty of human interaction is one area where the robots will never be able to beat the humans. It is a human nature that the people treat everyone differently. People develop a perception regarding the personality preferences of an individual and respond to their queries accordingly. On the other hand, a chatbot assistant will treat all human equally. The difference in responses based on the information and assistance needs of the individual is still beyond the capabilities of a chatbot. Some of the plagiarism checking websites such as turnitin can also detect if a given piece of text was written by a human or a chatbot. This capability makes it evident that the behavioral styles of a machine and a human are entirely different and a machine can never write with a human touch.

The use of AI in management is not a new phenomenon and some level of implementation was observed even as early as 1983. At that time, the database management tools such as oracle were used to process large amount of data and general intelligent reports and dashboard indicators. But the AI of today has found much more usage of the technology and this book takes one next step to highlight the benefits of an algorithmic CEO.

The current era is characterized by the management solutions where the machine learning technologies are used for an effective project management. In fact, the project management was the first area where the significance of an AI general manager was acknowledged. The next era is of autonomous AI where the management functions will be performed autonomously by robots. It is this era where the focus of the book is, i.e. how a general manager, which is an AI robot, can be appointed that could perform all the management roles and the performance is far superior to a human manager. The book argues that there is a huge significance of appointing an algorithmic CEO. However, it should be a hybrid model and the intent of the business managers should not be to replace humans.

In an AI-powered organization, you might see that the robots have taken control for almost all of the organization. They are performing routine tasks, management tasks, as well as surveillance tasks. The tasks are being executed in a robotic manner with an amazing level of accuracy. The queries will be responded promptly that will result in a happy customer and higher customer conversions. This task efficiency should be an ultimate goal of the organization and the human interface should still be used in conjunction with the robotic environment.

Another aspect that you may appreciate in the current model is that the setup of a robotic organization is highly sophisticated and based on the state-of-the-art technologies. This is one area where the business entities will have to focus. They will need to review the requirements of their organizations and present a strong case to the senior management for implementing a robotic organization. In the absence of sufficient funds, it will be difficult to transform the organizational outlook. The development of a robot CEO or an industrial CEO should not only be seen in the context of the development cost but also in the context of the running cost or the operation cost. The running cost involves the power consumption cost, downtime cost, and maintenance cost.

Another aspect that you might also notice is that robots appear to be ready for responding to the events. It is possible in an AI-based organization when the AI general manager has all the required data available and the quality of data is extremely good. For example, if there is not required number of CVs received, the shortlisting and interviewing process will suffer despite the availability of robot recruiters. It is a major challenge in the AI-based systems that the algorithms are data-driven. If the supplied data is of poor quality, no AI algorithm can give you good quality results.

The quality of a successful AI model is driven by both the training data and the new input data. If all the efforts are aimed at developing a successful algorithm, the required results may still not be achieved due to the poor quality of the data.

The need for an AI general manager has emerged due to multiple factors. There is more and more government ownership and encouragement for implementing AI tools and technologies. The employees can also be held more responsible for their work by facilitating them with AI tools and technologies. The AI concepts have successfully been used in developing the management solutions. The organizations also have a pressure from the competitors because if they become early adopters of AI, the organizations may lose their competitive advantage. The first AI boss was developed by Hitachi Company. It was introduced in 2015 that shows that the technology and management professionals were exploring the possibility of AI in management for quite long. They wanted more accuracy and objectivity in the decision-making process and provide more freedom of expression to the subordinates.

The robot CEO is appointed with the intent that the process flow of the business entity will be streamlined and the speed of task execution will improve substantially. However, at the implementation level, various challenges were also observed by the company. The employees tended to be always connected in the metaverse and the physical activity during the working hours reduced significantly. There was a reduced level of socialization because the CEO always got connected through Zoom calls. With this implementation, it emerged that the robot CEOs may increase the anxiety levels and depersonalization effect.

The robot CEO of Drinks Company in Poland that was experimented in November 2023. The CEO performed efficiently the tasks of project management, marketing, sales, and strategic management. From the lifecycle development, you will have noticed that the performance of AI-based systems significantly depend on two factors. The first is the quality and accuracy of the AI model. If the rules and feature extraction processes in AI algorithms are biased because the AI developer is convinced with a certain style of management, then the quality of the whole AI-based system will suffer. Another important factor is the quality of data. If the training examples in the dataset favor a certain segment of the population, then the AI model will learn wrong rules that will affect the algorithmic decision-making. Due to these limitations of the AI algorithms, professionals working in AI always prefer narrow AI over general AI.

There are benefits of using narrow AI for management-based AI algorithms. This technology has a binding to a specific task. The technology is based on fixed-domain models. It might come as a limitation for some general managers because the general-AI has a self-learning process and the system developed in general-AI today will have a far optimized version in the next 6 months based on self-learning. Another benefit of narrow AI is that the learning mechanism is based on a large number of examples and therefore, the concept development in the AI model is very strong. A limitation of narrow AI is that the system is reflexive instead of using cognitive abilities. In the above figure, the general AI has been designation as the future of the AI because the knowledge can be transferred to other domains. It is a highly significant feature particularly when the AI-based concepts are using in conjunction with an IoT environment.

AI general manager can also conduct performance appraisal effectively. Employees always have reservations and complaints that their efforts are not compensated adequately and the appraisals are always biased to the likes of the supervisor. Due to this reason, the management literature also suggests 360 degree feedback in addition to the straight line method of appraisal. There are numerous benefits of performance appraisals when conducted by robots. The risks of human errors are eliminated. The projects and training assessments are data-driven. A better level of employee engagement can be expected. However, the performance reviews by the robots gather too much information from the connected devices that the employees may find intrusive.

Performance appraisals are also a key source document for promoting the employees. The algorithmic performance appraisal evaluates each subordinate objectively and justly and only the most hardworking, competent, and devoted employee is selected for promotion and moving up the career ladder. The AI managers will make an impression in the organizations when their performances significantly outperform the human managers. Several successful implementations have been made in this regard so far.

If we visualize the blue-print of an AI-powered organization, we can see that the robots have taken control for almost all of the organization. They are performing routine tasks, management tasks, as well as surveillance tasks. The tasks are being executed in a robotic manner with an amazing level of accuracy. The queries will be responded promptly that will result in a happy customer and higher customer conversions.

Another aspect that you may appreciate in the current model is that the setup of a robotic organization is highly sophisticated and based on the state-of-the-art technologies. This is one area where the business entities will have to focus. They will need to review the requirements of their organizations and present a strong case to the senior management for implementing a robotic organization. In the absence of sufficient funds, it will be difficult to transform the organizational outlook.

Another aspect that you might also notice is that robots appear to be ready for responding to the events. It is possible in an AI-based organization when the AI general manager has all the required data available and the quality of data is extremely good. For example, if there is not required number of CVs received, the shortlisting and interviewing process will suffer despite the availability of robot recruiters.

The need for an AI general manager has emerged due to multiple factors. There is more and more government ownership and encouragement for implementing AI tools and technologies. The employees can also be held more responsible for their work by facilitating them with AI tools and technologies. The AI concepts have successfully been used in development the management solutions. The organizations also have a pressure from the competitors because if they become early adopters of AI, the organizations may lose their competitive advantage.

The most important benefit of an algorithmic CEO is the provision of an unbiased information. The CEO never controls or filters the information. This advantage was endorsed by the maximum number of managers (36%). The algorithms are also highly efficient in maintaining work schedules. The performance of humans is influenced by external factors as well such as family issues or illnesses. However, the algorithmic workers are always available for the task execution as long as the required IT infrastructure is available and connected.

The challenge faced in AI based management is that employees are accustomed to interacting with other humans. They miss the human touch and socialization aspect in robotic environment. The environment becomes too mechanistic. The second challenge is the issue of security and privacy of the data. There is so much connectivity of the devices for the efficient working of AI algorithms. The data exposure might be without consent or a data breach from a single device may aggravate to a massive data breach. Another challenge faced in the organizational setting is that as soon as the AI based implementation is announced, employees fear losing their jobs. Another challenge is the lack of understanding of the potential impact of AI. If the management itself is not convinced that the AI based systems will transform the management landscape, then the AI based interventions will always be a distant dream. An algorithmic CEO may select a candidate for the job that is highly competitive. However, the candidate may not fit well to the current organizational setting. These aspects can best be judged by humans because it constitutes a dynamic reality and has an element of subjectivity.

The AI-based management has also raised concerns because of the intrusive nature of the AI algorithms. As I explained earlier, the AI algorithms process a large amount of data for making an efficient AI model. The development of the data model may access those data sets for which explicit information has not been provided. The quality of algorithms gets improved but the question arises whether legitimate means have been used for improving the efficiency of algorithms.

AI has invaded all aspects of the humanity. In the absence of a standard regulatory framework, the fate of the AI-based systems is left to the integrity of the AI developers. As I explained earlier, it usually creates an algorithmic bias.

An algorithmic boss can be a real blessing for an organization if the implementation considers several key aspects and a formal strategy are developed for the transformation process. In the strategy phase, you will need to determine to what extent, the algorithmic management is needed in your organization. In the next step, you should develop a change management process. In this stage, you will have to train the existing staff for using algorithms instead of manual interventions. The management should still make the communication lines open because the change will be successful through an evolutionary process. Once the algorithmic management is in place, the management should constantly evaluate the management flow of the algorithms so that the algorithmic decision-making is not influenced by the algorithmic biases.

In the future, AI-based organizations, one may expect that the CEO is an algorithmic CEO and all key leadership positions are occupied by robots. Humans have been assigned only to the operational work, and the technology-driven aspect of the organization has been endorsed at the level of the organization chart. AI bosses are not limited to the human resource function and they are also being used in other management and business functions. There is also an implementation where the algorithmic managers have been used for an effective wealth management.

In order to understand the potential biases in AI algorithms, it is crucial to understand the complete lifecycle of AI algorithms. The lifecycle begins with the definition of a business problem. Then the relevant datasets are acquired and prepared in a consistent format. The next step is the development and training of an AI model. The quality of the AI model is continuously evaluated and refined based on new data and requirements. The system is deployed when the AI model has a sufficient level of maturity. Then machine learning operations are put into place.

From the lifecycle development, you will have noticed that the performance of AI-based systems significantly depend on two factors. The first is the quality and accuracy of the AI model. If the rules and feature extraction processes in AI algorithms are biased because the AI developer is convinced with a certain style of management, then the quality of the whole AI-based system will suffer. Another important factor is the quality of data. If the training examples in the dataset favor a certain segment of the population, then the AI model will learn wrong rules that will affect the algorithmic decision-making. This also applies to the CEO algorithm. An AI boss can be efficient only to the extent if the quality of the supplied data or the training set is good and all the technological resources are available to the AI boss for processing big data.

It should also be noted that that the risk of algorithmic bias is higher in supervised learning because the learning process is at the discretion of the AI developer. Moreover, when negative reinforcers are identified in reinforcement learning, it is based on how the negativity is defined in the system by the AI developer that creates an algorithmic bias.

Humans are generally more influenced by technology and they believe that the human biases will be overcome by the use of technology. However, the technology generates a new form of bias known as an algorithmic bias. These biases can be found in the algorithms as well as how the data is acquired for the training of these algorithms. The AI implementation forms a cycle, which is world, data, design, and use. If the AI developers are not the men of integrity, this cycle can become a vicious cycle.

5. AI Performing Executive Roles

The ultimate AI-based implementation can be achieved in an organization when an algorithmic CEO takes charge of the organization. In the other cases, the robots may be appointed for assisting the general manager as shown in Figure 78 below. It will also prove to be a good strategy because the robots in the execute roles will keep the manager focused and committed. The robot will also remind them about the meeting and the tasks that are to be submitted shortly. It will ensure that the manager executes all the tasks happily and never miss a task. The managers often struggle in multitasking. However, the robots will show them the best course of action and at any given point in time, the general managers will also perform the most relevant task in the organization.

Figure 78: AI Robot assisting the General Manager[lxxvii]

Figure 79 mentions another benefit of AI performing executive roles. The humans have limited capacities of working and they easily get tired when there are stretched timings or work overload. On the contrary, the robots can work stress-free throughout the day and they can also be made available 24/7. They work as per instructions without any demand of reward and compensation. They are also honest and candid in their responses because they do not have any job insecurity or personal motives.

Figure 79: Stress-Free, Always Available Robot[lxxviii]

5.1. AI CEO and the Organizational Structure

The organization of future will be a mix of human workers and robots. You might feel more comfortable reporting to a robot than a human. It is because the human decision-making is often influenced by biases and prejudices. There are complaints of favoritism and partially in every other organization. On the other hand, a robot CEO is highly objective and focused. It is available 24/7, never sleeps, and never gets ill. Despite the presence of an AI manager, there are still various tasks for which human presence will be needed in the organization.

If humans have biases, then AI-based algorithms are also influenced by algorithms biases of the AI developers. When AI-based systems perform the conventional tasks of humans, they provide more opportunity to the coworkers to focus more on strategic and managerial level tasks. If recruitment and performance appraisal are carried out by algorithms, the HR managers will have the options to utilize the workforce in field visits, market analysis, and finding strategies of gaining a competitive advantage. The workers can also focus on sustainability issues and implementing green human resources strategies. Think of the tools such as ChatGPT and Google Bard. The job of the programmers is not gone. These tools can generate the code but the code still needs to be consolidated and deployed, which can only be done by a professional computer programmer. Therefore, an AI general manager will ease the task of the employees and make them more productive and useful in the organizational context.

There are some roles that can be performed efficiently by AI and there are also other roles that humans can perform even better than AI. It is these roles where the needs of humans will still be felt. In the case of digital assistants, the training of these assistants will still be carried out by humans. The analysis of AI-robots will be a quantitative analysis, however, qualitative analysis will still be carried out by humans. This qualitative analysis will indicate why a certain trend is developing and how the current roles and responsibilities of the management professionals can be modified.

There are still some jobs where humans can demonstrate more impressive performance than AI robots. Humans are well-versed in critical thinking. For humans, everything is not just right and wrong. They also evaluate the grey areas and acknowledge the dynamic reality of the phenomenon. Humans can also become strategic thinkers through their visionary approach, whereas robots can only learn based on the available datasets. In creative jobs, humans can perform well. Drama and video scripts are being written by AI, but how about poetry. There will be only a few (if any) examples where a high-level creative, poetry work could be produced by a robot. The humans also show more empathy in the communication process and they may overlook the shortcomings of an employee based on the contextual, environmental, and personality factors. However, an AI general manager will be very objective in the communication. The good performances will be appreciated, but there will also be immediate and prompt feedback on the bad performance that may not be liked by those employees who are very sensitive and short-tempered.

Another aspect is the physical skills and the evaluation of the physical skills. An AI general manager might struggle in a factory setting where physical labor work is required. The robots could prove to be highly expensive in these tasks, and it might not be possible for them to evaluate the performance of the workers involved in the physical labor. Robots are being used in warehouses for the proper and efficient maintenance of the inventory. However, consider the construction sector. The robots will find it difficult to do the labor-intensive task in the construction sector. Therefore, physical skills is one area where humans still dominate the robots.

When the concept of AI general manager or AI CEO is implemented in the organizations, there will always be a need to create an organizational structure, which is a mix of both humans and robots. In the future, one might see an organizational chart where the humans and robots are working together. In this context, the AI CEO will also need to consider the human-robot interaction and ensure that it is executed in a smooth manner and humans are satisfied and comfortable working with robots.

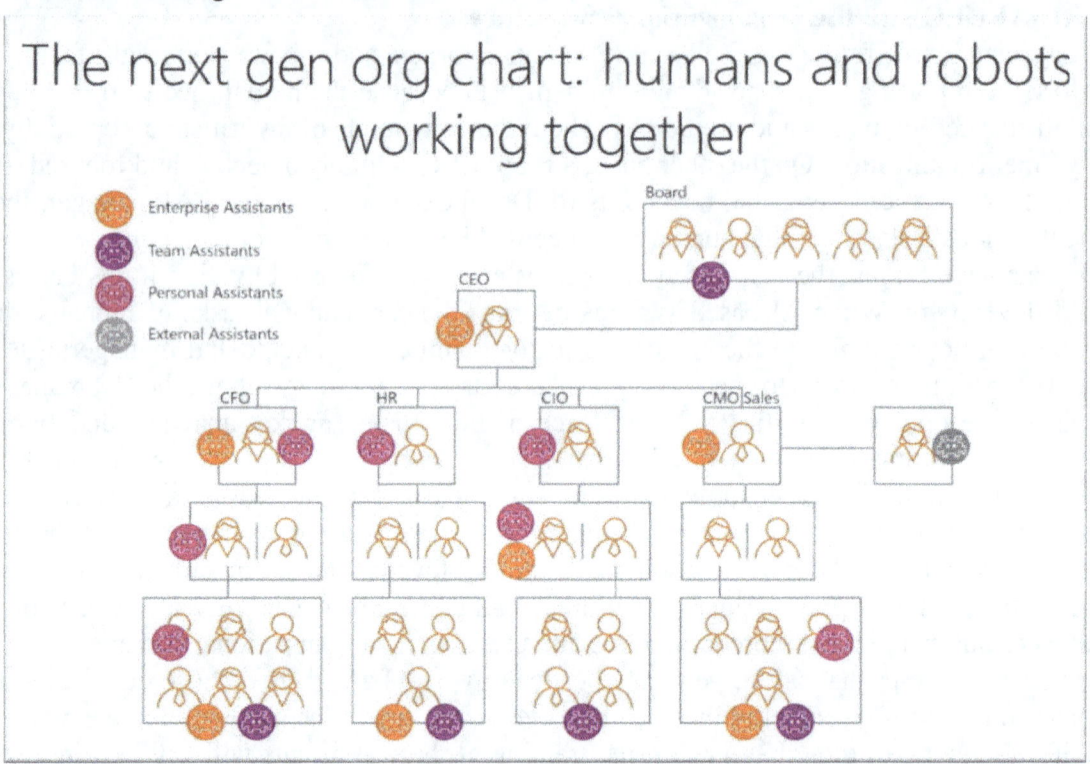

Figure 80: A Mix of Robot and Human Employees[lxxix]

Figure 81 shows an implementation in the healthcare setting in which the healthcare units are being managed by robotics. The robotics manages the social as well as the physical HRI departments. Social HRI is responsible for effective communication and coordination. Physical HRI is responsible for tele-operation and wearable systems. This example shows a full-scale implementation in which a subset of the healthcare facilities is entirely managed by the AI-based systems.

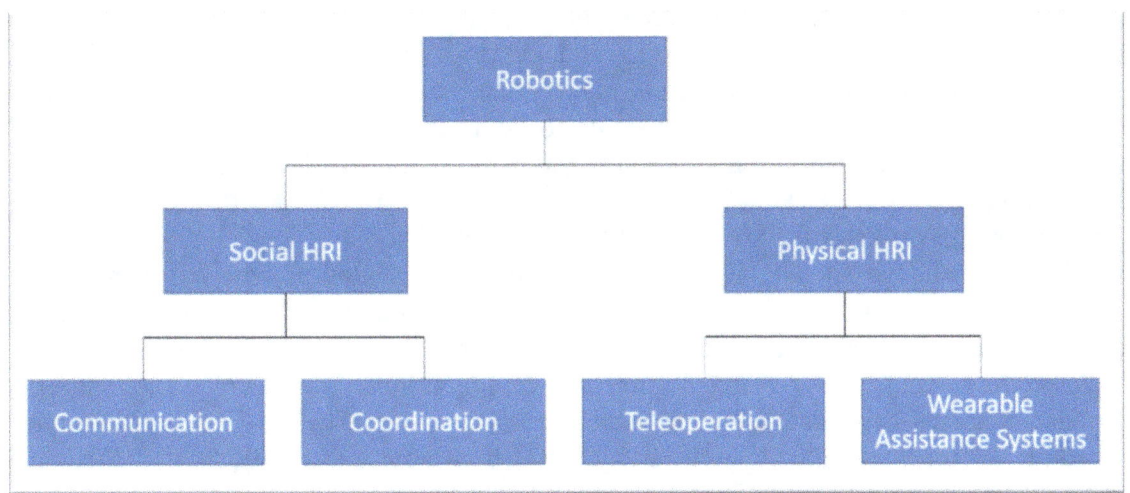

Figure 81: Robotics Organization Chart in Healthcare[lxxx]

5.2. Perception of Employees regarding AI CEO

The organizations are expected to receive mixed responses when they introduce AI CEO in their environments. Also, within the organization, the comfort level of the employees with the AI robots will vary significantly. The most important benefit of an algorithmic CEO is the provision of an unbiased information. The CEO never controls or filters the information. The algorithms are also highly efficient in maintaining work schedules. The performance of humans is influenced by external factors as well such as family issues or illnesses. However, the algorithmic workers are always available for the task execution as long as the required IT infrastructure is available and connected.

The algorithmic CEOs are also problem solvers and they can make an efficient utilization of the available budget. The algorithmic CEOs and workers will always be truthful because they do not have any fear of scrutiny or losing their jobs. The team performance can also be evaluated effectively by algorithmic CEOs.

Employees, however, have reported that the human CEOs have a better comprehension of the feelings. An algorithm will give a negative feedback to the employee without realizing the mental and emotional state of the employee. On the other hand, the humans will consider the environmental and contextual factors before issuing such remarks. The humans can also train other humans better than machines. An enabling work environment can also be ensured well by humans.

The real the benefits of AI in management can be seen by the mapping of AI technologies and the management support. The algorithmic managers are powered by machine learning technologies, neural networks, data mining, big data science, and business intelligence. All these AI-based concepts can provide immense support to the management. The benefits can be seen in the optimized decision-making and accurate decision-making. The benefit can also be observed in the improved functionality of the organization. The tasks such as recruitment, performance appraisal, wealth management, and supply chain management can all be automated.

Robo-CEO is an algorithmic CEO that selects the most suitable candidate based on the available data. Unlike traditional CEO, the employee is most likely to move up the career ladder due to the objective decision-making of the algorithmic CEO.

Despite the promising outcomes of an AI general manager, there are still only a few successful case studies of an algorithmic CEO. This raises the question why organizations are reluctant to make the optimum utilization of the AI. It is because the employees are fearful of losing their jobs due to a high level of automation. There are problems and difficulties in the business processes due to which the employees have been hired. If all these issues are resolved by the AI manager in an automated fashion, all these employees will become redundant.

A key benefit of an algorithmic CEO that employees are reporting happily to them. They know that the behavior of the boss will be unbiased and the interaction will be limited to the assigned job responsibilities. There will be no favors and additional tasks asked by the boss. Moreover, the working day end within the working hour and there will be no stretched timings and late duties. The future organizations are expected to be a nice blend of AI workers and human workers. It will also affect how the organograms will be presented and reported in different statutory reports.

5.3. How to Prepare Employees for AI-based Transition

The biggest challenge for an AI general manager implementation will be to prepare the employees for the algorithmic transition. As I have explained earlier, the employees all over the world are highly fearful that the AI-based implementations will automate the tasks for which they have been hired. As a result, they may lose their jobs. Their fears are not unfounded and these concerns have also been endorsed and acknowledged by IMF in its recent report. According to a recent report[lxxxi] published by IMF, AI will make a significant influence on the global job market and approximately 40% of the jobs may be affected by AI-based implementations in different organizations. Therefore, organizations need to evaluate the pros and cons of AI-based implementations and manage effectively the motivation and morale of the employees.[lxxxii] The growing AI exposure in different countries and regions have been illustrated by IMF as shown in Figure 82 below. The figure indicates that the share of AI is higher in advanced economies and emerging markets. It is because there is a high cost associated with developing an IT infrastructure for AI implementations.

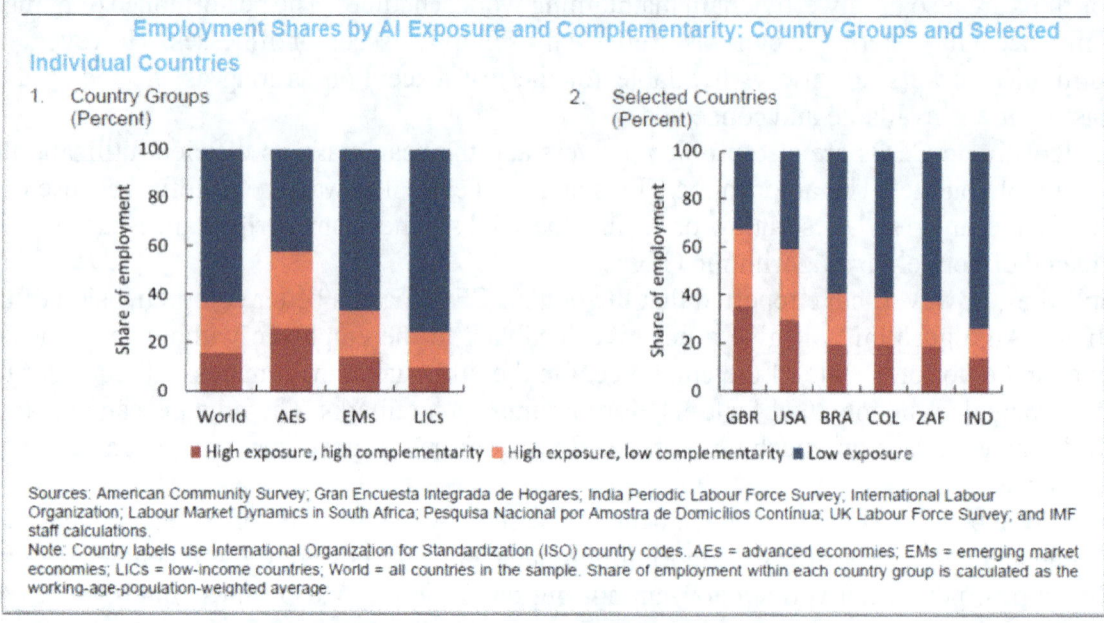

Figure 82: AI-Based Employment Share[lxxxiii]

Figure 83 highlights another prediction of IMF that the implementation of AI will influence professional and managerial positions higher than elementary occupations. Therefore, there is another type of preparation needed for the AI-based transitions. The senior management and leaders will be required to train for AI-based implementations. The current book also presents the case of an AI general manager that will manage the overall structure of the whole organization. Therefore, senior managers should get them updated as to how they will cope with the new challenges and emerging realities of the management and organizational behavior.

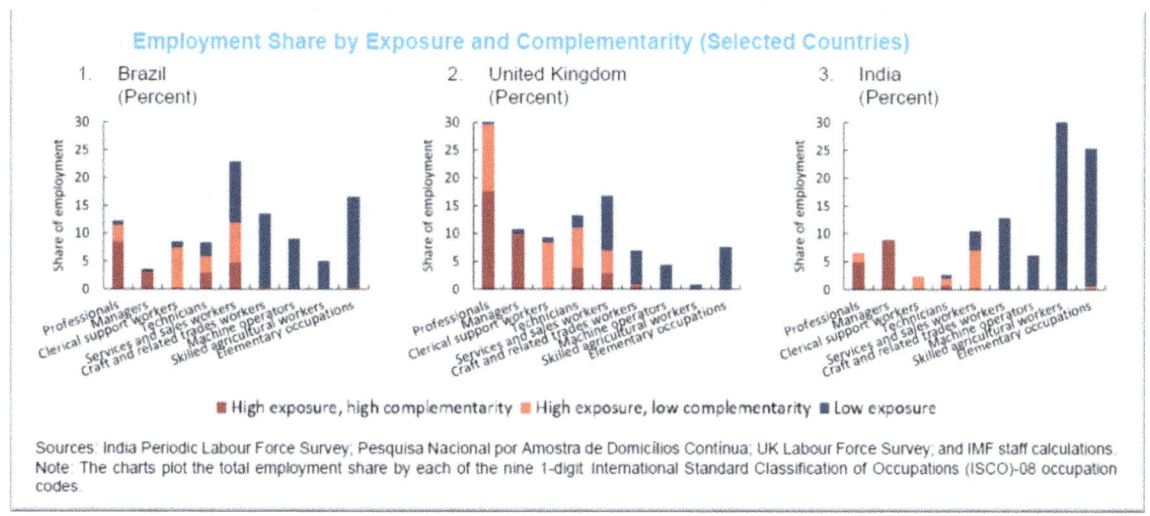

Figure 83: AI Exposure based on Employment Types[lxxxiv]

Figure 84 indicates some interesting facts based on the demographic variables. The AI-based implementations will influence female employees more than males. Similarly, more qualified individuals are more prone to losing their jobs based on AI implementations because AI algorithms are targeting to solve the complex tasks of the organization. In terms of age group, the AI exposure will be observed more in the age bracket of 45 years and more.

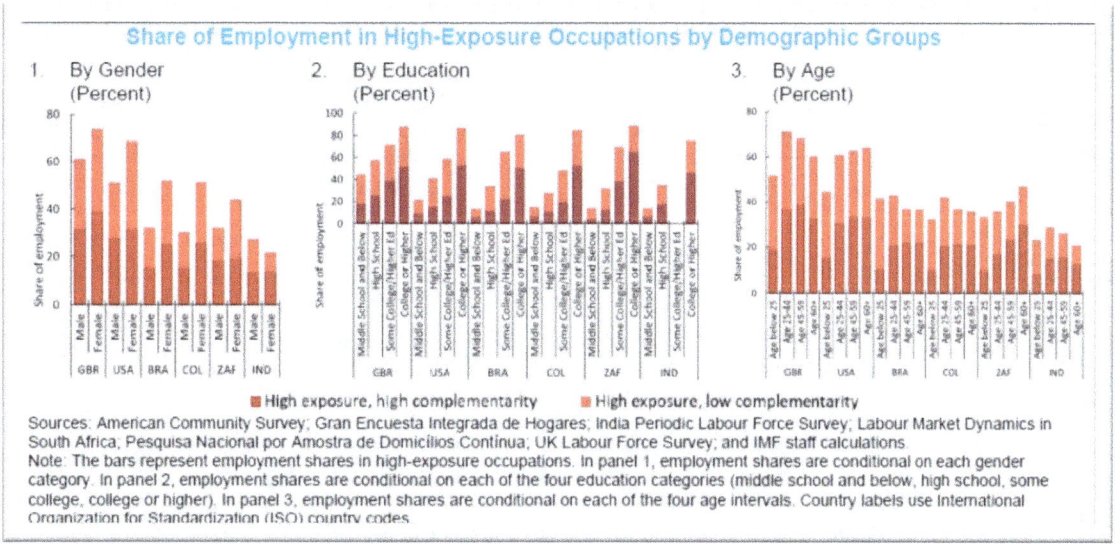

Figure 84: AI-based Exposure based on Demographic Variables[lxxxv]

Figure 85 shows that that AI-based exposure will influence employees of all income groups. There is even a higher impact with the increase in the earnings. It may become a serious concern for the employees because they may struggle in finding the same job with that level of compensation package if the AI-based implementations may result in losing their jobs. It may also create resentment among them and they may not cooperate with the owners in implementing the AI-based systems and robot employees

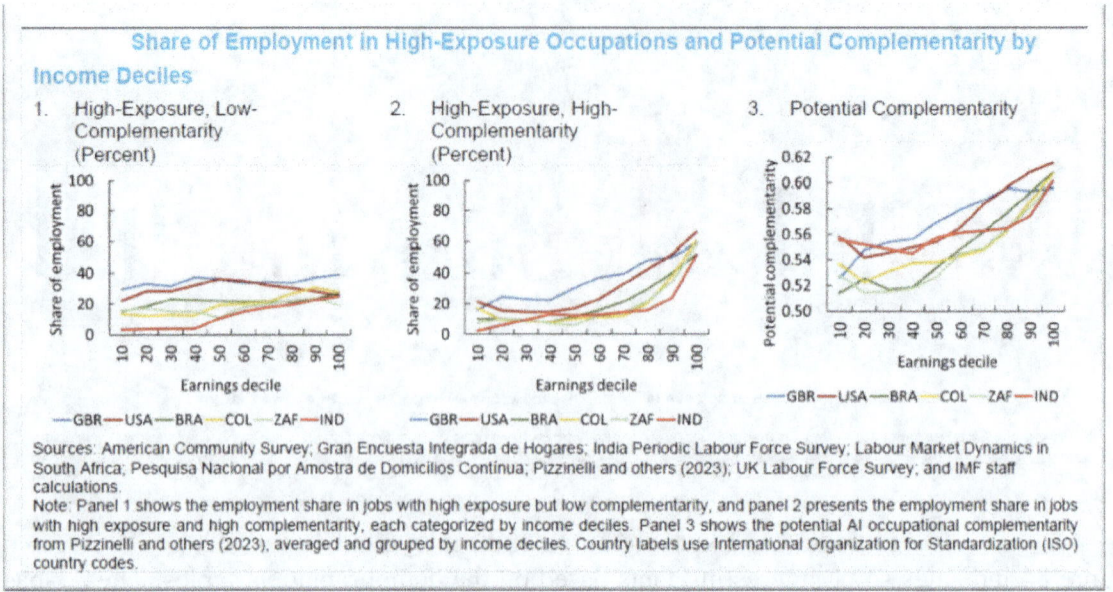

Figure 85: AI-Based Exposure based on Employees' Earnings[lxxxvi]

The IMF report also mentioned the preparedness level of the employees and the business entities from different dimensions. As shown in Figure 86 below, in all the cases of digital infrastructure, human resource policies, innovation, and ethical dimensions, advanced economies have made a considerable progress. On the other hand, there is a reduced level of interest in lower income countries and a moderate level of interest in emerging economies.

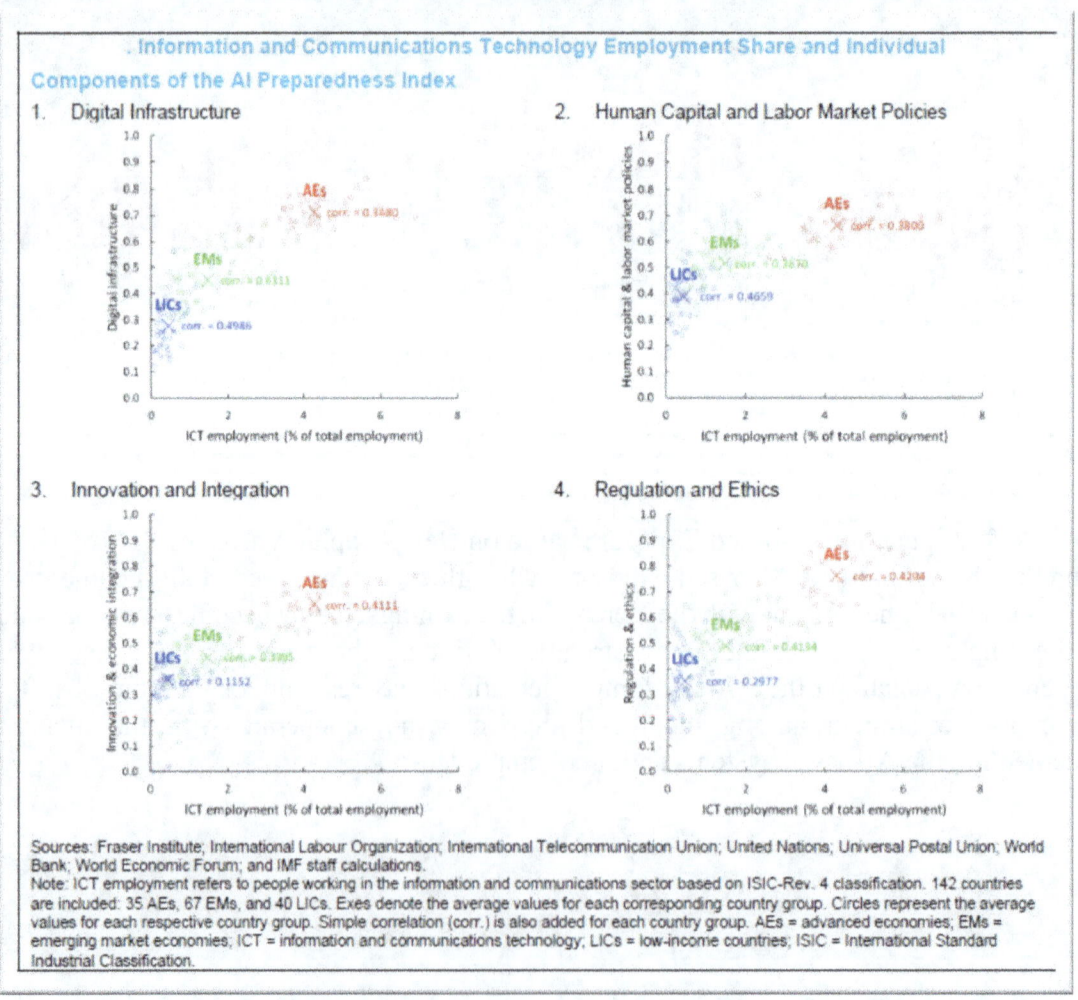

Figure 86: Preparedness Level for AI Implementations[lxxxvii]

From the above insights provided in the IMF report, it becomes evident that preparing employees for AI-based transition is a highly complex task. These implementations will affect the managerial positions and higher income groups more than the junior employees. Moreover, the employees might not cooperate in the implementation in the fear that these implementations are challenging their very existence in the organization.

Considering these factors, the owners and directors of the organizations should make a careful analysis of the whole situation and create a win-win situation in the organization. They should find ways of engaging the employees in more strategic tasks to improve the productivity of the organization. They should also make the employees realize that the sustainability of the organization will be at stake if the organization does not embrace AI. If the competitors become the early adopters, the organization may lose its competitive advantage. The employees should also be made to realize the significance of learning AI tools and technologies. Working with an AI general manager will be a significant boost on their CVs and their skills of working efficiently with machines will be highly valued and regarded in the AI-based world of today and tomorrow.

5.4. Implications for Organizational Structures and Decision-Making Processes

The organizational managers and CEOs might be looking at the AI implementation with a sense of fear and reservation. The world leaders recently gathered in the meeting of the World Economic Forum where AI implementation was the key theme of the meeting. The leaders from the key technology organizations used this opportunity to remove the concerns and fears regarding AI implementation. Here I am presenting the thoughts of some of these leaders as to how they see the future landscape of AI in the domain of management.

Open AI CEO acknowledged the concerns shown by the users of AI-based systems. However, he was positive and highly confident about the future of AI as mentioned in Figure 87 below:

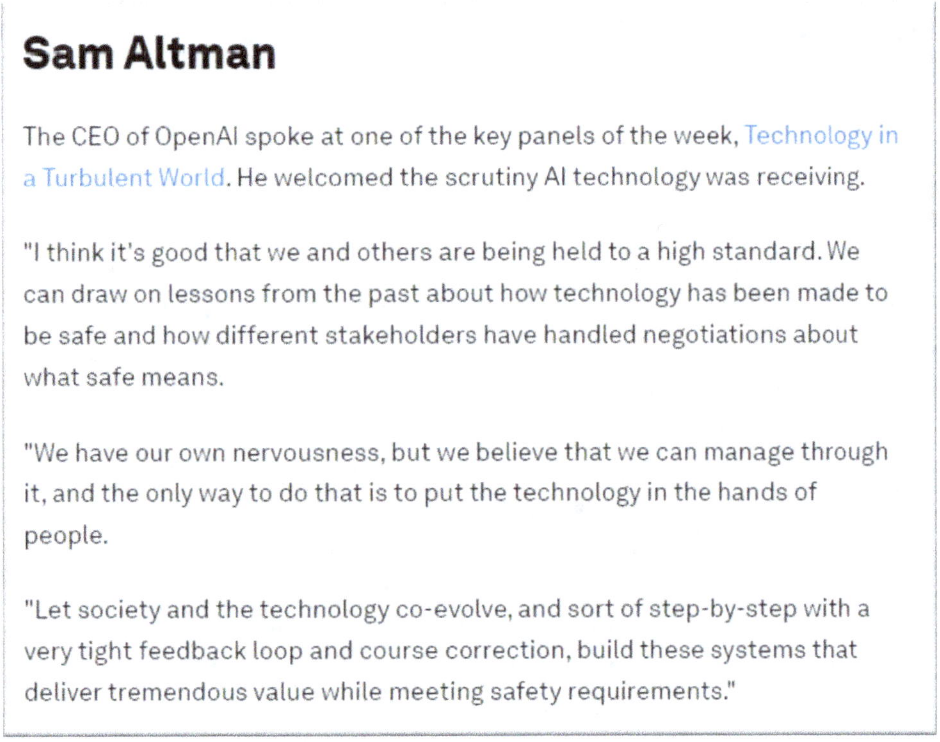

Sam Altman

The CEO of OpenAI spoke at one of the key panels of the week, Technology in a Turbulent World. He welcomed the scrutiny AI technology was receiving.

"I think it's good that we and others are being held to a high standard. We can draw on lessons from the past about how technology has been made to be safe and how different stakeholders have handled negotiations about what safe means.

"We have our own nervousness, but we believe that we can manage through it, and the only way to do that is to put the technology in the hands of people.

"Let society and the technology co-evolve, and sort of step-by-step with a very tight feedback loop and course correction, build these systems that deliver tremendous value while meeting safety requirements."

Figure 87: OpenAI View Point[lxxxviii]

EU president was also hopeful regarding the future of AI as mentioned in Figure 88 below. He stressed the need of being the early adopters because the business viability may become at stake if the organizations become complacent in AI adoption.

Ursula von der Leyen

"AI is a very significant opportunity – if used in a responsible way," the President of the European Commission said in her special address.

"I am a tech optimist and, as a medical doctor by training, I know that AI is already revolutionizing healthcare. That's good. AI can boost productivity at unprecedented speed. First movers will be rewarded, and the global race is already on without any question.

"Our future competitiveness depends on AI adoption in our daily businesses, and Europe must up its game and show the way to responsible use of AI. That is AI that enhances human capabilities, improves productivity and serves society."

Figure 88: EU President Perspective[lxxxix]

UN Secretary General was of the opinion that the growing inequalities in the world will further exacerbate by AI-based implementations as mentioned in Figure 89 below. The risk management and governance models are two areas that should be considered by the AI developers, AI adopters, and the governments.

António Guterres

The UN Secretary-General used his Davos address to warn of the "existential threat" posed by "the runaway development of AI without guard rails" and its potential to increase inequality in the world.

He called for the full engagement of the private sector in the UN's multi-stakeholder effort to "develop a governance model that is networked and adaptive" and that can "tap the benefits of this incredible new technology while mitigating its risks".

"We need governments urgently to work with tech companies on risk management frameworks for current AI development, and on monitoring and mitigating future harms.

"And we need a systematic effort to increase access to AI so that developing economies can benefit from its enormous potential. We need to bridge the digital divide instead of deepening it."

Figure 89: UN Secretary General Viewpoint[xc]

The leader from China appreciated the role played by AI technologies as mentioned in Figure 90 below. However, he also warned about the security risks and ethical implications associated with AI implementations.

Li Qiang

"Generative AI, represented by ChatGPT, has caused a lot of discussion. People love it, but there are also surprises and fear in certain quarters," said the Premier of the State Council of the People's Republic of China in his special address.

"AI is everywhere, it seems omnipotent, but people are still taking time to get used to it. Like other technologies, AI is a double-edged sword.

"If it is applied well, it can do good and bring opportunities to the progress of human civilization and provide great impetus to the industrial and scientific revolution.

"But at the same time, it also poses risks to security and ethics. China believes technology must serve the common good of humanity, it must do good, and the same applies to AI."

Figure 90: Perspective from Chinese Leadership[xci]

Microsoft CEO highlighted that the technology developers should also consider the consequences of introducing new technology as mentioned in Figure 91 below. The notions of equity, trust, and safety cannot be overlooked.

Satya Nadella

"The biggest lesson learned is we have to take the unintended consequences of any new technology along with all the benefits, and think about them simultaneously – as opposed to waiting for the unintended consequences to show up and *then* address them," the Microsoft CEO said in his annual fireside chat with the Forum's Founder and Executive Chairman Klaus Schwab.

"I don't think the world will put up anymore with any of us coming up with something where we haven't thought through safety, equity and trust – these are big issues for the world."

Figure 91: Microsoft Perspective[xcii]

The ILO Director highlighted that AI-based implementations should not be seen as a threat to employment opportunities as shown in Figure 92 below. It is just that the workers need to upskill and reskill them to compete in the emerging job market.

Gilbert Fossoun Houngbo

"We do not believe that AI is going to [cause] an employment apocalypse," said the Director-General of the International Labour Organization in a session on What to Expect from the Labour Markets?

"Although it is true that millions of jobs are going to be lost and millions of jobs are going to be created, the augmentation side is the transformation side."

For this reason, reskilling, upskilling and lifelong learning would be crucial, he added.

Figure 92: ILO ViewPoint[xciii]

CEO code.org highlighted another dimension that the competition in the world of tomorrow will be between AI knowers and AI don't knowers as mentioned in Figure 93 below. If people have a good know-how of AI, there will be even more job opportunities available to them.

Hadi Partovi

During a session on Education Meets AI, the Founder and CEO of Code.org said when people think about job losses due to AI, the risk isn't people losing their job to AI.

"It's losing their job to somebody else who knows how to use AI. That is going to be a much greater displacement.

"It's not that the worker gets replaced by just a robot or a machine in most cases, especially for desk jobs, it's that some better educated or more modernly educated worker can do that job because they can be twice as productive or three times as productive."

"The imperative is to teach how AI tools work to every citizen, and especially to our young people."

Figure 93: Code.org Perspective[xciv]

The state secretary from Switzerland launched a new initiative related to AI networks as mentioned in Figure 94 below. However, he warned that the AI adoption can increase inequalities in the world. The IMF report that I explained earlier also indicates that advanced economies are much more prepared and receptive to AI tools and technologies than low-income countries.

Alexandre Fasel, State Secretary, Switzerland

The Swiss State Secretary launched the new International Computation and AI Network of Excellence initiative at Davos, which aims to develop and test AI models to advance the UN Sustainable Development Goals and humanitarian aid.

He said: "AI is amongst the key technologies of our time and will have a lasting impact on society, economies and politics and an important role to play in tackling the global challenges we face.

"Not all countries have the same access to the resources needed to implement these. If we do not address this, AI could become a driver of inequality. We must avoid opening an AI gap. We must ensure all voices are heard and AI solutions are a global public good."

Figure 94: Switzerland Perspective[xcv]

All the above perspectives from the renowned world leaders indicate the future of management in an AI-based world. The AI implementations will be increasingly prominent in the organizational setting and the managers will have to address the challenge so that the organizations remain sustainable, competitive, and resilient.

Chapter **6**

Demystifying
the Robot Boss

Now that I have unfolded various aspects of a robot CEO, it's time to get you a feel of the robot boss. It's time to summarize and consolidate the learning so far and see how human-AI interaction works. If the human employees see it as an opportunity, then this interaction can be highly productive and interesting. However, if the employees are fearful about their job prospects, then these interactions will not be meaningful.

6.   Simulation of the Boss in Various Setups

In a blue-print of an AI-powered organization, you can see that the robots have taken control for almost all of the organization. They are performing routine tasks, management tasks, as well as surveillance tasks. The tasks are being executed in a robotic manner with an amazing level of accuracy. The queries will be responded promptly that will result in a happy customer and higher customer conversions. The robot boss will be the CEO of the organization. However, it will not mean a strict bureaucratic control in the organization. The robot CEO may follow a centralized or a decentralized structure based on the logic and intelligence built into the AI model.

Another aspect that you may appreciate in the AI model is that the setup of a robotic organization is highly sophisticated and based on the state-of-the-art technologies. This is one area where the business entities will have to focus. They will need to review the requirements of their organizations and present a strong case to the senior management for implementing a robotic organization. In the absence of sufficient funds, it will be difficult to transform the organizational outlook.

Another aspect that you might also notice is that robots appear to be ready for responding to the events. It is possible in an AI-based organization when the AI general manager has all the required data available and the quality of data is extremely good. For example, if there is not required number of CVs received, the shortlisting and interviewing process will suffer despite the availability of robot recruiters. Therefore, the employees should not expect that the AI general manager will be the master of all aspects. It will depend on the quality of human-robot relationship and how accurate and quick, the required information is made available to the robot CEO.

The need for an AI general manager has emerged due to multiple factors. There is more and more government ownership and encouragement for implementing AI tools and technologies. The employees can also be held more responsible for their work by facilitating them with AI tools and technologies. The AI concepts have successfully been used in development the management solutions. The organizations also have a pressure from the competitors because if they become early adopters of AI, the organizations may lose their competitive advantage. However, as I explained in the section on success stories, the stories of successful humanoid robots are limited. The good aspect is that the AI models can learn and improve over time. Therefore, the employees should wait and allow AI managers to build intelligent AI models. Then, they will see the significance and benefits of an AI general manager.

There is a fear factor among employees that robots in the management domain will eat their jobs and they will become redundant. However, there are some roles that can be performed efficiently by AI and there are also other roles that humans can perform even better than AI. It is these roles where the needs of humans will still be felt. Therefore, it should not be expected from the AI boss that s/he will only hire or prefer robots. In some cases, the AI CEO might prefer humans over robots.

The algorithmic CEOs are also problem solvers and they can make an efficient utilization of the available budget. The algorithmic CEOs and workers will always be truthful because they do not have any fear of scrutiny or losing their jobs. The team performance can also be evaluated effectively by algorithmic CEOs. Therefore, the employees can be comfortable that the CEO will respond honestly and will always be available to them.

It is argued in the management literature that the data-based decision-making is possible only if the decisions of the managers are based on seven key pillars. The first aspect is leadership. The decision-making process should provide leadership regarding the strategic directions of the organization. The second aspect is trust. The human managers as well as AI general manager can use the data only if it is trustworthy and is relied upon by all the stakeholders of the organization. If the quality of the data is very low, then the data-driven decision-making may prove to be counterproductive. The third aspect is the commitment level of the managers. They should keep their personal biases aside and follow the patterns and trends in data for effective decision-making. The other aspect is the use of metrics. An AI general manager should have the availability of all key metrics and dashboard indicators. These indicators should provide the real-time view of the organization. Another dimension is data literacy. It is a common argument against the AI algorithms that the users do not know how the algorithms arrived at a particular decision. An AI general manager should also consider this aspect and it should be able to explain the rationale of the decision-making to its human subordinates. Moreover, staff training and awareness are also essential in data-based approach to decision-making. The AI developers should consider all these seven pillars in the development of a robot CEO.

A landmark achievement was observed in 2016, when chatbots assistant were introduced. A chatbot assistant such as a WhatsApp chatbot remembers the solutions of the frequently asked questions by the clients. The queries are then responded by the chatbot in an automated manner without any intervention by the human. The beauty of this chatbot was that the support services became highly effective and were made available 24/7. Moreover, the accuracy of the responses was phenomenal because the responses are generated based on the processing of a large dataset. However, the users of the technology are also much aware of the potential and limitations of the technology. They know that they are talking to a chatbot that might give them general purpose answer but may not answer their specific queries and concerns. Even at the level of call centers, if the caller has the option of using automated menu options or calling to an operator, many callers would prefer calling to an operator because it provides a human touch and a personalized interaction.

The beauty of human interaction is one area where the robots will never be able to beat the humans. It is a human nature that the people treat everyone differently. People develop a perception regarding the personality preferences of an individual and respond to their queries accordingly. On the other hand, a chatbot assistant will treat all human equally. The difference in responses based on the information and assistance needs of the individual is still beyond the capabilities of a chatbot. Some of the plagiarism checking websites such as turnitin can also detect if a given piece of text was written by a human or a chatbot. This capability makes it evident that the behavioral styles of a machine and a human are entirely different and a machine can never write with a human touch.

6.1. How Human-AI Interaction Works

The first AI boss was developed by Hitachi Company. It was introduced in 2015 that shows that the technology and management professionals were exploring the possibility of AI in management for quite long. They wanted more accuracy and objectivity in the decision-making process and provide more freedom of expression to the subordinates.

The use of AI in management is not a new phenomenon and some level of implementation was observed even as early as 1983. At that time, the database management tools such as oracle were used to process large amount of data and general intelligent reports and dashboard indicators. But the AI of today has found much more usage of the technology and this book takes one next step to highlight the benefits of an algorithmic CEO.

The employees should also be confident that it is not always the case that algorithms will outperform humans. There are also instances where human managers perform better than algorithms. One of these aspects is a better comprehension of the feelings. An algorithm will give a negative feedback to the employee without realizing the mental and emotional state of the employee. On the other hand, the humans will consider the environmental and contextual factors before issuing such remarks. The humans can also train other humans better than machines. An enabling work environment can also be ensured well by humans.

The benefits of AI in management can be seen by the mapping of AI technologies and the management support. The algorithmic managers are powered by machine learning technologies, neural networks, data mining, big data science, and business intelligence. All these AI-based concepts can provide immense support to the management. The benefits can be seen in the optimized decision-making and accurate decision-making. The benefit can also be observed in the improved functionality of the organization. The tasks such as recruitment, performance appraisal, wealth management, and supply chain management can all be automated.

Another benefit of AI-based management is that a robot selects the most suitable candidate based on the available data. Unlike traditional CEO, the employee is most likely to move up the career ladder due to the objective decision-making of the algorithmic CEO.

Despite the promising outcomes of an AI general manager, there are still only a few successful case studies of an algorithmic CEO. This raises the question why organizations are reluctant to make the optimum utilization of the AI.

The first challenge faced in AI based management is that employees are accustomed to interacting with other humans. They miss the human touch and socialization aspect in robotic environment. The environment becomes too mechanistic. The algorithmic CEOs assume that the receivers of their instructions are also robots and they will be able to follow each and every word of their instructions. The humans do not work that way and their rationality is always bounded by various constraints including the family constraints and technical constraints. It is the biggest challenge faced by robot CEO. If the human employees do not perform the tasks as expected, what should a robot CEO do? The CEO will respond as per the programming or the learning made based on the supplied datasets. Therefore, the normative and human aspect will be missing from the decision-making of the robot CEO.

The second challenge is the issue of security and privacy of the data. There is so much connectivity of the devices for the efficient working of AI algorithms. The data exposure might be without consent or a data breach from a single device may aggravate to a massive data breach. The skill set of professionals regarding the maintenance of AI systems is limited. Therefore, hackers can exploit this opportunity and compromise the sanctity and integrity of the data. It also raises a concern regarding the rights of the employees. If an employer or a supervisor abuse the rights of the employees, the employee may file a lawsuit in the labor court. But what if the robot CEO does something wrong? Will it face any legal punishment? The courts are yet to give a punishment or verdict against the robots.

Another challenge faced in the organizational setting is that as soon as the AI based implementation is announced, employees fear losing their jobs. The tasks for which they had established the timelines of two to three days can be done by robots in two to three hours. So, they anticipate that they will soon become redundant. The employees may also consider them as worthless because there is nothing to offer to the organization that the robots cannot do. Therefore, robot CEOs will also be a challenge to the self-esteem of the employees.

Another challenge is the lack of understanding of the potential impact of AI. If the management itself is not convinced that the AI based systems will transform the management landscape, then the AI based interventions will always be a distant dream. Moreover, an algorithmic CEO may select a candidate for the job that is highly competitive. However, the candidate may not fit well to the current organizational setting. These aspects can best be judged by humans because it constitutes a dynamic reality and has an element of subjectivity. The subjectivity notion will be the biggest challenge for the robot CEO because the machine will assume that there is always a solution for the problem at hand, which is objective and straightforward. As we know, it is not the case in the real world, and there are always grey areas and dynamic realities in the world.

The AI-based management has also raised concerns because of the intrusive nature of the AI algorithms. As I explained earlier, the AI algorithms process a large amount of data for making an efficient AI model. The development of the data model may access those data sets for which explicit information has not been provided. The quality of algorithms gets improved but the question arises whether legitimate means have been used for improving the efficiency of algorithms. This is one area where the implementation team will have to focus because the robot CEOs will be information greedy. They will try to get more and more data to improve their learning and make informed recommendations.

6.2. Boss Communications

The AI-based resource allocation can offer various advantages to the senior management. These benefits are further optimized when the CEO or the general manager of the company is an AI robot and not a human. It is because the resource allocation management software based on AI concepts assume that the user of these tools will also be well versed in executing the different functions and interfaces of the software. In the case of an AI CEO, this intelligence is built into the CEO algorithms that increases the benefits of an AI-based resource allocation.

When the resource allocation takes advantage of the AI concepts, the efficiency and productivity of the workforce increases because the system learns from the mistakes and makes continuous adaptations to the resource allocation process. The resource planning is also optimized because it is based on the predefined rules and criteria and alternate plans and strategies are also made part of the algorithmic process. The burden of the administration is reduced significantly because the resource allocation is accomplished automatically and everyone is aware of their roles and possible tasks that might be assigned in the near future. The organizations can also reduce costs and gain a competitive advantage through AI-based resource allocation.

Various features and options that are offered by different AI vendors in the resource allocation software. The resource allocation becomes entirely automated in the AI-based software. The predictive management is also a well-known feature of the AI where the issues and problems in the existing strategies are tracked by the system proactively and alternate strategies are recommended. The dashboard indicators also show the real-time availability of all available resources. There are also options for time tracking and project management. The resources needed for future projects and future years can also be forecasted by the system and then the algorithmic CEO can initiate the hiring process for meeting the higher demand of resources in the future. The resources may also be needed in the form of financial resources and material resources. In those cases, the procurement department may be intimated for acquiring the materials and funding agencies may be contacted for receiving the required funds for the future projects.

The benefits of resource allocation can also be viewed from the technology paradigm. When the organizations opt for AI-based resource allocation in management, the quality of data analysis improves significantly. The entered data is not only used for reporting and descriptive statistics, but inferences are also drawn and future state of the organization is also predicted based on the current data. In this way, if there are loopholes in any strategy, they can be rectified well before their occurrence. The real-time monitoring of the resource allocation is also possible because the resource allocation is carried out by the systems and all the decision-making steps are recorded and reported by the system. The collaboration process is also improved significantly and the resource allocation can also cover remote workers through the use of virtualization hardware, software, and systems.

The learning mechanism ensures that the quality of experience is at an optimum level when the output is sent to the end users. Between the users and the physical servers, there is a whole system of network topologies and AI-based systems. When the tasks are received by the task receiver, the intelligent agent is used for generating rewards and assigning resources. This information is stored in the mapping table. The intelligent agent also receives the feedback from the end users regarding the quality of experience and then the improvements are made by reinforcement learning. This whole AI-based resource allocation system not only ensures an efficient allocation of resources but also learns from the feedback of the users and make improvements in the resource allocation tasks for the future scenarios.

AI algorithms can prove to be an effective general manager because of their abilities of enabling a process of continued learning. For the humans, the management has to ask them to go for continued professional development. Moreover, some managers do not have the required aptitude for the leadership positions, and they are successful in securing the positions based on the tenure of their employment. All these aspects can be addressed effectively by an AI general manager because it does not require an aptitude and interest for learning. The algorithms will learn in an automated, mechanistic style.

To fully understand the potential of AI learning in resource allocation, project management, and risk assessment, it is crucial to gain a basic understanding of how the learning process works in the AI-based systems. Active learning in AI is a function of Label, Enrich, Train, and Query processes. First, a given sample or a resource will be assigned a label by the system. It facilitates in identifying the sample and assigning it to a class or a category. The training dataset is enriched by the inclusion of the newly labelled sample because the system sees it as an opportunity of learning and strengthening the system protocols. In the Train phase, the AI model receives the training based on the available dataset. This dataset includes the past, historical data as well as the newly added samples. The query process can also be used by the learning function to view and select different samples available in the dataset. This simple example shows the power of AI-based algorithms that they are always ready for the new learning. As soon as they receive the newly added samples, they trigger the training phase and train the AI model based on the current and new data.

As I explained earlier, the algorithmic managers are powered by machine learning technologies, neural networks, data mining, big data science, and business intelligence. All these AI-based concepts can provide immense support to the management. The benefits can be seen in the optimized decision-making and accurate decision-making. The benefit can also be observed in the improved functionality of the organization. The tasks such as recruitment, performance appraisal, wealth management, and supply chain management can all be automated.

I had also highlighted that the learning process can be effective if there are no algorithmic biases in the AI-based systems. The key factor in AI systems is the quality of data. If the training examples in the dataset favor a certain segment of the population, then the AI model will learn wrong rules that will affect the algorithmic decision-making. Due to these limitations of the AI algorithms, professionals working in AI always prefer narrow AI over general AI.

While considering the benefits of AI learning in resource allocation, project management, and risk management, another key area of consideration is the distinction between supervised and unsupervised learning. The first form is supervised learning in which the self-learning system is not built into the model. The learning process is initiated at various time intervals and a trigger is generated in the system to initiate the learning process. The second form is unsupervised learning in which the algorithms enable learning as soon as they encounter new data points and interactions. The third form is reinforcement learning in which the learned data points are categorized into positive or negative reinforcers. It is easier to understand that the risk of algorithmic bias is higher in supervised learning because the learning process is at the discretion of the AI developer. Moreover, when negative reinforcers are identified in reinforcement learning, it is based on how the negativity is defined in the system by the AI developer that creates an algorithmic bias.

A survey was recently conducted in which the managers were asked to respond what they think they would do better and which tasks can be performed more appropriately by the robots. From the survey, it emerged that the most important benefit of an algorithmic CEO is the provision of an unbiased information. The CEO never controls or filters the information. This advantage was endorsed by the maximum number of managers (36%). The algorithms are also highly efficient in maintaining work schedules. The performance of humans is influenced by external factors as well such as family issues or illnesses. However, the algorithmic workers are always available for the task execution as long as the required IT infrastructure is available and connected.

AI has invaded all aspects of the humanity. In the absence of a standard regulatory framework, the fate of the AI-based systems is left to the integrity of the AI developers. As I mentioned earlier, there is no single management style followed by the robot CEOs. They may operate as authoritarian bosses as well as laissez faire bosses. It is up to the AI developers how they construct a robot CEO. The boss communications will also depend on the communication tone and style set by the developers. Therefore, there is a high risk of algorithmic bias in the construction of a robot CEO.

An algorithmic boss can be a real blessing for an organization if the implementation considers several key aspects and a formal strategy are developed for the transformation process. In the strategy phase, you will need to determine to what extent, the algorithmic management is needed in your organization. In the next step, you should develop a change management process. In this stage, you will have to train the existing staff for using algorithms instead of manual interventions. The management should still make the communication lines open because the change will be successful through an evolutionary process. Once the algorithmic management is in place, the management should constantly evaluate the management flow of the algorithms so that the algorithmic decision-making is not influenced by the algorithmic biases.

From the AI boss, you will get a feel that the individual is very much focused on the work and there will be complete impartiality in the decision-making process. You may also discuss your concerns and issues with an open heart to an AI boss because there is no fear of retaliation and anger on the part of the boss. The boss is instructed to listen to the issues of the subordinates calmly and openly. The performance of the team will be measured strictly against the assigned objectives quarterly and annually.

In order to understand the significance of data-driven decision-making, it is crucial to know the evolutionary process of AI-based systems. The AI-based systems for data-driven decision-making were first presented as assisted intelligence systems. The key selling point of the systems at that time was that these systems can learn in an organized manner, whereas the humans do not take the learning process so seriously. In the next phase, it was realized that a good AI system is a product of human-machine interaction. It was argued that the quality of an AI system is influenced by the data model and if a good quality data is not provided by the humans, the algorithms cannot work effectively. Therefore, there was a gradual shift to augmented intelligence where machines facilitate humans and humans facilitate machines.

The third phase or the current phase is regarded as autonomous intelligence. In this era, the nature of tasks changes very rapidly. Therefore, the decisions need to be taken by the AI manager in an automated manner based on data and predefined rules, policies, and procedures of the organization. The machines should have a mechanism of a continued learning. It means that the AI CEO that the subordinates are interacting with today will not have the same responses in the future because it is a machine. Based on a continued learning, the responses and the behavioral disposition of the algorithmic CEO will also change. It is one area where the AI boss will simulate the human behavior exceptionally well. From the humans too, the expectation is that they will be wiser over time. An experienced professional will respond more prudently than a new comer.

As I explained earlier that the organization of future will be a mix of human workers and robots. You might feel more comfortable reporting to a robot than a human. It is because the human decision-making is often influenced by biases and prejudices. There are complaints of favoritism and partially in every other organization. On the other hand, a robot CEO is highly objective and focused. It is available 24/7, never sleeps, and never gets ill. Despite the presence of an AI manager, there are still various tasks for which human presence will be needed in the organization.

If humans have biases, then AI-based algorithms are also influenced by algorithms biases of the AI developers. When AI-based systems perform the conventional tasks of humans, they provide more opportunity to the coworkers to focus more on strategic and managerial level tasks. If recruitment and performance appraisal are carried out by algorithms, the HR managers will have the options to utilize the workforce in field visits, market analysis, and finding strategies of gaining a competitive advantage. The workers can also focus on sustainability issues and implementing green human resources strategies. Think of the tools such as ChatGPT and Google Bard. The job of the programmers is not gone. These tools can generate the code but the code still needs to be consolidated and deployed, which can only be done by a professional computer programmer. Therefore, an AI general manager will ease the task of the employees and make them more productive and useful in the organizational context.

6.3. Boss Interaction with Employees

In the project management paradigm, there are several key processes and the AI systems should be able to optimize all these processes. A typical project will involve the estimation of tasks and resources. Then the costing and resource scheduling should be done. The project manager also needs to do sequencing and collating of data. They also identify risks and trends in the projects. The AI-based systems should assist in all these areas. Good AI-based systems offer automated scheduling, optimization of all tasks, predictive analytics features, and machine learning algorithms for all AI types.

This book highlights the role of AI general manager and beyond. Therefore, the benefits of AI-based project management should also be viewed as to how AI can assist general managers if it is not possible to appoint an AI general manager altogether. Various benefits can be gained in those cases. The training and development of the employees will be based on the analysis of their learning habits by the AI software. The resource allocation will be optimized due to which it will be easier to release the employees from the operational tasks and depute them to the project activities. The project team will be able not only to track the progress of the project but also predict the future activities of the project. The budgeting and scheduling tasks will all be automated. The complex, employee-based analytics will be handled smoothly by the AI software. Therefore, AI algorithms will sever as a virtual assistant of the project manager in cases where it is not possible to appoint an AI project manager.

Robo-CEO is an algorithmic CEO that selects the most suitable candidate based on the available data. Unlike traditional CEO, the employee is most likely to move up the career ladder due to the objective decision-making of the algorithmic CEO. The higher level of automation in robots may also cause serious issues in an automated workplace. In a recent incident, a robot in the famous Tesla Company launched an attack on the human engineer of the company. Tesla later explained that it was due to a violent malfunction of the robot. It was a critical case because the unintended action of the robot could have harmed the lives of the employees.

Due to these incidents, despite the promising outcomes of an AI general manager, there are still only a few successful case studies of an algorithmic CEO. This raises the question why organizations are reluctant to make the optimum utilization of the AI. The first challenge faced in AI based management is that employees are accustomed to interacting with other humans. They miss the human touch and socialization aspect in robotic environment. The environment becomes too mechanistic. The algorithmic CEOs assume that the receivers of their instructions are also robots and they will be able to follow each and every word of their instructions. The humans do not work that way and their rationality is always bounded by various constraints including the family constraints and technical constraints.

In an ideal scenario, there should be an algorithmic CEO such that employees are reporting happily to them. They know that the behavior of the boss will be unbiased and the interaction will be limited to the assigned job responsibilities. There will be no favors and additional tasks asked by the boss. Moreover, the working day end within the working hour and there will be no stretched timings and late duties. It will be the biggest blessing of a robot boss that there will be no distractions and time wastage. A focused work will be executed by the employees and the AI boss will ensure the availability of an enabling environment.

The future organizations are expected to be a nice blend of AI workers and human workers. It will also affect how the organograms will be presented and reported in different statutory reports. Therefore, be prepared to interact simultaneously with humans and robots in the organization.

In a hybrid environment, the CEO is an algorithmic CEO and all key leadership positions are occupied by robots. Humans have been assigned only to the operational work, and the technology-driven aspect of the organization has been endorsed at the level of the organization chart.

The AI managers will make an impression in the organizations when their performances significantly outperform the human managers. Several successful implementations have been made in this regard so far. An algorithmic CEO was tested in a Hong Kong based company. The boss is named Tang Yu and she is the CEO of mobile and gaming company. The model proved highly successful in the organization and there was a marked improvement in the speed of execution and the quality of work. The company where this model was successfully tested is NetDragon.

AI general manager will also need some tools for effective decision-making. The managerial aspect requires a high level of collaboration and effective business communication. There, AI humanoid CEO should be supported with various emerging and on-demand AI services. The chat services can be managed effectively by ChatGPT and Bard services. The document management systems and chatbots also assist in the effective management of the workspace by the AI manager.

In an AI-powered organization, you might see that the robots have taken control for almost all of the organization. They are performing routine tasks, management tasks, as well as surveillance tasks. The tasks are being executed in a robotic manner with an amazing level of accuracy. The queries will be responded promptly that will result in a happy customer and higher customer conversions. This task efficiency should be an ultimate goal of the organization and the human interface should still be used in conjunction with the robotic environment.

The quality of a successful AI model is driven by both the training data and the new input data. If all the efforts are aimed at developing a successful algorithm, the required results may still not be achieved due to the poor quality of the data.

The need for an AI general manager has emerged due to multiple factors. There is more and more government ownership and encouragement for implementing AI tools and technologies. The employees can also be held more responsible for their work by facilitating them with AI tools and technologies. The AI concepts have successfully been used in developing the management solutions. The organizations also have a pressure from the competitors because if they become early adopters of AI, the organizations may lose their competitive advantage. The first AI boss was developed by Hitachi Company. It was introduced in 2015 that shows that the technology and management professionals were exploring the possibility of AI in management for quite long. They wanted more accuracy and objectivity in the decision-making process and provide more freedom of expression to the subordinates. In the current context, a robot CEO was appointed by a Chinese firm NetDragon.

The robot CEO was appointed with the intent that the process flow of the business entity will be streamlined and the speed of task execution will improve substantially. However, at the implementation level, various challenges were also observed by the company. The employees tended to be always connected in the metaverse and the physical activity during the working hours reduced significantly. There was a reduced level of socialization because the CEO always got connected through Zoom calls. With this implementation, it emerged that the robot CEOs may increase the anxiety levels and depersonalization effect.

6.4. Workforce Adaptation Requirements

There are benefits of using narrow AI for management-based AI algorithms. This technology has a binding to a specific task. The technology is based on fixed-domain models. It might come as a limitation for some general managers because the general-AI has a self-learning process and the system developed in general-AI today will have a far optimized version in the next 6 months based on self-learning.

Another benefit of narrow AI is that the learning mechanism is based on a large number of examples and therefore, the concept development in the AI model is very strong. A limitation of narrow AI is that the system is reflexive instead of using cognitive abilities. The general AI has been designated as the future of the AI because the knowledge can be transferred to other domains. It is a highly significant feature particularly when the AI-based concepts are using in conjunction with an IoT environment.

In order to fully understand the algorithmic bias, it is also important to know the different nature of AI algorithms. AI algorithms are implemented in three key ways in the system.

The first form is supervised learning in which the self-learning system is not built into the model. The learning process is initiated at various time intervals and a trigger is generated in the system to initiate the learning process. The second form is unsupervised learning in which the algorithms enable learning as soon as they encounter new data points and interactions. The third form is reinforcement learning in which the learned data points are categorized into positive or negative reinforcers.

From these examples, it is easier to understand that the risk of algorithmic bias is higher in supervised learning because the learning process is at the discretion of the AI developer. Moreover, when negative reinforcers are identified in reinforcement learning, it is based on how the negativity is defined in the system by the AI developer that creates an algorithmic bias. As I highlighted earlier, there are not always right and wrong answers in the management. The human managers use their experience to make decisions in those cases. The robot CEO may struggle in arriving at the best decision under given circumstances.

There is a successful implementation by a firm in which AI manager was used for talent acquisition and talent management. This robot was given the responsibility of managing a $100 billion firm. The entire human resources of the company will be handled by the algorithmic CEO. The company aims to replace more and more humans with robots in key leadership positions.

Recruitment was one of the first HR functions where the algorithms were introduced in the form of a robot recruiter. The robots have been highly successful in conducting interviews and candidates express them comfortably in front of a robot. The responses are also processed efficiently by the robots and the same processing strategy is applied for all candidates.

The function of a robot does not end at conducting an interview. The algorithms can also participate in the entire process of recruitment and selection. They can evaluate all the interview results and select the right and the most suitable candidate by matching the organizational requirements with the candidate skill sets. The workforce adaption requirements are higher in these cases because the robots can fully automate the process with minimal or no human intervention.

With the growth of the automated screening process, the job candidates should also update their CVs so that the robots do not discard their resumes. The traditional CVs might not be considered worthy by the robots.

The candidates will now have to ensure that their CVs and job applications include the keywords of the positions. The AI algorithms match the CVs with the internal dictionary and job descriptors. If the relevant keywords are not found then even the CV of a highly qualified individual might be overlooked.

AI general manager can also conduct performance appraisal effectively. Employees always have reservations and complaints that their efforts are not compensated adequately and the appraisals are always biased to the likes of the supervisor. Due to this reason, the management literature also suggests 360 degree feedback in addition to the straight line method of appraisal. An AI general manager will record all the efforts of the employees objectively. Therefore, employees can be confident that none of their efforts will go unnoticed. The employees can also be assured that the performance will always be evaluated on merit and there will not be any cases of favoritism.

In an ideal scenario, the performance appraisal should begin with the Plan stage. At this stage, the annual objectives of an employee should be set. The next stage is the Act stage where the employee applies the skill set to achieve those objectives. The third stage is the Track stage where the supervisor should periodically monitor the performance of the subordinate and provide feedback. The last stage is review where the performance of the employee should be evaluated, the achievements should be appreciated and the deficiencies should be highlighted. To overcome those deficiencies, the key learning opportunities should be identified for the employees. It will be easier for the senior leadership to follow the recommendations of the robot CEO because these recommendations are based on objective analysis.

This appraisal cycle looks promising; however, in the real world environment, the supervisors are so busy in the regular tasks that they do not focus on the appraisal cycle. Moreover, due to the severe economic conditions, the employees are more worried regarding the survival of their jobs than the growth opportunities and performance appraisals. All these issues will be addressed effectively by the robot CEO and the employees can be confident about the prospects with the current organization.

An algorithmic CEO can optimize the appraisal systems by using strength-based appraisals. In this strategy, the performance ratings are based on the strengths and competencies of the employees. When there is a fairness and equity in the appraisal process, the motivation and morale of the workforce also improves and the employees are always motivated to improve their skill set.

Performance appraisals are also a key source document for promoting the employees. The algorithmic performance appraisal evaluates each subordinate objectively and justly and only the most hardworking, competent, and devoted employee is selected for promotion and moving up the career ladder.

Another aspect is the physical skills and the evaluation of the physical skills. An AI general manager might struggle in a factory setting where physical labor work is required. The robots could prove to be highly expensive in these tasks, and it might not be possible for them to evaluate the performance of the workers involved in the physical labor. Robots are being used in warehouses for the proper and efficient maintenance of the inventory. However, consider the construction sector. The robots will find it difficult to do the labor-intensive task in the construction sector. Therefore, physical skills is one area where humans still dominate the robots.

The resource allocation based on AI learning is executed in a highly sophisticated manner. Considering this aspect, the AI developers recommend that various parameters should be reviewed by the technology team before implementing resource allocation. In a study, these considerations have been considered into three key categories of task, approach, and computing paradigm. The first area of consideration is that how many resource allocation strategies will be input into the system and how the power consumption can be optimized during the algorithmic decision-making. The efficient power management is always crucial in AI-based software because the AI models process huge datasets that might consume energy beyond the available resources of the organization. The second factor is the AI approach in which the technology team should select from the available machine learning techniques and deep learning techniques. The third factor is the computing paradigm. Ideally, the resource allocation should be processed in the cloud computing environment because various nodes and parameters will be processed that will require extensive storage space and the computing power. Other options may also be considered such as the IoT environment, edge computing, or mobile edge computing.

It should be noted that at the technical level, different AI types provide varied level of benefits to the project managers. Therefore, the technology team in the organizations should build understanding of all the AI types that they are anticipating for the implementation. There is a relevance of each AI type in the project management paradigm. The machine learning algorithms are more beneficial in project analytics and risk assessment. The deep learning algorithms can be utilized for the optimization of task scheduling. The supervised learning should be used for project costing and budgeting. The unsupervised learning should be utilized for team creating and team management. The reinforcement learning is a good strategy for the resource allocation tasks. The natural language processing algorithms should be utilized for the sentiment analysis of the team performance. The computer vision technology should be used for the summarization of the educational videos related to the project. The adversarial networks should be utilized for the testing of projects in a safe and secure environment. The expert systems will be needed when risk management is to be carried out based on historical data.

Risk assessment has become a highly crucial activity for the general managers because the projects in the organizations incur significant costs. In the competitive world, the costs should be justified and risk mitigation strategies should also be developed by the management to keep the organization sustainable.

The risk assessment activities usually begin with the identification of risks in the internal and external environment. Then the risks are analyzed and their severity level are ascertained. In the final stage, strategies are developed for the management of these risks. A good AI-based system automates all these three processes of risk management. The net outcomes is the development of more relevant and efficient risk management strategies.

AI tools can be successfully used for the assessment of underwriting. The accuracy level is improved because AI algorithms analyze huge datasets. The efficient AI algorithms process big data speedily and generate meaningful results. The systems provide the details of the most profitable market segments. The fraudulent claims are quickly identified based on the historical data. The system also offers personalized recommendations to the customers based on their needs. The overall cost of operation is reduced due to accuracy and protecting fraudulent claims.

The ultimate AI-based implementation can be achieved in an organization when an algorithmic CEO takes charge of the organization. In the other cases, the robots may be appointed for assisting the general manager. It will also prove to be a good strategy because the robots in the execute roles will keep the manager focused and committed. The robot will also remind them about the meeting and the tasks that are to be submitted shortly. It will ensure that the manager executes all the tasks happily and never miss a task. The managers often struggle in multitasking. However, the robots will show them the best course of action and at any given point in time, the general managers will also perform the most relevant task in the organization. The humans have limited capacities of working and they easily get tired when there are stretched timings or work overload. On the contrary, the robots can work stress-free throughout the day and they can also be made available 24/7. They work as per instructions without any demand of reward and compensation. They are also honest and candid in their responses because they do not have any job insecurity or personal motives.

When the concept of AI general manager or AI CEO is implemented in the organizations, there will always be a need to create an organizational structure, which is a mix of both humans and robots. In the future, one might see an organizational chart where the humans and robots are working together. In this context, the AI CEO will also need to consider the human-robot interaction and ensure that it is executed in a smooth manner and humans are satisfied and comfortable working with robots.

The organizations are expected to receive mixed responses when they introduce AI CEO in their environments. Also, within the organization, the comfort level of the employees with the

AI robots will vary significantly. The most important benefit of an algorithmic CEO is the provision of an unbiased information. The CEO never controls or filters the information. The algorithms are also highly efficient in maintaining work schedules. The performance of humans is influenced by external factors as well such as family issues or illnesses. However, the algorithmic workers are always available for the task execution as long as the required IT infrastructure is available and connected.

Employees, however, have reported that the human CEOs have a better comprehension of the feelings. An algorithm will give a negative feedback to the employee without realizing the mental and emotional state of the employee. On the other hand, the humans will consider the environmental and contextual factors before issuing such remarks. The humans can also train other humans better than machines. An enabling work environment can also be ensured well by humans.

The biggest challenge for an AI general manager implementation will be to prepare the employees for the algorithmic transition. As I have explained earlier, the employees all over the world are highly fearful that the AI-based implementations will automate the tasks for which they have been hired. As a result, they may lose their jobs. Their fears are not unfounded and these concerns have also been endorsed and acknowledged by IMF in its recent report. According to a recent report[xcvi] published by IMF, AI will make a significant influence on the global job market and approximately 40% of the jobs may be affected by AI-based implementations in different organizations. Therefore, organizations need to evaluate the pros and cons of AI-based implementations and manage effectively the motivation and morale of the employees.

6.5. Ethical Concerns and Impact on Employee Morale

To understand the potential biases in AI algorithms, it is crucial to understand the complete lifecycle of AI algorithms. The lifecycle begins with the definition of a business problem. Then the relevant datasets are acquired and prepared in a consistent format. The next step is the development and training of an AI model. The quality of the AI model is continuously evaluated and refined based on new data and requirements. The system is deployed when the AI model has a sufficient level of maturity. Then machine learning operations are put into place.

From the lifecycle development, you will have noticed that the performance of AI-based systems significantly depend on two factors. The first is the quality and accuracy of the AI model. If the rules and feature extraction processes in AI algorithms are biased because the AI developer is convinced with a certain style of management, then the quality of the whole AI-based system will suffer. Another important factor is the quality of data. If the training examples in the dataset favor a certain segment of the population, then the AI model will learn wrong rules that will affect the algorithmic decision-making. It can make a significant negative impact on the employee morale because employees will know that the algorithms are making wrong decisions but they cannot do anything about it because the management has embraced an AI boss as a strategic move.

Humans are generally more influenced by technology and they believe that the human biases will be overcome by the use of technology. However, the technology generates a new form of bias known as an algorithmic bias. These biases can be found in the algorithms as well as how the data is acquired for the training of these algorithms. I gave you the example of a cycle, which is world, data, design, and use. If the AI developers are not the men of integrity, this cycle can become a vicious cycle.

Six strategies are used for overcoming algorithmic biases. They can be addressed by having an awareness of the context, establishing key processes, fact-based communications, a good human-machine interaction, more investment in research, and more research in the AI field.

As I highlighted earlier that the use of AI is influencing all aspects of a business entity. The multinational companies are fearful that if they do not embrace AI, they may lose their competitive advantage. However, the limited knowledge of the AI algorithms makes them hesitant in embracing AI at a mass scale. When there was a widespread adoption of AI tools and technologies in multinational organizations, the management professionals also thought that the AI concepts can be useful and significant in the managerial tasks as well because the emerging requirement of the management was to enable data-driven decision-making, and AI algorithms have the potential to process a huge amount of data quickly. However, the business entities are also not in favor that they do things where the decision-making is quick but they do not have any clue how a particular course of action was selected.

The current era is characterized by the management solutions where the machine learning technologies are used for an effective project management. In fact, the project management was the first area where the significance of an AI general manager was acknowledged. The next era is of autonomous AI where the management functions will be performed autonomously by robots. It is this era where the focus of the book is, i.e. how a general manager, which is an AI robot, can be appointed that could perform all the management roles and the performance is far superior to a human manager. The book argues that there is a huge significance of appointing an algorithmic CEO. However, it should be a hybrid model and the intent of the business managers should not be to replace humans.

A key challenge is the issue of security and privacy of the data. There are so many applications of AI in the organizational context and there is so much connectivity of the devices for the efficient working of AI algorithms. The data exposure might be without consent or a data breach from a single device may aggravate to a massive data breach. The skill set of professionals regarding the maintenance of AI systems is limited. Therefore, hackers can exploit this opportunity and compromise the sanctity and integrity of the data.

When the organizations opt for AI-based systems, they have to make a tradeoff between data exposure and intelligent decision-making. The benefits are experienced in the form of good decision-making, sensing, and sound reasoning. However, the organizations may lose their control over data in a highly interconnected environment. As I explained earlier, the AI systems process such a large amount of data, then the users of the system are even unable to comprehend how the algorithms arrived at a particular conclusion or recommendation. They have to trust the expertise of the system. If the systems have committed errors, then it is almost impossible for the users to find out those errors.

Another challenge faced in the organizational setting is that as soon as the AI based implementation is announced, employees fear losing their jobs. The tasks for which they had established the timelines of two to three days can be done by robots in two to three hours. So, they anticipate that they will soon become redundant. Another challenge highlighted in the survey is the lack of understanding of the potential impact of AI. If the management itself is not convinced that the AI based systems will transform the management landscape, then the AI based interventions will always be a distant dream. The current report by IMF has also endorsed these fears that the AI systems can take away almost 40% of the current jobs.

Another key challenge is that an algorithmic CEO may select a candidate for the job that is highly competitive. However, the candidate may not fit well to the current organizational setting. These aspects can best be judged by humans because it constitutes a dynamic reality and has an element of subjectivity. The humans may not work with the same level of accuracy as the machine, but there is one aspect in which they are unbeatable. They know other humans better than machines. They can identify if a task was executed successfully or not. However, the bigger aspect is that they can also evaluate why a person failed to perform a given task despite having all the capabilities of performing that task.

The CEO robot NAO was introduced in 2018 in Germany. It was claimed that these robots will operate in a human-like way and the human jobs will be replaced significantly. However, most of the times, the robot was seen watching and observing the employees and the employees felt that they have lost their freedom at work. In an article by vox, it was mentioned that an employee in Bangladesh complained that the robot CEO monitors him so closely that a picture of him is taken after every ten minutes to confirm that the employee is sitting at his computer.

The AI-based management has raised concerns because of the intrusive nature of the AI algorithms. As I explained earlier, the AI algorithms process a large amount of data for making an efficient AI model. The development of the data model may access those data sets for which explicit information has not been provided. The quality of algorithms gets improved but the question arises whether legitimate means have been used for improving the efficiency of algorithms. AI has invaded all aspects of the humanity. In the absence of a standard regulatory framework, the fate of the AI-based systems is left to the integrity of the AI developers. As I explained earlier, it usually creates an algorithmic bias.

The robot CEO of Drinks Company in Poland was experimented in November 2023. The CEO performed efficiently the tasks of project management, marketing, sales, and strategic management. From the lifecycle development, you will have noticed that the performance of AI-based systems significantly depend on two factors. The first is the quality and accuracy of the AI model. If the rules and feature extraction processes in AI algorithms are biased because the AI developer is convinced with a certain style of management, then the quality of the whole AI-based system will suffer. Another important factor is the quality of data. If the training examples in the dataset favor a certain segment of the population, then the AI model will learn wrong rules that will affect the algorithmic decision-making. Due to these limitations of the AI algorithms, professionals working in AI always prefer narrow AI over general AI.

There is a successful implementation by a firm in which AI manager was used for talent acquisition and talent management. This robot was given the responsibility of managing a $100 billion firm. The entire human resources of the company will be handled by the algorithmic CEO. The company aims to replace more and more humans with robots in key leadership positions. If this experiment is successful, then from the ethical perspective, there will again be questions if the AI will eventually replace the humans as job holders.

Another drawback is the time and resources needed for AI implementation. Although the automation and quick processing will be achieved by using AI algorithms, these benefits will only be seen in the long run. In the short run, more time will be consumed in implementing the systems and training the workforce. In some organizations, there is a high employee turnover rate that further increases the time to learn.

One more drawback is to interpret the results produced by the AI algorithms. The algorithms process huge datasets before providing recommendations. A human general manager may find it difficult to know the rationale behind a specific recommendation. If the things do not go as expected, the human manager may struggle in justifying their moves.

Another aspect is the risk of error in the absence of data. There is no doubt that AI algorithms will provide accurate results when the relevant data is available. However, when the relevant data is not available, there is a general tendency of the algorithms to produce the results based on whatever is available to them. You might have observed it while using ChatGPT or Google Bard. If these chatbots do not have the relevant data, they still respond you with irrelevant and inaccurate results. It can become a serious limitation in the organizational context when the processes will have automated and there will be a huge reliance on the AI based systems.

There are also some more issues with machine learning in management. The organizations may face cost overruns because appointment an AI general manager and automating all tasks require a complete overhaul of the current IT infrastructure. The training of the remaining human workforce will also incur a significant cost. There is also limited capabilities of AI developers available in the IT industry that are particularly proficient in AI based implementations. There is also a great potential of misuse of the technology because as I mentioned earlier, the AI-based systems also suffer with the algorithmic bias. Moreover, the end users can manipulate the system by benefitting from the limited expertise of the senior management in using AI-based systems.

The setup of a robotic organization is highly sophisticated and based on the state-of-the-art technologies. This is one area where the business entities will have to focus. They will need to review the requirements of their organizations and present a strong case to the senior management for implementing a robotic organization. In the absence of sufficient funds, it will be difficult to transform the organizational outlook.

The use of AI is influencing all aspects of a business entity. The multinational companies are fearful that if they do not embrace AI, they may lose their competitive advantage. However, the limited knowledge of the AI algorithms makes them hesitant in embracing AI at a mass scale. When there was a widespread adoption of AI tools and technologies in multinational organizations, the management professionals also thought that the AI concepts can be useful and significant in the managerial tasks as well because the emerging requirement of the management was to enable data-driven decision-making, and AI algorithms have the potential to process a huge amount of data quickly. However, the business entities are also not in favor that they do things where the decision-making is quick but they do not have any clue how a particular course of action was selected.

A challenge faced in AI based management is that employees are accustomed to interacting with other humans. They miss the human touch and socialization aspect in robotic environment. The environment becomes too mechanistic. The algorithmic CEOs assume that the receivers of their instructions are also robots and they will be able to follow each and every word of their instructions. The humans do not work that way and their rationality is always bounded by various constraints including the family constraints and technical constraints.

Another challenge is the lack of understanding of the potential impact of AI. If the management itself is not convinced that the AI based systems will transform the management landscape, then the AI based interventions will always be a distant dream.

Another challenge faced in the organizational setting is that as soon as the AI based implementation is announced, employees fear losing their jobs. The tasks for which they had established the timelines of two to three days can be done by robots in two to three hours. So, they anticipate that they will soon become redundant.

Another key challenge is that an algorithmic CEO may select a candidate for the job that is highly competitive. However, the candidate may not fit well to the current organizational setting. These aspects can best be judged by humans because it constitutes a dynamic reality and has an element of subjectivity.

AI has invaded all aspects of the humanity. In the absence of a standard regulatory framework, the fate of the AI-based systems is left to the integrity of the AI developers. As I explained earlier, it usually creates an algorithmic bias.

In the future, AI-based organizations, one may expect that the CEO is an algorithmic CEO and all key leadership positions are occupied by robots. Humans have been assigned only to the operational work, and the technology-driven aspect of the organization has been endorsed at the level of the organization chart. AI bosses are not limited to the human resource function and they are also being used in other management and business functions. There is also an implementation where the algorithmic managers have been used for an effective wealth management.

Employee motivation and morale management is going to be highly challenging for the business owners in an AI-based world. The employees are motivated to work because they expect that their efforts will be appreciated and rewarded. Moreover, they will gain an expert power by working hard and showing their commitment. In the new AI paradigm, there will not be such motivation available to them. Why should an employee work hard if the same work can be done by a robot in a much less time? It means that there will be no more appreciation of the work.

These are some of the ethical dilemmas that the managers of today or tomorrow will have to face. On the one hand, the world is getting highly efficient robots. But on the other hand, the world will lose the committed, dedicated, and experienced human employees. There will be a high turnover rate because employees will have a constant fear of insecurity. As I mentioned in the IMF report, the AI adoption poses more dangers to managerial jobs and the jobs of highly qualified individuals. Moreover, advanced economies are more prepared for AI adoption.

In this context, an interesting phenomenon might occur in the future. People might move to low-income countries for lucrative jobs. In those countries, as per the IMF reports, people are not prepared and not much convinced about the use of AI. Therefore, they will value those professionals that are highly skilled. These facts suggest that there are interesting times ahead where not only the whole job environment is going to be transformed but also there will be changes in the migration patterns of the workforce.

As also highlighted by the world leaders in economic forum, the future will be a battle between the AI experts and non-experts. So, your best move will be to learn more and more AI tools and technologies to establish a sound future for yourself and your future generations. If you do not do so, there will come one day where the AI technologies will also 'attack' your domain of expertise and challenge your significance through the automation of tasks performed by you. So, you are better off by learning AI tools and technologies and also learning to work with robots in addition to humans.

Chapter 7

The Beneficial Management Landscape of AI

The future of management can be made highly beneficial by the use of AI general manager. The current era is characterized by the management solutions where the machine learning technologies are used for an effective project management. In fact, the project management was the first area where the significance of an AI general manager was acknowledged. The next era is of autonomous AI where the management functions will be performed autonomously by robots. It is this era where the focus of the book is, i.e. how a general manager, which is an AI robot, can be appointed that could perform all the management roles and the performance is far superior to a human manager.

In an AI-powered organization, you can see that the robots have taken control for almost all of the organization. They are performing routine tasks, management tasks, as well as surveillance tasks. The tasks are being executed in a robotic manner with an amazing level of accuracy. The queries will be responded promptly that will result in a happy customer and higher customer conversions. Another aspect that you may appreciate in the current model is that the setup of a robotic organization is highly sophisticated and based on the state-of-the-art technologies. This is one area where the business entities will have to focus. They will need to review the requirements of their organizations and present a strong case to the senior management for implementing a robotic organization. In the absence of sufficient funds, it will be difficult to transform the organizational outlook.

In the AI-powered organizations, you will notice that robots appear to be ready for responding to the events. It is possible in an AI-based organization when the AI general manager has all the required data available and the quality of data is extremely good. For example, if there is not required number of CVs received, the shortlisting and interviewing process will suffer despite the availability of robot recruiters.

The need for an AI general manager has emerged due to multiple factors. There is more and more government ownership and encouragement for implementing AI tools and technologies. The employees can also be held more responsible for their work by facilitating them with AI tools and technologies. The AI concepts have successfully been used in development the management solutions. The organizations also have a pressure from the competitors because if they become early adopters of AI, the organizations may lose their competitive advantage.

7. AI-Powered Company

There is a fear factor among employees that robots in the management domain will eat their jobs and they will become redundant. It is not going to be the case at least in the near future. There are some roles that can be performed efficiently by AI and there are also other roles that humans can perform even better than AI. It is these roles where the needs of humans will still be felt.

In the case of digital assistants, the training of these assistants will still be carried out by humans. The AI models will give specific and task-centered information. The generalization of this information and articulating the data to the organizational context will still be done by humans. The robots can code the knowledge into high-level and low-level processes. However, the handling of complex, exceptional tasks and social interactions will still be managed by humans. The analysis of AI-robots will be a quantitative analysis, however, qualitative analysis will still be carried out by humans. This qualitative analysis will indicate why a certain trend is developing and how the current roles and responsibilities of the management professionals can be modified.

As shown in Figure 95 below, the AI powered companies will be challenged to manage the machine level interactions by ensuring real-time connectivity and seamless availability of data.

Figure 95: AI-Powered Corporate Interactions[xcvii]

If the general manager is an AI CEO, it will have to interact with machines as well as humans. The humans might feel happy and comfortable regarding the objectivity and impartiality, but they may feel pressurized when the external environment such as the domestic issues or the health conditions do not favor them. In those testing times, the humanoid CEO might not extend the favors that might be expected from a human CEO.

Figure 96 shows how the robotics implementation in a company has automated the inventory management and shipment process. However, the proper execution of these processes will require that the AI-based systems are implemented properly and robots are well-trained to perform the required tasks.

Figure 96: Robotics Implementation in Companies[xcviii]

The above figure shows a promising outlook of an AI-powered organization. However, from the technology perspective, it should be noted that the performance of these robots is dependent on how well these robots have been trained. As I gave you a recent example of an incident in Tesla Company, the robots even began to attack the employees in that organization. Therefore, poor programming and algorithmic biases can make a negative impact on the usefulness of an AI-based setup in the organizations.

7.1. Trust Relationship between AI and Humans

The organization of future will be a mix of human workers and robots. You might feel more comfortable reporting to a robot than a human. It is because the human decision-making is often influenced by biases and prejudices. There are complaints of favoritism and partially in every other organization. On the other hand, a robot CEO is highly objective and focused. It is available 24/7, never sleeps, and never gets ill. Despite the presence of an AI manager, there are still various tasks for which human presence will be needed in the organization.

The biggest challenge for an AI general manager implementation will be to prepare the employees for the algorithmic transition. As I have explained earlier, the employees all over the world are highly fearful that the AI-based implementations will automate the tasks for which they have been hired. As a result, they may lose their jobs. Their fears are not unfounded and these concerns have also been endorsed and acknowledged by IMF in its recent report. According to a recent report[xcix] published by IMF, AI will make a significant influence on the global job market and approximately 40% of the jobs may be affected by AI-based implementations in different organizations. Therefore, organizations need to evaluate the pros and cons of AI-based implementations and manage effectively the motivation and morale of the employees.[c] The growing AI exposure in different countries and regions have been illustrated by IMF. The figure indicates that the share of AI is higher in advanced economies and emerging markets. It is because there is a high cost associated with developing an IT infrastructure for AI implementations.

Considering these factors, the owners and directors of the organizations should make a careful analysis of the whole situation and create a win-win situation in the organization. They should find ways of engaging the employees in more strategic tasks to improve the productivity of the organization. They should also make the employees realize that the sustainability of the organization will be at stake if the organization does not embrace AI. If the competitors become the early adopters, the organization may lose its competitive advantage. The employees should also be made to realize the significance of learning AI tools and technologies. Working with an AI general manager will be a significant boost on their CVs and their skills of working efficiently with machines will be highly valued and regarded in the AI-based world of today and tomorrow.

The organizational managers and CEOs might be looking at the AI implementation with a sense of fear and reservation. The world leaders recently gathered in the meeting of the World Economic Forum where AI implementation was the key theme of the meeting. The leaders from the key technology organizations used this opportunity to remove the concerns and fears regarding AI implementation. The perspectives from the renowned world leaders indicate the future of management in an AI-based world. The AI implementations will be increasingly prominent in the organizational setting and the managers will have to address the challenge so that the organizations remain sustainable, competitive, and resilient.

The beauty of human interaction is one area where the robots will never be able to beat the humans. It is a human nature that the people treat everyone differently. People develop a perception regarding the personality preferences of an individual and respond to their queries accordingly. On the other hand, a chatbot assistant will treat all human equally. The difference in responses based on the information and assistance needs of the individual is still beyond the capabilities of a chatbot. Some of the plagiarism checking websites such as turnitin can also detect if a given piece of text was written by a human or a chatbot. This capability makes it evident that the behavioral styles of a machine and a human are entirely different and a machine can never write with a human touch.

If humans have biases, then AI-based algorithms are also influenced by algorithms biases of the AI developers. When AI-based systems perform the conventional tasks of humans, they provide more opportunity to the coworkers to focus more on strategic and managerial level tasks. If recruitment and performance appraisal are carried out by algorithms, the HR managers will have the options to utilize the workforce in field visits, market analysis, and finding strategies of gaining a competitive advantage. The workers can also focus on sustainability issues and implementing green human resources strategies. Think of the tools such as ChatGPT and Google Bard. The job of the programmers is not gone. These tools can generate the code but the code still needs to be consolidated and deployed, which can only be done by a professional computer programmer. Therefore, an AI general manager will ease the task of the employees and make them more productive and useful in the organizational context.

There are some roles that can be performed efficiently by AI and there are also other roles that humans can perform even better than AI. It is these roles where the needs of humans will still be felt. In the case of digital assistants, the training of these assistants will still be carried out by humans. The analysis of AI-robots will be a quantitative analysis, however, qualitative analysis will still be carried out by humans. This qualitative analysis will indicate why a certain trend is developing and how the current roles and responsibilities of the management professionals can be modified.

Figure 97: AI-Human Trust Building[ci]

Figure 97 above highlights a strategy that should be highlighted and promoted by an AI manager. The AI manager should build a healthy partnership where the AI tools and technologies are seen as means of achieving more rather than replacing the humans altogether. There are still some jobs where humans can demonstrate more impressive performance than AI robots. Humans are well-versed in critical thinking. For humans, everything is not just right and wrong. They also evaluate the grey areas and acknowledge the dynamic reality of the phenomenon. Humans can also become strategic thinkers through their visionary approach, whereas robots can only learn based on the available datasets. In creative jobs, humans can perform well. Drama and video scripts are being written by AI, but how about poetry. There will be only a few (if any) examples where a high-level creative, poetry work could be produced by a robot. The humans also show more empathy in the communication process and they may overlook the shortcomings of an employee based on the contextual, environmental, and personality factors. However, an AI general manager will be very objective in the communication. The good performances will be appreciated, but there will also be immediate and prompt feedback on the bad performance that may not be liked by those employees who are very sensitive and short-tempered.

Another aspect is the physical skills and the evaluation of the physical skills. An AI general manager might struggle in a factory setting where physical labor work is required. The robots could prove to be highly expensive in these tasks, and it might not be possible for them to evaluate the performance of the workers involved in the physical labor. Robots are being used in warehouses for the proper and efficient maintenance of the inventory. However, consider the construction sector. The robots will find it difficult to do the labor-intensive task in the construction sector. Therefore, physical skills is one area where humans still dominate the robots.

Figure 98 shows the paradox of AI-human trust relationship. The humans view the AI as someone that will hit them from the back and kill/remove them from the jobs. On the other hand, the fact of the matter is that humans are struggling in a highly competitive job market of today. They might give up in their struggles at some point in their lives. However, embracing AI tools and technologies will enable the humans to become stable in their jobs. Moreover, AI tools will ensure that humans never give up and become incompetent in their jobs.

Figure 98: Paradox of AI-Human Trust[cii]

The paradox highlighted in the above figure can be the biggest challenge for an AI general manager. Although an AI general manager does not need to make itself happy because the machine has no emotions, but the AI general manager will also be dealing with humans and these humans should be happy and satisfied workers. Motivation and morale management is a crucial HR function and the AI general manager should be well programmed to perform this function efficiently. If the productivity of the employees do not increase and there is a high turnover rate in the organization, the AI general manager model will not be sustainable. The case studies that I have mentioned in this book, some of these implementations were halted because they could not produce the desired results. Therefore, the performance of the AI general manager will also be evaluated critically by the senior management.

The use of AI is influencing all aspects of a business entity. The multinational companies are fearful that if they do not embrace AI, they may lose their competitive advantage. However, the limited knowledge of the AI algorithms makes them hesitant in embracing AI at a mass scale. When there was a widespread adoption of AI tools and technologies in multinational organizations, the management professionals also thought that the AI concepts can be useful and significant in the managerial tasks as well because the emerging requirement of the management was to enable data-driven decision-making, and AI algorithms have the potential to process a huge amount of data quickly. However, the business entities are also not in favor that they do things where the decision-making is quick but they do not have any clue how a particular course of action was selected.

A landmark achievement was observed in 2016, when chatbots assistant were introduced. A chatbot assistant such as a WhatsApp chatbot remembers the solutions of the frequently asked questions by the clients. The queries are then responded by the chatbot in an automated manner without any intervention by the human. The beauty of this chatbot was that the support services became highly effective and were made available 24/7. Moreover, the accuracy of the responses was phenomenal because the responses are generated based on the processing of a large dataset. However, the users of the technology are also much aware of the potential and limitations of the technology. They know that they are talking to a chatbot that might give them general purpose answer but may not answer their specific queries and concerns. Even at the level of call centers, if the caller has the option of using automated menu options or calling to an operator, many callers would prefer calling to an operator because it provides a human touch and a personalized interaction. The beauty of human interaction is one area where the robots will never be able to beat the humans. It is a human nature that the people treat everyone differently. People develop a perception regarding the personality preferences of an individual and respond to their queries accordingly. On the other hand, a chatbot assistant will treat all human equally. The difference in responses based on the information and assistance needs of the individual is still beyond the capabilities of a chatbot. Some of the plagiarism checking websites such as turnitin can also detect if a given piece of text was written by a human or a chatbot. This capability makes it evident that the behavioral styles of a machine and a human are entirely different and a machine can never write with a human touch.

A survey was recently conducted in which the managers were asked to respond what they think they would do better and which tasks can be performed more appropriately by the robots. From the survey, it emerged that the most important benefit of an algorithmic CEO is the provision of an unbiased information. The CEO never controls or filters the information. This advantage was endorsed by the maximum number of managers (36%). The algorithms are also highly efficient in maintaining work schedules. The performance of humans is influenced by external factors as well such as family issues or illnesses. However, the algorithmic workers are always available for the task execution as long as the required IT infrastructure is available and connected.

The algorithmic CEOs are also problem solvers and they can make an efficient utilization of the available budget. The algorithmic CEOs and workers will always be truthful because they do not have any fear of scrutiny or losing their jobs. The team performance can also be evaluated effectively by algorithmic CEOs. The findings of this survey also indicated that it is not always the case that algorithms will outperform humans. There are also instances where human managers perform better than algorithms. One of these aspects is a better comprehension of the feelings. An algorithm will give a negative feedback to the employee without realizing the mental and emotional state of the employee. On the other hand, the humans will consider the environmental and contextual factors before issuing such remarks. The humans can also train other humans better than machines. An enabling work environment can also be ensured well by humans.

Employee motivation and morale management is going to be highly challenging for the business owners in an AI-based world. The employees are motivated to work because they expect that their efforts will be appreciated and rewarded. Moreover, they will gain an expert power by working hard and showing their commitment. In the new AI paradigm, there will not be such motivation available to them. Why should an employee work hard if the same work can be done by a robot in a much less time? It means that there will be no more appreciation of the work.

7.2. Objective Decision-Making

The AI managers will make an impression in the organizations when their performances significantly outperform the human managers. Several successful implementations have been made in this regard so far. Figure 30 below shows an implementation of an algorithmic CEO that was tested in a Hong Kong based company. The boss is named Tang Yu and she is the CEO of mobile and gaming company. The model proved highly successful in the organization and there was a marked improvement in the speed of execution and the quality of work. The company where this model was successfully tested is NetDragon.

AI general manager can also conduct performance appraisal effectively. Employees always have reservations and complaints that their efforts are not compensated adequately and the appraisals are always biased to the likes of the supervisor. Due to this reason, the management literature also suggests 360 degree feedback in addition to the straight line method of appraisal. In an ideal scenario, the performance appraisal should begin with the Plan stage as shown in Figure 27 below. At this stage, the annual objectives of an employee should be set. The next stage is the Act stage where the employee applies the skill set to achieve those objectives. The third stage is the Track stage where the supervisor should periodically monitor the performance of the subordinate and provide feedback. The last stage is review where the performance of the employee should be evaluated, the achievements should be appreciated and the deficiencies should be highlighted. To overcome those deficiencies, the key learning opportunities should be identified for the employees.

This appraisal cycle looks promising; however, in the real world environment, the supervisors are so busy in the regular tasks that they do not focus on the appraisal cycle. Moreover, due to the severe economic conditions, the employees are more worried regarding the survival of their jobs than the growth opportunities and performance appraisals. An algorithmic CEO can optimize the appraisal systems by using strength-based appraisals. In this strategy, the performance ratings are based on the strengths and competencies of the employees. When there is a fairness and equity in the appraisal process, the motivation and morale of the workforce also improves and the employees are always motivated to improve their skill set.

Performance appraisals are also a key source document for promoting the employees. The algorithmic performance appraisal evaluates each subordinate objectively and justly and only the most hardworking, competent, and devoted employee is selected for promotion and moving up the career ladder.

The AI-based systems will facilitate the AI manager in objective decision-making. Resource allocation, data analytics, and fraud detection will all be based on AI algorithms. The recommender and decision support systems will process huge data to provide the best options under given circumstances.

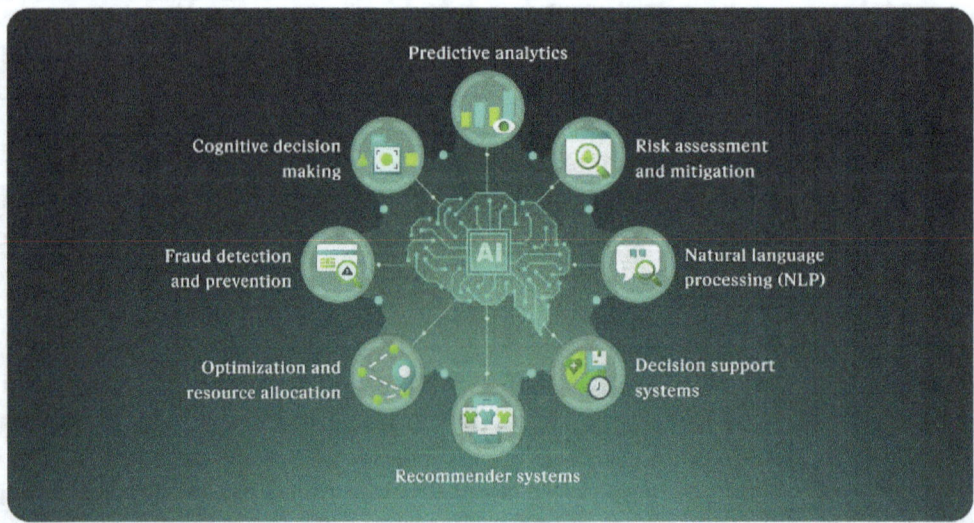

Figure 99: AI Systems for Objective Decision-Making[ciii]

Objective decision-making based on AI tools will also pose some challenges for the AI manager. As shown in Figure 100 below, one of the key challenges of AI is that the AI has a black box problem. The algorithmic decision-making makes it difficult for the humans to understand the logic and working of the AI programs. Therefore, the humans will take time to trust the recommendations of the AI systems. AI manager should be trained to provide this time flexibility to the human workers.

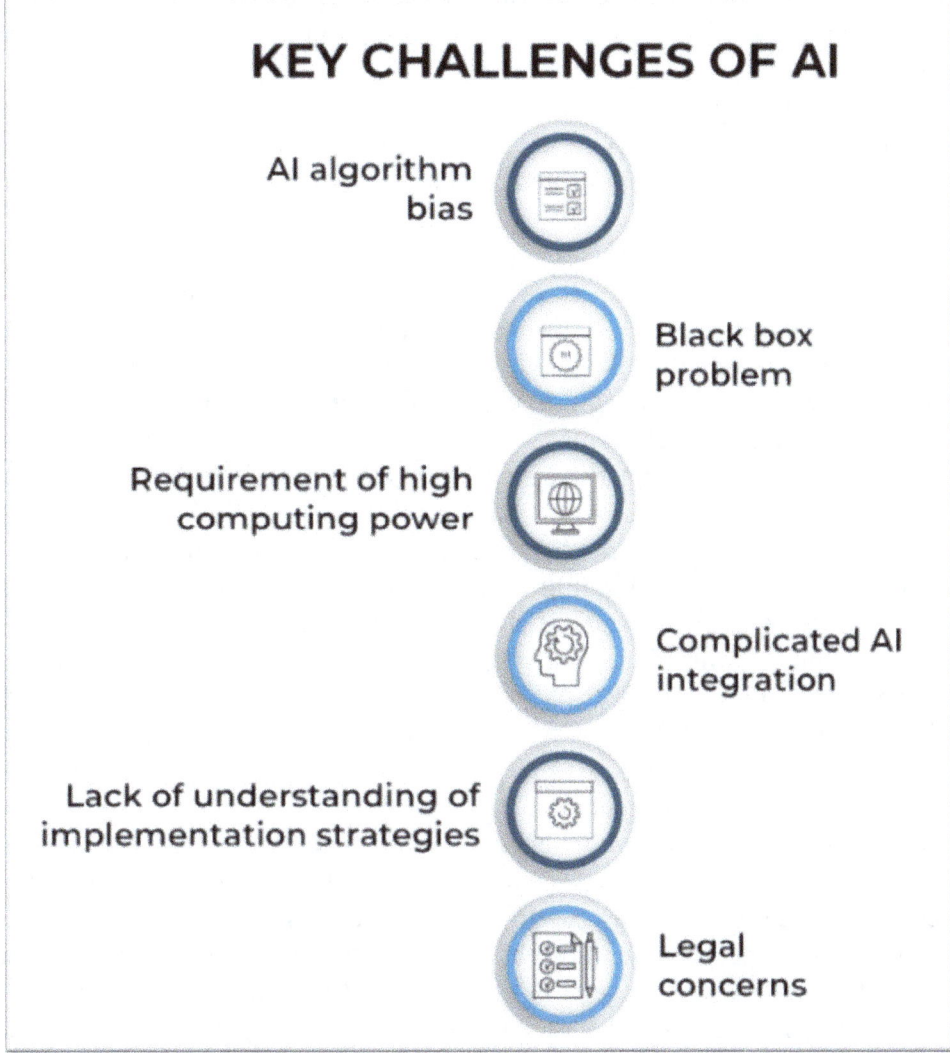

Figure 100: Challenges in Objective Decision-Making[civ]

Another challenge mentioned in the above figure is the complicated nature of AI integration. Most of the corporate organizations have some form of computer and software applications already in place. Some of the multinational organizations are also using ERP systems from Oracle, SAP, Microsoft, and other renowned vendors. They will not be in a position to completely replace their current systems with AI based systems. Therefore, the AI general manager will need to be integrated with the current business processes of the organization. It can be a real challenge because the current systems were not developed with the consideration of AI integration. They can handle big amount and volume of data, but the AI algorithms operate at an entirely different layer. The processing of huge data of AI algorithms that is incomparable with the current software systems. Moreover, the programming logic of the current systems is significantly different from the AI-based systems. Therefore, the integration of these systems with the AI systems will be a real challenge.

Another important challenge is the requirement of high computing power. The AI algorithms provide good results and recommendations at a cost, and this cost is high computing power. The algorithms process a huge volume of data, and therefore, consume far more energy than the conventional systems. Across the globe, there is an emphasis on conserving the energy sources and using renewable sources of energy. When there is a higher use of energy, the energy bills of the organization will also increase due to the use of the AI general manager. Therefore, the overall model of AI general manager might be revisited by the senior management. Therefore, before the implementation, the AI developers should make a good estimate of the required energy resources and present to the management the clear picture of the future energy utilization of the corporation. Then the owners should weigh the pros and cons of implementing the AI general manager in the light of the energy cost associated with the implementation.

The use of AI is influencing all aspects of a business entity. The multinational companies are fearful that if they do not embrace AI, they may lose their competitive advantage. However, the limited knowledge of the AI algorithms makes them hesitant in embracing AI at a mass scale. When there was a widespread adoption of AI tools and technologies in multinational organizations, the management professionals also thought that the AI concepts can be useful and significant in the managerial tasks as well because the emerging requirement of the management was to enable data-driven decision-making, and AI algorithms have the potential to process a huge amount of data quickly. However, the business entities are also not in favor that they do things where the decision-making is quick but they do not have any clue how a particular course of action was selected.

In the project management paradigm, there are several key processes and the AI systems should be able to optimize all these processes. A typical project will involve the estimation of tasks and resources. Then the costing and resource scheduling should be done. The project manager also needs to do sequencing and collating of data. They also identify risks and trends in the projects. The AI-based systems should assist in all these areas. Good AI-based systems offer automated scheduling, optimization of all tasks, predictive analytics features, and machine learning algorithms for all AI types.

This book highlights the role of AI general manager and beyond. Therefore, the benefits of AI-based project management should also be viewed as to how AI can assist general managers if it is not possible to appoint an AI general manager altogether. Various benefits can be gained in those cases. The training and development of the employees will be based on the analysis of their learning habits by the AI software. The resource allocation will be optimized due to which it will be easier to release the employees from the operational tasks and depute them to the project activities. The project team will be able not only to track the progress of the project but also predict the future activities of the project. The budgeting and scheduling tasks will all be automated. The complex, employee-based analytics will be handled smoothly by the AI software. Therefore, AI algorithms will sever as a virtual assistant of the project manager in cases where it is not possible to appoint an AI project manager.

7.3. Strategic Planning based on Intelligent Data

AI benefits in management by the mapping of AI technologies and the management support. The algorithmic managers are powered by machine learning technologies, neural networks, data mining, big data science, and business intelligence. All these AI-based concepts can provide immense support to the management. The benefits can be seen in the optimized decision-making and accurate decision-making. The benefit can also be observed in the improved functionality of the organization. The tasks such as recruitment, performance appraisal, wealth management, and supply chain management can all be automated. It should be noted that various individual components make up an AI robot and the unique, mechanistic blend of these components improve the processing capabilities of an AI manager.

Field	Technique	Analytics	Human Intelligence		Artificial Intelligence
			Insights	Decisions	Actions
Data Strategy	Data Visualization	Descriptive: What happened?			
Business Intelligence	Business Intelligence	Diagnostic: Why did it happen?			
Data Science and Machine Learning	Predictive Analytics and Modeling	Predictive: What will happen?			
	Machine Learning and Optimization	Prescriptive: What should I do?		Decision Support	
				Decision Automation	
Artificial Intelligence		Artificial Intelligence: How can I enhance or replace human reasoning?			

Figure 101: AI-Based Strategic Planning[cv]

Figure 101 shows that intelligent data gathering for strategic planning requires considering different dimensions of AI. At the level of field, the AI manager should consider data strategies, business intelligence, data science methods, and machine learning techniques. At the analytics level, the data insights should be gained regarding the descriptive, predictive, as well as prescriptive dimensions. The decision support systems should be developed based on the three key variables of insights, decisions, and actions.

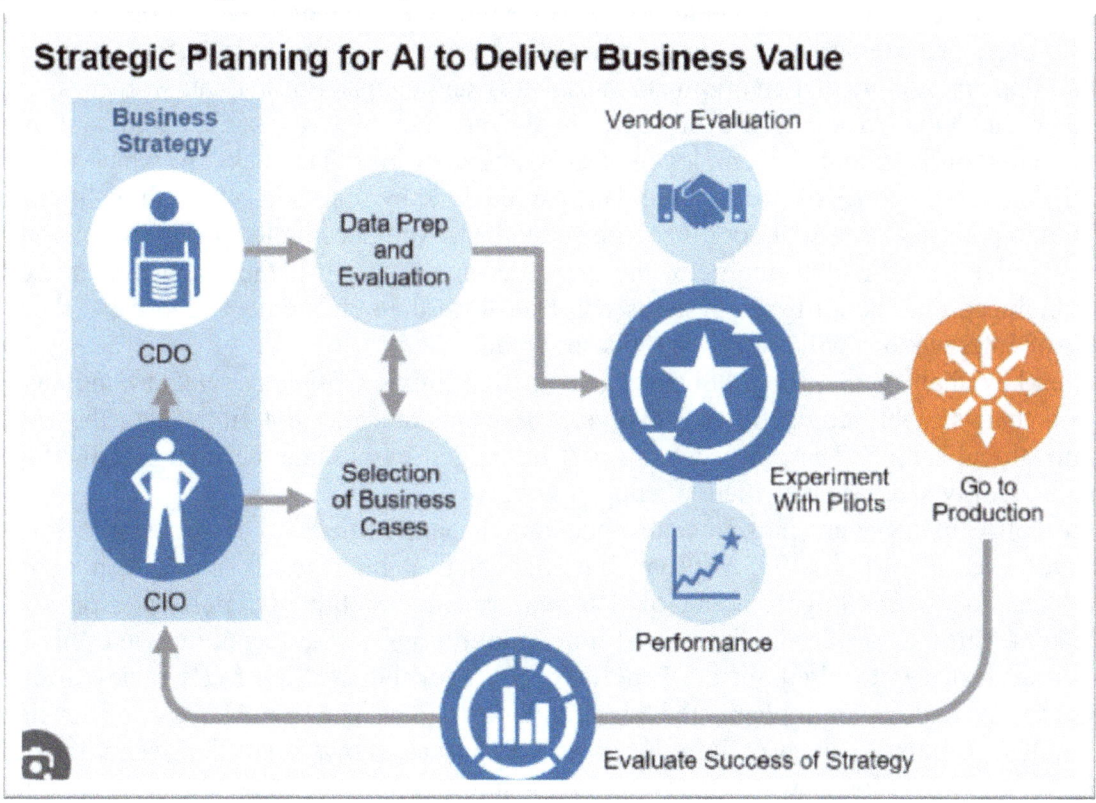

Figure 102: Artificial Intelligence and Strategic Planning[cvi]

Figure 102 above shows that when AI is used in the process of strategic planning, higher business value can be achieved. An active role should be played in this regard by the information officer and data officer. The data officer should prepare and make the critical evaluation of the data. The information officer should produce and select the relevant business cases. Pilot testing should be made by the systems for the evaluation of different strategies.

This step should also be supported by vendor evaluation and performance evaluation. After this rigorous process, any new business strategy should be finalized and go to the production stage.

In the project management paradigm, there are several key processes and the AI systems should be able to optimize all these processes. A typical project will involve the estimation of tasks and resources. Then the costing and resource scheduling should be done. The project manager also needs to do sequencing and collating of data. They also identify risks and trends in the projects. The AI-based systems should assist in all these areas. Good AI-based systems offer automated scheduling, optimization of all tasks, predictive analytics features, and machine learning algorithms for all AI types.

7.4. Success Stories

Despite the promising outcomes of an AI general manager, there are still only a few successful case studies of an algorithmic CEO. This raises the question why organizations are reluctant to make the optimum utilization of the AI. The managers have expressed their concerns and challenges in AI management.

The first challenge faced in AI based management is that employees are accustomed to interacting with other humans. They miss the human touch and socialization aspect in robotic environment. The environment becomes too mechanistic. The algorithmic CEOs assume that the receivers of their instructions are also robots and they will be able to follow each and every word of their instructions. The humans do not work that way and their rationality is always bounded by various constraints including the family constraints and technical constraints. The second challenge is the issue of security and privacy of the data. There is so much connectivity of the devices for the efficient working of AI algorithms. The data exposure might be without consent or a data breach from a single device may aggravate to a massive data breach. The skill set of professionals regarding the maintenance of AI systems is limited. Therefore, hackers can exploit this opportunity and compromise the sanctity and integrity of the data.

Another challenge faced in the organizational setting is that as soon as the AI based implementation is announced, employees fear losing their jobs. The tasks for which they had established the timelines of two to three days can be done by robots in two to three hours. So, they anticipate that they will soon become redundant. Another challenge highlighted in the survey is the lack of understanding of the potential impact of AI. If the management itself is not convinced that the AI based systems will transform the management landscape, then the AI based interventions will always be a distant dream.

Another key challenge in using AI boss is that an algorithmic CEO may select a candidate for the job that is highly competitive. However, the candidate may not fit well to the current organizational setting. These aspects can best be judged by humans because it constitutes a dynamic reality and has an element of subjectivity.

The use of AI in management is not a new phenomenon and some level of implementation was observed even as early as 1983. At that time, the database management tools such as oracle were used to process large amount of data and general intelligent reports and dashboard indicators. But the AI of today has found much more usage of the technology and this book takes one next step to highlight the benefits of an algorithmic CEO. Let's review how the organizations have so far implemented humanoid robo CEOs. The first AI boss was developed by Hitachi Company. It was introduced in 2015 that shows that the technology and management professionals were exploring the possibility of AI in management for quite long. They wanted more accuracy and objectivity in the decision-making process and provide more freedom of expression to the subordinates. Robo-CEO is an algorithmic CEO that selects the most suitable candidate based on the available data. Unlike traditional CEO, the employee is most likely to move up the career ladder due to the objective decision-making of the algorithmic CEO.

AI bosses are not limited to the human resource function and they are also being used in other management and business functions. There is also an implementation where the algorithmic managers have been used for an effective wealth management.

There is a successful implementation by a firm in which AI manager was used for talent acquisition and talent management. This robot was given the responsibility of managing a $100 billion firm. The entire human resources of the company will be handled by the algorithmic CEO. The company aims to replace more and more humans with robots in key leadership positions.

Recruitment was one of the first HR functions where the algorithms were introduced in the form of a robot recruiter. The robots have been highly successful in conducting interviews and candidates express them comfortably in front of a robot. The responses are also processed efficiently by the robots and the same processing strategy is applied for all candidates.

With the growth of the automated screening process, the job candidates should also update their CVs so that the robots do not discard their resumes. The traditional CVs might not be considered worthy by the robots. Performance appraisals are also a key source document for promoting the employees. The algorithmic performance appraisal evaluates each subordinate objectively and justly and only the most hardworking, competent, and devoted employee is selected for promotion and moving up the career ladder.

There is also an implementation of an algorithmic CEO that was tested in a Hong Kong based company. The boss is named Tang Yu and she is the CEO of mobile and gaming company. The model proved highly successful in the organization and there was a marked improvement in the speed of execution and the quality of work. The company where this model was successfully tested is NetDragon.

In the current context, a robot CEO was appointed by a Chinese firm NetDragon. The robot CEO was appointed with the intent that the process flow of the business entity will be streamlined and the speed of task execution will improve substantially.

Mika became the CEO of a Drinks Company. She promised the availability of 24/7 for their subordinates and told them that there would not be any layoffs in the company. She performs the tasks of identifying the potential customers and the artists for the new and innovative designs of the bottles.

A robot was developed by a Japanese company and this robot is planned to be deployed for managing the manufacturing operations in Japan. It has been developed by Ryo Yoshida, who himself is a CEO of a Japanese company.

In a landmark event at telecommunication conference, there was also a press talk of robots. The robots emphasized in this press conference that humans should not fear losing their jobs due to robots. Moreover, they do not have any plans to rebel against humans.

All these success stories indicate that AI has a significant role in improve the managerial aspects of an organization. AI systems can become a CEO of the organization. In the other cases, the robots can assist the general managers and make them more productive and working smartly.

A landmark achievement was observed in 2016, when chatbots assistant were introduced. A chatbot assistant such as a WhatsApp chatbot remembers the solutions of the frequently asked questions by the clients. The queries are then responded by the chatbot in an automated manner without any intervention by the human. The beauty of this chatbot was that the support services became highly effective and were made available 24/7. Moreover, the accuracy of the responses was phenomenal because the responses are generated based on the processing of a large dataset. However, the users of the technology are also much aware of the potential and limitations of the technology. They know that they are talking to a chatbot that might give them general purpose answer but may not answer their specific queries and concerns.

Even at the level of call centers, if the caller has the option of using automated menu options or calling to an operator, many callers would prefer calling to an operator because it provides a human touch and a personalized interaction. The beauty of human interaction is one area where the robots will never be able to beat the humans. It is a human nature that the people treat everyone differently. People develop a perception regarding the personality preferences of an individual and respond to their queries accordingly. On the other hand, a chatbot assistant will treat all human equally. The difference in responses based on the information and assistance needs of the individual is still beyond the capabilities of a chatbot. Some of the plagiarism checking websites such as turnitin can also detect if a given piece of text was written by a human or a chatbot. This capability makes it evident that the behavioral styles of a machine and a human are entirely different and a machine can never write with a human touch.

Chapter 8

AI Management Roadmap

8. Future of AI Manager

The future organizations are expected to be a nice blend of AI workers and human workers. It will also affect how the organograms will be presented and reported in different statutory reports. In a typical organization, the CEO might be an algorithmic CEO and all key leadership positions are occupied by robots. Humans have been assigned only to the operational work, and the technology-driven aspect of the organization has been endorsed at the level of the organization chart. AI bosses are not limited to the human resource function and they are also being used in other management and business functions.

From an AI boss, you will get a feel that the individual is very much focused on the work and there will be complete impartiality in the decision-making process. You may also discuss your concerns and issues with an open heart to an AI boss because there is no fear of retaliation and anger on the part of the boss. The boss is instructed to listen to the issues of the subordinates calmly and openly. The performance of the team will be measured strictly against the assigned objectives quarterly and annually.

Recruitment was one of the first HR functions where the algorithms were introduced in the form of a robot recruiter. The robots have been highly successful in conducting interviews and candidates express them comfortably in front of a robot. The responses are also processed efficiently by the robots and the same processing strategy is applied for all candidates. The function of a robot does not end at conducting an interview. The algorithms can also participate in the entire process of recruitment and selection. They can evaluate all the interview results and select the right and the most suitable candidate by matching the organizational requirements with the candidate skill sets.

Figure 103 shows a blue-print of an AI-powered organization in which cloud-based platforms will play a dominant role. There will be interconnected devices all over the place and the whole setup will be powered by Internet of Things infrastructure. This will require a highly trained and technology advanced AI manager that can efficiently manage all the technological and human resources.

Figure 103: AI-Based Future Organizations[cvii]

Figure 104: AI CEO Responsibilities[cviii]

Figure 104 shows an AI futuristic CEO, and as I explained earlier, the AI CEO will have huge responsibilities. It is true that AI CEO is just a machine and can bear all burdens and pressures. However, the efficiency of the AI general manager will be measured by the quality of its decisions. This quality is dependent on how well the robot is trained to manage the machine interactions as well as human interactions.

8.1. How to Implement AI Manager Effectively

An algorithmic boss can be a real blessing for an organization if the implementation considers several key aspects and a formal strategy are developed for the transformation process. There are several recommendations in this regard. In the strategy phase, you will need to determine to what extent, the algorithmic management is needed in your organization. In the next step, you should develop a change management process. In this stage, you will have to train the existing staff for using algorithms instead of manual interventions. The management should still make the communication lines open because the change will be successful through an evolutionary process. Once the algorithmic management is in place, the management should constantly evaluate the management flow of the algorithms so that the algorithmic decision-making is not influenced by the algorithmic biases.

From the AI boss, you will get a feel that the individual is very much focused on the work and there will be complete impartiality in the decision-making process. You may also discuss your concerns and issues with an open heart to an AI boss because there is no fear of retaliation and anger on the part of the boss. The boss is instructed to listen to the issues of the subordinates calmly and openly. The performance of the team will be measured strictly against the assigned objectives quarterly and annually. A key benefit of an algorithmic CEO that employees are reporting happily to them. They know that the behavior of the boss will be unbiased and the interaction will be limited to the assigned job responsibilities. There will be no favors and additional tasks asked by the boss. Moreover, the working day end within the working hour and there will be no stretched timings and late duties.

Figure 105 shows how the AI CEO, Ms. Tang Yu, is managing the human resources at a Chinese company. The employees are interacting happily with the CEO, and they trust the directions and recommendations of the CEO.

Figure 105: AI CEO Managing the Team[cix]

As highlighted in Figure 105, AI general manager will also need some tools for effective decision-making. The managerial aspect requires a high level of collaboration and effective business communication. There, AI humanoid CEO should be supported with various emerging and on-demand AI services. Some of the technologies have gained a huge prominence in the AI world. The chat services can be managed effectively by ChatGPT and Bard services. The document management systems and chatbots also assist in the effective management of the workspace by the AI manager.

In order to understand the significance of data-driven decision-making, it is crucial to know the evolutionary process of AI-based systems. The AI-based systems for data-driven decision-making were first presented as assisted intelligence systems. The key selling point of the systems at that time was that these systems can learn in an organized manner, whereas the humans do not take the learning process so seriously. In the next phase, it was realized that a good AI system is a product of human-machine interaction. It was argued that the quality of an AI system is influenced by the data model and if a good quality data is not provided by the humans, the algorithms cannot work effectively. Therefore, there was a gradual shift to augmented intelligence where machines facilitate humans and humans facilitate machines. The third phase or the current phase is regarded as autonomous intelligence. In this era, the nature of tasks changes very rapidly.

Therefore, the decisions need to be taken by the AI manager in an automated manner based on data and predefined rules, policies, and procedures of the organization. The machines should have a mechanism of a continued learning. It means that the AI CEO that the subordinates are interacting with today will not have the same responses in the future because it is a machine. Based on a continued learning, the responses and the behavioral disposition of the algorithmic CEO will also change.

It is argued in the management literature that the data-based decision-making is possible only if the decisions of the managers are based on seven key pillars. The first aspect is leadership. The decision-making process should provide leadership regarding the strategic directions of the organization. The second aspect is trust. The human managers as well as AI general manager can use the data only if it is trustworthy and is relied upon by all the stakeholders of the organization. If the quality of the data is very low, then the data-driven decision-making may prove to be counterproductive. The third aspect is the commitment level of the managers. They should keep their personal biases aside and follow the patterns and trends in data for effective decision-making. The other aspect is the use of metrics. An AI general manager should have the availability of all key metrics and dashboard indicators. These indicators should provide the real-time view of the organization. Another dimension is data literacy. It is a common argument against the AI algorithms that the users do not know how the algorithms arrived at a particular decision. An AI general manager should also consider this aspect and it should be able to explain the rationale of the decision-making to its human subordinates. Moreover, staff training and awareness are also essential in data-base approach to decision-making.

Figure 106: A Machine Governing the Humans[cx]

Figure 106 shows that the AI general manager is leading the whole organization and the humans are at the lower career ladder following the instructions and commands of a machine. To fully understand the potential of AI learning in resource allocation, project management, and risk assessment, it is crucial to gain a basic understanding of how the learning process works in the AI-based systems. Active learning in AI is a function of Label, Enrich, Train, and Query processes. First, a given sample or a resource will be assigned a label by the system. It facilitates in identifying the sample and assigning it to a class or a category. The training dataset is enriched by the inclusion of the newly labelled sample because the system sees it as an opportunity of learning and strengthening the system protocols. In the Train phase, the AI model receives the training based on the available dataset. This dataset includes the past, historical data as well as the newly added samples. The query process can also be used by the learning function to view and select different samples available in the dataset. This simple example shows the power of AI-based algorithms that they are always ready for the new learning. As soon as they receive the newly added samples, they trigger the training phase and train the AI model based on the current and new data.

As I explained earlier, the algorithmic managers are powered by machine learning technologies, neural networks, data mining, big data science, and business intelligence. All these AI-based concepts can provide immense support to the management. The benefits can be seen in the optimized decision-making and accurate decision-making. The benefit can also be observed in the improved functionality of the organization. The tasks such as recruitment, performance appraisal, wealth management, and supply chain management can all be automated. I had also highlighted that the learning process can be effective if there are no algorithmic biases in the AI-based systems. The key factor in AI systems is the quality of data. If the training examples in the dataset favor a certain segment of the population, then the AI model will learn wrong rules that will affect the algorithmic decision-making. Due to these limitations of the AI algorithms, professionals working in AI always prefer narrow AI over general AI.

While considering the benefits of AI learning in resource allocation, project management, and risk management, another key area of consideration is the distinction between supervised and unsupervised learning. The first form is supervised learning in which the self-learning system is not built into the model. The learning process is initiated at various time intervals and a trigger is generated in the system to initiate the learning process. The second form is unsupervised learning in which the algorithms enable learning as soon as they encounter new data points and interactions. The third form is reinforcement learning in which the learned data points are categorized into positive or negative reinforcers. It is easier to understand that the risk of algorithmic bias is higher in supervised learning because the learning process is at the discretion of the AI developer. Moreover, when negative reinforcers are identified in reinforcement learning, it is based on how the negativity is defined in the system by the AI developer that creates an algorithmic bias.

The resource allocation based on AI learning is executed in a highly sophisticated manner. Considering this aspect, the AI developers recommend that various parameters should be reviewed by the technology team before implementing resource allocation. In a study, these considerations have been considered into three key categories of task, approach, and computing paradigm as shown in Figure 60 below. The first area of consideration is that how many resource allocation strategies will be input into the system and how the power consumption can be optimized during the algorithmic decision-making. The efficient power management is always crucial in AI-based software because the AI models process huge datasets that might consume energy beyond the available resources of the organization. The second factor is the AI approach in which the technology team should select from the available machine learning techniques and deep learning techniques. The third factor is the computing paradigm. Ideally, the resource allocation should be processed in the cloud computing environment because various nodes and parameters will be processed that will require extensive storage space and the computing power. Other options may also be considered such as the IoT environment, edge computing, or mobile edge computing.

The AI-based resource allocation can offer various advantages to the senior management. These benefits are further optimized when the CEO or the general manager of the company is an AI robot and not a human. It is because the resource allocation management software based on AI concepts assume that the user of these tools will also be well versed in executing the different functions and interfaces of the software. In the case of an AI CEO, this intelligence is built into the CEO algorithms that increases the benefits of an AI-based resource allocation. When the resource allocation takes advantage of the AI concepts, the efficiency and productivity of the workforce increases because the system learns from the mistakes and makes continuous adaptations to the resource allocation process. The resource planning is also optimized because it is based on the predefined rules and criteria and alternate plans and strategies are also made part of the algorithmic process. The burden of the administration is reduced significantly because the resource allocation is accomplished automatically and everyone is aware of their roles and possible tasks that might be assigned in the near future. The organizations can also reduce costs and gain a competitive advantage through AI-based resource allocation.

As I explained earlier, various features and options that are offered by different AI vendors in the resource allocation software. The resource allocation becomes entirely automated in the AI-based software. The predictive management is also a well-known feature of the AI where the issues and problems in the existing strategies are tracked by the system proactively and alternate strategies are recommended. The dashboard indicators also show the real-time availability of all available resources. There are also options for time tracking and project management. The resources needed for future projects and future years can also be forecasted by the system and then the algorithmic CEO can initiate the hiring process for meeting the higher demand of resources in the future. The resources may also be needed in the form of financial resources and material resources. In those cases, the procurement department may be intimated for acquiring the materials and funding agencies may be contacted for receiving the required funds for the future projects.

There are also the benefits of resource allocation from the technology paradigm. When the organizations opt for AI-based resource allocation in management, the quality of data analysis improves significantly. The entered data is not only used for reporting and descriptive statistics, but inferences are also drawn and future state of the organization is also predicted based on the current data. In this way, if there are loopholes in any strategy, they can be rectified well before their occurrence. The real-time monitoring of the resource allocation is also possible because the resource allocation is carried out by the systems and all the decision-making steps are recorded and reported by the system. The collaboration process is also improved significantly and the resource allocation can also cover remote workers through the use of virtualization hardware, software, and systems.

There can be a model of AI resource allocation software in which reinforcement learning can be used. The learning mechanism ensures that the quality of experience is at an optimum level when the output is sent to the end users. Between the users and the physical servers, there is a whole system of network topologies and AI-based systems. When the tasks are received by the task receiver, the intelligent agent is used for generating rewards and assigning resources. This information is stored in the mapping table. The intelligent agent also receives the feedback from the end users regarding the quality of experience and then the improvements are made by reinforcement learning. This whole AI-based resource allocation system not only ensures an efficient allocation of resources but also learns from the feedback of the users and make improvements in the resource allocation tasks for the future scenarios.

In a study, 152 cognitive projects were studied. It was found that robotics and automation are being used extensively in cognitive projects and it significantly increases the power of resource allocation, AI-based software. Currently, general managers spend significant time in identifying the best fit for a project or a management task. Even during the course of the project, they might find out that they erred in the decision-making and did not find the right person for the right job. These limitations in the decision-making has a lot to do with the cognitive potential of a leader. However, an AI-based general manager can improve the cognitive potential of an AI CEO due to objective decision making and using the cognitive thinking facilities of the latest AI-based software. As a result, the managers can always be confident that they have the best team available and each employee has been assigned the tasks based on the person-organization fit. The assigned person possesses all the capabilities and skills for executing the assigned task.

Various tools and technologies can be used in AI-based resource allocation. The data points are classified by the algorithms for feature extraction. The regression analysis indicate the contribution of each resources in the accomplishment of overall organizational objectives. The forecasting models predict the future demand of resources based on the objectives and goals set by the organization. The clustering mechanism uses the features and highlights groups and patterns in the data. The process of machine translation codifies the strategies for algorithmic decision-making. The computer vision technology may also be used for identifying and recommending the resources. The generative AI can be used in the process of collaboration and communication. The reinforcement learning makes it possible that the system improves over time based on the bottlenecks emerged in the current strategies of resource allocation.

Risk assessment has become a highly crucial activity for the general managers because the projects in the organizations incur significant costs. In the competitive world, the costs should be justified and risk mitigation strategies should also be developed by the management to keep the organization sustainable. The risk assessment activities usually begin with the identification of risks in the internal and external environment. Then the risks are analyzed and their severity level are ascertained. In the final stage, strategies are developed for the management of these risks. A good AI-based system automates all these three processes of risk management. The net outcomes is the development of more relevant and efficient risk management strategies.

I have given you an example of risk assessment using AI tools and how it can be successfully used for the assessment of underwriting. The accuracy level is improved because AI algorithms analyze huge datasets. The efficient AI algorithms process big data speedily and generate meaningful results. The systems provide the details of the most profitable market segments. The fraudulent claims are quickly identified based on the historical data. The system also offers personalized recommendations to the customers based on their needs. The overall cost of operation is reduced due to accuracy and protecting fraudulent claims.

I have highlighted various benefits of AI learning for resource allocation, project management, and risk management. However, similar to other technological advancements, the use of machine learning in management may also be associated with various issues and problems. I am highlighting these issues so that you are more aware about all that AI has to offer and the associated pitfalls. I would still urge you to go for an AI general manager because in the overall analysis, the benefits still significantly outweigh the pitfalls. The first drawback of using machine learning is the acquisition of data. The quality of AI data model is reliant on the quality of training data, and in many cases, acquiring the data may become a cumbersome activity. There may also be issues regarding the legitimate rights of accessing and using those datasets. If the dataset is limited, then AI algorithms will not give you the desired results because their key strength lies in big data processing and providing meaningful results based on the comprehensive analysis of data.

The second drawback is the time and resources needed for AI implementation. Although the automation and quick processing will be achieved by using AI algorithms, these benefits will only be seen in the long run. In the short run, more time will be consumed in implementing the systems and training the workforce. In some organizations, there is a high employee turnover rate that further increases the time to learn. The third drawback is to interpret the results produced by the AI algorithms. The algorithms process huge datasets before providing recommendations. A human general manager may find it difficult to know the rationale behind a specific recommendation. If the things do not go as expected, the human manager may struggle in justifying their moves.

The fourth drawback is the risk of error in the absence of data. There is no doubt that AI algorithms will provide accurate results when the relevant data is available. However, when the relevant data is not available, there is a general tendency of the algorithms to produce the results based on whatever is available to them. You might have observed it while using ChatGPT or Google Bard. If these chatbots do not have the relevant data, they still respond you with irrelevant and inaccurate results. It can become a serious limitation in the organizational context when the processes will have automated and there will be a huge reliance on the AI based systems.

There are also some more issues with machine learning in management. The organizations may face cost overruns because appointment an AI general manager and automating all tasks require a complete overhaul of the current IT infrastructure. The training of the remaining human workforce will also incur a significant cost. There is also limited capabilities of AI developers available in the IT industry that are particularly proficient in AI based implementations. There is also a great potential of misuse of the technology because as I mentioned earlier, the AI-based systems also suffer with the algorithmic bias. Moreover, the end users can manipulate the system by benefitting from the limited expertise of the senior management in using AI-based systems.

The ultimate AI-based implementation can be achieved in an organization when an algorithmic CEO takes charge of the organization. In the other cases, the robots may be appointed for assisting the general manager. It will also prove to be a good strategy because the robots in the execute roles will keep the manager focused and committed. The robot will also remind them about the meeting and the tasks that are to be submitted shortly. It will ensure that the manager executes all the tasks happily and never miss a task. The managers often struggle in multitasking. However, the robots will show them the best course of action and at any given point in time, the general managers will also perform the most relevant task in the organization. There is another benefit of AI performing executive roles. The humans have limited capacities of working and they easily get tired when there are stretched timings or work overload. On the contrary, the robots can work stress-free throughout the day and they can also be made available 24/7. They work as per instructions without any demand of reward and compensation. They are also honest and candid in their responses because they do not have any job insecurity or personal motives.

When the concept of AI general manager or AI CEO is implemented in the organizations, there will always be a need to create an organizational structure, which is a mix of both humans and robots. In the future, one might see an organizational chart where the humans and robots are working together. In this context, the AI CEO will also need to consider the human-robot interaction and ensure that it is executed in a smooth manner and humans are satisfied and comfortable working with robots.

8.2. Workforce Training and Development

Figure 107 shows that there are numerous benefits of workforce training and development and these benefits also apply to AI-based training and development. The employees are the end-users of all tools and technologies. They should not only be aware of using all the tools and systems but also know the working of AI algorithms to the best extent possible.

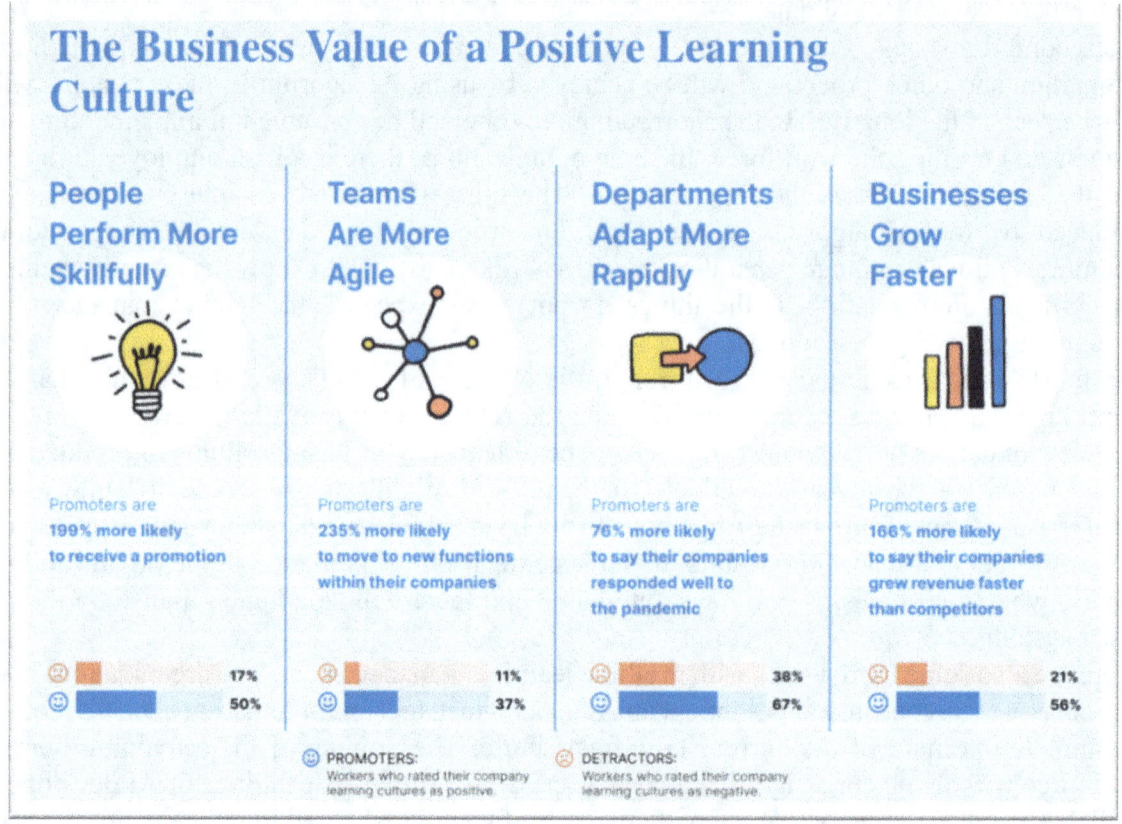

Figure 107: Training and Development Benefits[cxi]

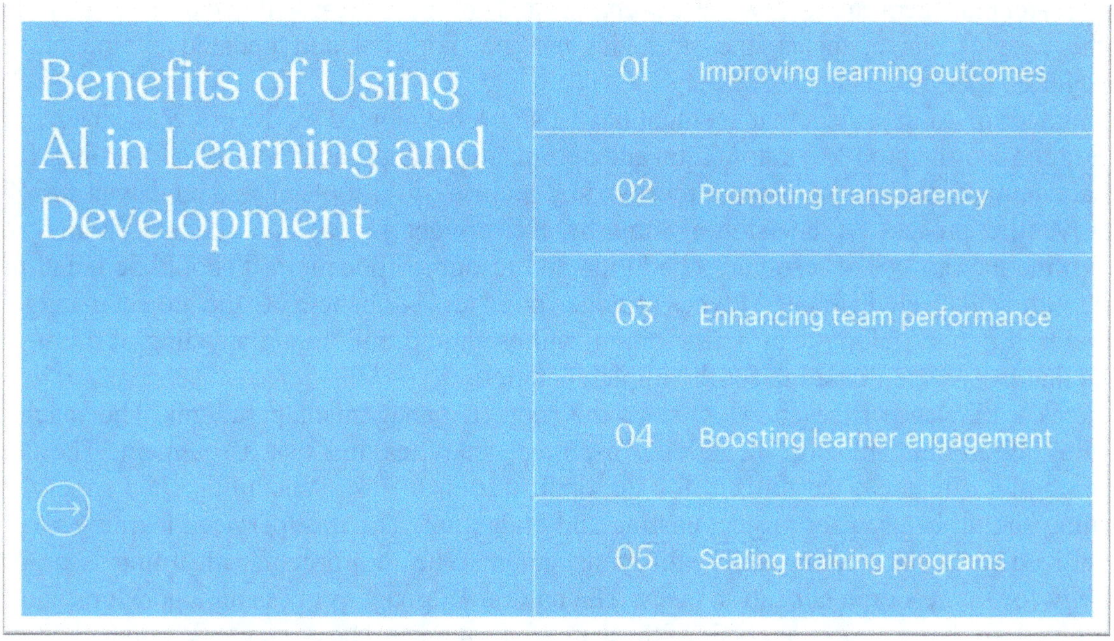

Figure 108: AI Utilization in Training and Development[cxii]

Figure 108 shows how AI itself can be used in the training and development process to enrich the learning environment. This level of integration will promote transparency and team performance. There will be higher level of learner engagement and the scaling of training programs. AI algorithms can prove to be an effective general manager because of their abilities of enabling a process of continued learning. For the humans, the management has to ask them to go for continued professional development. Moreover, some managers do not have the required aptitude for the leadership positions, and they are successful in securing the positions based on the tenure of their employment. All these aspects can be addressed effectively by an AI general manager because it does not require an aptitude and interest for learning. The algorithms will learn in an automated, mechanistic style. The AI learning can benefit in executing the management process successfully and what its specific benefits are in the context of resource allocation, project management, and risk assessment.

A successful AI learning in project management should result in task automation, efficient resource allocation, advanced predictive analytics, and effective natural language processing. The project planning is improved significantly because the project managers can take advantage of the recommendations and data-based suggestions provided by the AI algorithms. The project monitoring also becomes easier because AI keeps track of all the project tasks and provides alerts on those tasks where the deadlines might be missed. Hence, the project managers can focus on those tasks that require their immediate attention and leave the monitoring of those tasks where there is a good report given by the AI systems. In this way, an enhanced efficiency of the project managers can be ensured.

The predictive analytics feature provides an edge to the AI-based software to the conventional project management software. The AI-based software also predict and simulate the future state of the project and alert the project managers if there are any complications and issues in achieving the desired outcomes. A marked improvement in the overall decision-making process can be observed by implementing AI in project management. It is imperative to understand how the AI models develop a predictive model for an efficient project management. The complete flow of the machine learning algorithms can be depicted. With the help of the training set, the algorithms perform both supervised and unsupervised learning. The new data is also continuously added in the training data. Features are then extracted from the training set. Then the machine learning algorithms work on the developed AI model and the annotated data. Ultimately, the grouping of objects is accomplished and predictive models are developed. These predictive models inform the project managers regarding the future state of the project.

The project managers can review these scenarios and compare them with the desired scenarios. In the case of discrepancies, the strategies can be modified and updated by the project managers.

Advantages of AI in project management have also been endorsed by the Project Management Institute. According to PMI, automation and optimization can be achieved by AI learning. Risk management strategies can also be improved by the use of AI tools. The data-driven insights improve the process of decision-making by the project managers. The algorithms also streamline the process of resource scheduling and resource allocation. It should be noted that at the technical level, different AI types provide varied level of benefits to the project managers. Therefore, the technology team in the organizations should build understanding of all the AI types that they are anticipating for the implementation.

There is a relevance of each AI type in the project management paradigm. The machine learning algorithms are more beneficial in project analytics and risk assessment. The deep learning algorithms can be utilized for the optimization of task scheduling. The supervised learning should be used for project costing and budgeting. The unsupervised learning should be utilized for team creating and team management. The reinforcement learning is a good strategy for the resource allocation tasks. The natural language processing algorithms should be utilized for the sentiment analysis of the team performance. The computer vision technology should be used for the summarization of the educational videos related to the project. The adversarial networks should be utilized for the testing of projects in a safe and secure environment. The expert systems will be needed when risk management is to be carried out based on historical data.

8.3. Ethical Frameworks for AI Implementation

The AI-based management has raised concerns because of the intrusive nature of the AI algorithms. As I explained earlier, the AI algorithms process a large amount of data for making an efficient AI model. The development of the data model may access those data sets for which explicit information has not been provided. The quality of algorithms gets improved but the question arises whether legitimate means have been used for improving the efficiency of algorithms. AI has invaded all aspects of the humanity. In the absence of a standard regulatory framework, the fate of the AI-based systems is left to the integrity of the AI developers. As I explained earlier, it usually creates an algorithmic bias.

Figure 109 shows that how AI implementation can follow an ethical paradigm. It will require following the human rights and civil rights regulatory frameworks. Data security and algorithmic biases should also be considered and addressed. Transparency, accessibility, and accountability should also be ensured.

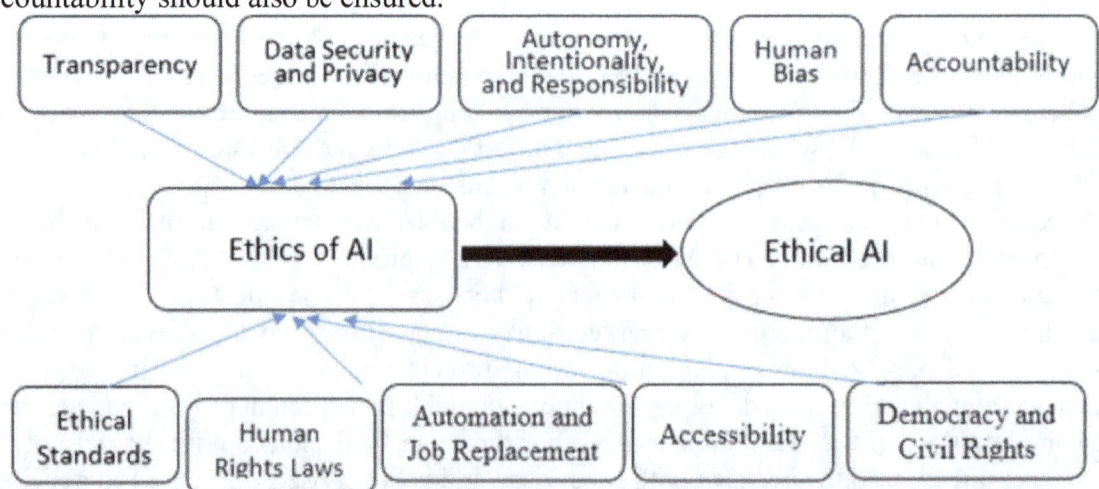

Figure 109: Ethical Premise for AI Implementation[cxiii]

In order to understand the potential biases in AI algorithms, it is crucial to understand the complete lifecycle of AI algorithms. The lifecycle begins with the definition of a business problem. Then the relevant datasets are acquired and prepared in a consistent format. The next step is the development and training of an AI model. The quality of the AI model is continuously evaluated and refined based on new data and requirements. The system is deployed when the AI model has a sufficient level of maturity. Then machine learning operations are put into place. From the lifecycle development, you will have noticed that the performance of AI-based systems significantly depend on two factors. The first is the quality and accuracy of the AI model. If the rules and feature extraction processes in AI algorithms are biased because the AI developer is convinced with a certain style of management, then the quality of the whole AI-based system will suffer. Another important factor is the quality of data. If the training examples in the dataset favor a certain segment of the population, then the AI model will learn wrong rules that will affect the algorithmic decision-making. Due to these limitations of the AI algorithms, professionals working in AI always prefer narrow AI over general AI. The choices available to the AI developers are shown in Figure 110 below:

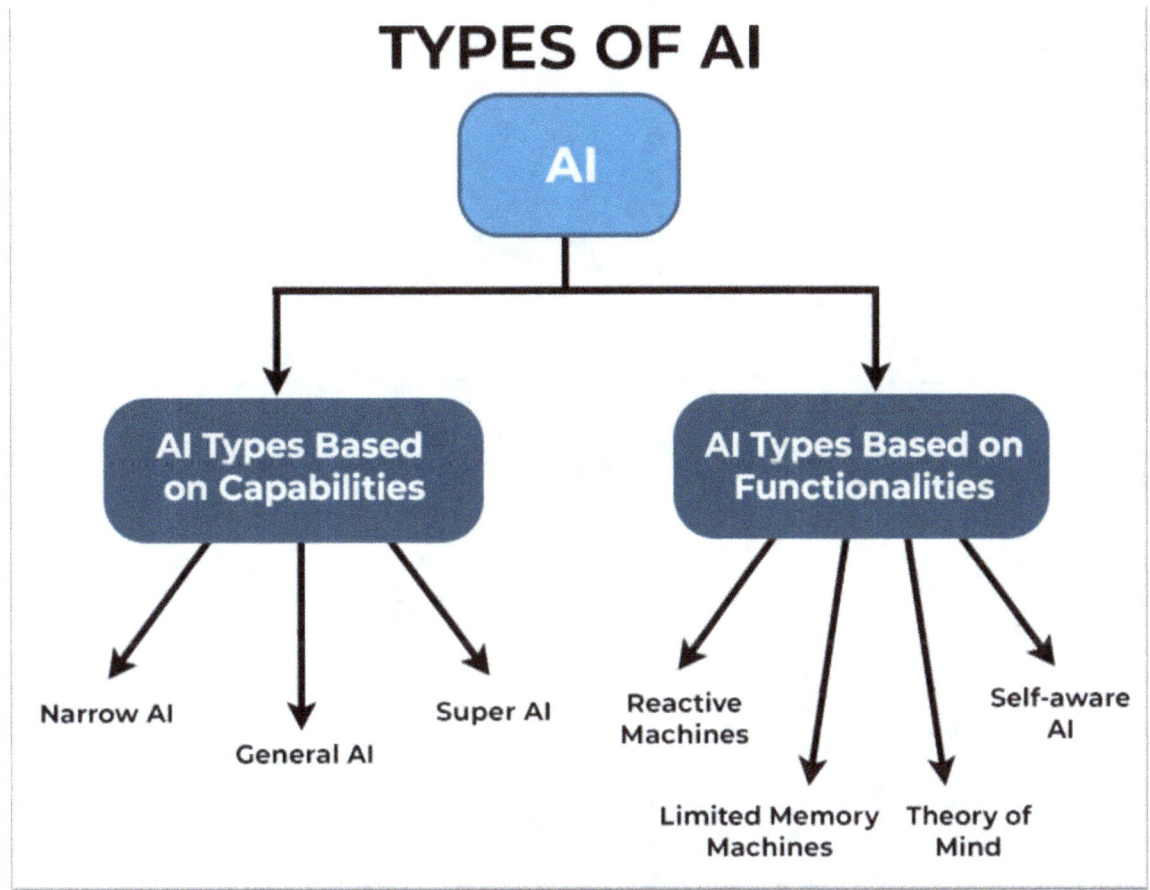

Figure 110: AI Dimensions and Approaches[cxiv]

There are benefits of using narrow AI for management-based AI algorithms. This technology has a binding to a specific task. The technology is based on fixed-domain models. It might come as a limitation for some general managers because the general-AI has a self-learning process and the system developed in general-AI today will have a far optimized version in the next 6 months based on self-learning. Another benefit of narrow AI is that the learning mechanism is based on a large number of examples and therefore, the concept development in the AI model is very strong. A limitation of narrow AI is that the system is reflexive instead of using cognitive abilities. In the above figure, the general AI has been designation as the future of the AI because the knowledge can be transferred to other domains. It is a highly significant feature particularly when the AI-based concepts are using in conjunction with an IoT environment.

In order to fully understand the algorithmic bias, it is also important to know the different nature of AI algorithms. AI algorithms are implemented in three key ways in the system. The first form is supervised learning in which the self-learning system is not built into the model. The learning process is initiated at various time intervals and a trigger is generated in the system to initiate the learning process. The second form is unsupervised learning in which the algorithms enable learning as soon as they encounter new data points and interactions. The third form is reinforcement learning in which the learned data points are categorized into positive or negative reinforcers.

From these examples, it is easier to understand that the risk of algorithmic bias is higher in supervised learning because the learning process is at the discretion of the AI developer. Moreover, when negative reinforcers are identified in reinforcement learning, it is based on how the negativity is defined in the system by the AI developer that creates an algorithmic bias. Humans are generally more influenced by technology and they believe that the human biases will be overcome by the use of technology. However, the technology generates a new form of bias known as an algorithmic bias. These biases can be found in the algorithms as well as how the data is acquired for the training of these algorithms. There is a cycle, which is world, data, design, and use. If the AI developers are not the men of integrity, this cycle can become a vicious cycle.

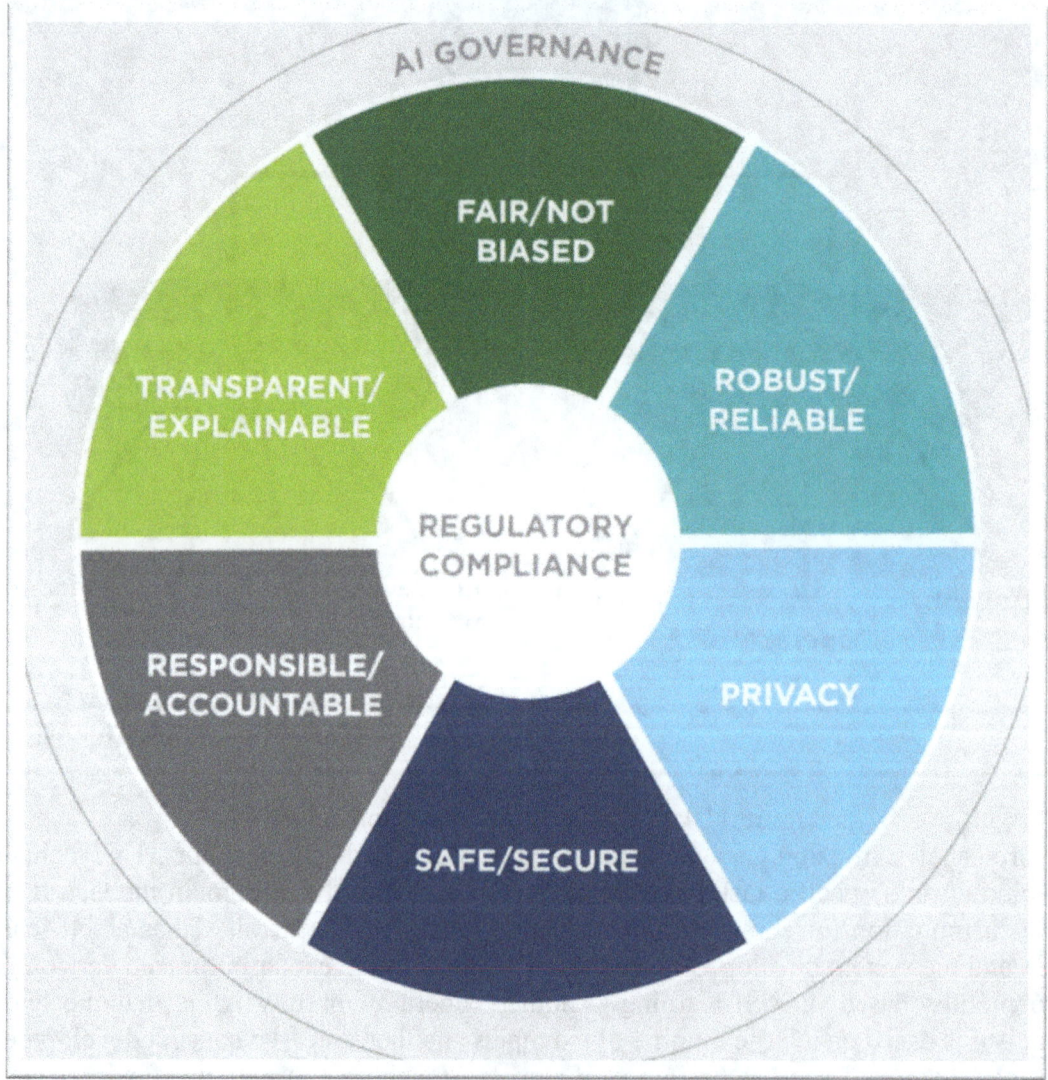

Figure 111: Key Pillars of Ethical Framework[cxv]

Figure 111 shows another strategy for building an ethical framework. The regulatory compliance and a good AI governance can be developed by using this framework. The framework should focus on the areas of algorithmic bias and reliability. The privacy and security of the corporate data should be ensured by the AI manager. The employees should be hold accountable for their tasks and there should be more and more explainable AI so that the human managers could understand the rationale behind the AI-based recommendations.

McKinsey recommends six strategies for overcoming algorithmic biases. They can be addressed by having an awareness of the context, establishing key processes, fact-based communications, a good human-machine interaction, more investment in research, and more research in the AI field.

These are some of the ethical dilemmas that the managers of today or tomorrow will have to face. On the one hand, the world is getting highly efficient robots. But on the other hand, the world will lose the committed, dedicated, and experienced human employees. There will be a high turnover rate because employees will have a constant fear of insecurity. As I mentioned in the IMF report, the AI adoption poses more dangers to managerial jobs and the jobs of highly qualified individuals. Moreover, advanced economies are more prepared for AI adoption.

In this context, an interesting phenomenon might occur in the future. People might move to low-income countries for lucrative jobs. In those countries, as per the IMF reports, people are not prepared and not much convinced about the use of AI. Therefore, they will value those professionals that are highly skilled. These facts suggest that there are interesting times ahead where not only the whole job environment is going to be transformed but also there will be changes in the migration patterns of the workforce.

As also highlighted by the world leaders in economic forum, the future will be a battle between the AI experts and non-experts. So, your best move will be to learn more and more AI tools and technologies to establish a sound future for yourself and your future generations. If you do not do so, there will come one day where the AI technologies will also 'attack' your domain of expertise and challenge your significance through the automation of tasks performed by you. So, you are better off by learning AI tools and technologies and also learning to work with robots in addition to humans.

In the context of management and the AI general manager, the consideration of ethical frameworks is highly crucial. It is because the employees will have limited avenues to lodge their complaints. If the CEO is a human, the employees also have the right to go to the labor courts if they are not satisfied with the behavior and treatment of the human CEO. However, what to do if the CEO is a robot? The employees will be extremely helpless because the CEO might exhibit a cruel behavior from the employee's perspective but still cannot be punished. The robot CEO will always be available, but as I explained earlier, this all-time availability may also be considered as an intrusion to privacy by the employees. Employees need some space to carry out their work and come up with new and innovative ideas. This type of micromanagement may not be welcomed by the employees.

Another crucial aspect in the ethical paradigm is the acquisition of data. When the data is required from third party providers, the human CEOs make a formal request to the concerned parties. When the consent is obtained, the relevant data is utilized by the CEOs. However, when the CEOs are robots, will the third parties entertain their requests? It will be interesting to see how this works in the real-life scenarios, because as I said, there are only a few implementations on the ground where humanoid CEOs have been used by the organizations.

In the case of AI-based systems, the data acquisition becomes automated once the data sources are integrated into the system. There is a constant and continued process of learning by the AI model based on the receiving of new and updated data. Therefore, there is a higher exposure of data to the AI-based systems. The data acquisition becomes continuous and perpetual, which might not be desirable for the data providers. If the concerned parties do not provide the required data, the quality of the AI systems will be compromised significantly. Therefore, it is also an ethical dilemma that needs to be dealt by the AI developers.

The AI general manager may also struggle in conflict resolution, which is a crucial function of management. There are so much variations in the emergence of conflicts, and the conflict management strategies also vary by regions and countries. The encapsulation of all these strategies and selecting the best outcomes will be a huge challenge for an AI general manager.

The managers demonstrate an ideal leadership when their conflict management strategies result in a win-win solution. The AI general manager might take some time to learn the best conflict management strategies in a given organizational circumstances.

Another area where an AI general manager might face an ethical dilemma is when a human worker is not performing as expected. The AI general manager might demonstrate a reactive approach where the help is extended to an employee only when asked. On the other hand, the humans are generous enough that they can know the feelings of others on their own and help the needy individuals proactively. These are areas where the humans have an edge over the machines and it may not be expected in the near future that the same level of performance will be demonstrated by an AI general manager.

The AI general manager might also face an ethical dilemma when the organizations themselves do not want to behave ethically in the corporate environment. For example, if there is an intention on the part of the management to hide the facts regarding the lower performance or exaggerate the performance in certain areas, then this is something that will be difficult to be accepted by the AI general manager. The general manager will operate as per the instructions and in most of the cases, the instructions will be to behave objectively and as per the laws and universal principles. The humans are good to handle exceptions in the organizational interest, but it is an area where it will be impossible to 'convince' an AI general manager for such favors and support.

In summary, the AI general manager will be a person of the highest integrity and it will be objective and prudent in the decision-making process. In some instances, the circumstances demand that the organizations desist from the rational behavior and adopt some precautionary measures. Incorporating such intelligence in the algorithmic CEO can pose ethical challenges to the organizations.

Chapter 9

Conclusion

The journey of this book regarding the future of management is about to end. You will have observed by now that similar to other fields, the future of management is all about AI. AI General Manager can be regarded as a peak of AI implementation in any organization because it means that every policy will be governed and managed by a humanoid CEO and not a human CEO. As I mentioned throughout this book, there are only a few success stories of organizations opting for an AI CEO. They have started implementing AI tools, systems, and technologies, but surrendering the entire fate of the organization to a robot requires bold and committed efforts and a high risk-taking approach. Once this goal is accomplished, as I explained in various parts of this book, its benefits will not only be seen in the improved level of productivity and objective decision-making but also 24/7 availability of the CEO who is always available and never becomes ill. The CEO does not have any domestic or work-life balance issues. All this sounds really interesting and it will surely drive the future of management.

9. Summary of the Key Ideas

I have presented to you numerous ideas, concepts, and themes regarding the future of management, AI general manager and beyond. Here I am presenting a summary of the key ideas and concepts presented in this book.

The use of AI in management is not a new phenomenon and some level of implementation was observed even as early as 1983. At that time, the database management tools such as oracle were used to process large amount of data and general intelligent reports and dashboard indicators. The current era is characterized by the management solutions where the machine learning technologies are used for an effective project management. In fact, the project management was the first area where the significance of an AI general manager was acknowledged. The next era is of autonomous AI where the management functions will be performed autonomously by robots. It is this era where the focus of the book is, i.e. how a general manager, which is an AI robot, can be appointed that could perform all the management roles and the performance is far superior to a human manager.

According to a recent survey, the most important benefit of an algorithmic CEO is the provision of an unbiased information. The CEO never controls or filters the information. This advantage was endorsed by the maximum number of managers (36%). The algorithms are also highly efficient in maintaining work schedules. The performance of humans is influenced by external factors as well such as family issues or illnesses. However, the algorithmic workers are always available for the task execution as long as the required IT infrastructure is available and connected. The algorithmic CEOs are also problem solvers and they can make an efficient utilization of the available budget. The algorithmic CEOs and workers will always be truthful because they do not have any fear of scrutiny or losing their jobs. The team performance can also be evaluated effectively by algorithmic CEOs.

From the AI boss, you will get a feel that the individual is very much focused on the work and there will be complete impartiality in the decision-making process. You may also discuss your concerns and issues with an open heart to an AI boss because there is no fear of retaliation and anger on the part of the boss. The boss is instructed to listen to the issues of the subordinates calmly and openly. The performance of the team will be measured strictly against the assigned objectives quarterly and annually.

The findings of the survey also indicated that it is not always the case that algorithms will outperform humans. There are also instances where human managers perform better than algorithms. One of these aspects is a better comprehension of the feelings. An algorithm will give a negative feedback to the employee without realizing the mental and emotional state of the employee. On the other hand, the humans will consider the environmental and contextual factors before issuing such remarks. The humans can also train other humans better than machines. An enabling work environment can also be ensured well by humans.

The algorithmic managers are powered by machine learning technologies, neural networks, data mining, big data science, and business intelligence. All these AI-based concepts can provide immense support to the management. The benefits can be seen in the optimized decision-making and accurate decision-making. The benefit can also be observed in the improved functionality of the organization. The tasks such as recruitment, performance appraisal, wealth management, and supply chain management can all be automated. Robo-CEO is an algorithmic CEO that selects the most suitable candidate based on the available data. Unlike traditional CEO, the employee is most likely to move up the career ladder due to the objective decision-making of the algorithmic CEO.

There is a fear factor among employees that robots in the management domain will eat their jobs and they will become redundant. It is not going to be the case at least in the near future. There are some roles that can be performed efficiently by AI and there are also other roles that humans can perform even better than AI. It is these roles where the needs of humans will still be felt. Despite the promising outcomes of an AI general manager, there are still only a few successful case studies of an algorithmic CEO. This raises the question why organizations are reluctant to make the optimum utilization of the AI. In a survey, the managers have expressed their concerns and challenges in AI management.

The first challenge faced in AI based management is that employees are accustomed to interacting with other humans. They miss the human touch and socialization aspect in robotic environment. The environment becomes too mechanistic. The algorithmic CEOs assume that the receivers of their instructions are also robots and they will be able to follow each and every word of their instructions. The humans do not work that way and their rationality is always bounded by various constraints including the family constraints and technical constraints. The second challenge is the issue of security and privacy of the data. There is so much connectivity of the devices for the efficient working of AI algorithms. The data exposure might be without consent or a data breach from a single device may aggravate to a massive data breach. The skill set of professionals regarding the maintenance of AI systems is limited. Therefore, hackers can exploit this opportunity and compromise the sanctity and integrity of the data.

Another challenge faced in the organizational setting is that as soon as the AI based implementation is announced, employees fear losing their jobs. The tasks for which they had established the timelines of two to three days can be done by robots in two to three hours. So, they anticipate that they will soon become redundant. Another challenge highlighted in the survey is the lack of understanding of the potential impact of AI. If the management itself is not convinced that the AI based systems will transform the management landscape, then the AI based interventions will always be a distant dream. Moreover, an algorithmic CEO may select a candidate for the job that is highly competitive. However, the candidate may not fit well to the current organizational setting. These aspects can best be judged by humans because it constitutes a dynamic reality and has an element of subjectivity.

A key benefit of an algorithmic CEO that employees are reporting happily to them. They know that the behavior of the boss will be unbiased and the interaction will be limited to the assigned job responsibilities. There will be no favors and additional tasks asked by the boss. Moreover, the working day end within the working hour and there will be no stretched timings and late duties.

The AI-based management has raised concerns because of the intrusive nature of the AI algorithms. The AI algorithms process a large amount of data for making an efficient AI model. The development of the data model may access those data sets for which explicit information has not been provided. The quality of algorithms gets improved but the question arises whether legitimate means have been used for improving the efficiency of algorithms. In this context, AI has invaded all aspects of the humanity. In the absence of a standard regulatory framework, the fate of the AI-based systems is left to the integrity of the AI developers.

In order to understand the potential biases in AI algorithms, it is crucial to understand the complete lifecycle of AI algorithms. The lifecycle begins with the definition of a business problem. Then the relevant datasets are acquired and prepared in a consistent format. The next step is the development and training of an AI model. The quality of the AI model is continuously evaluated and refined based on new data and requirements. The system is deployed when the AI model has a sufficient level of maturity. Then machine learning operations are put into place.

From the lifecycle development, you will have noticed that the performance of AI-based systems significantly depend on two factors. The first is the quality and accuracy of the AI model. If the rules and feature extraction processes in AI algorithms are biased because the AI developer is convinced with a certain style of management, then the quality of the whole AI-based system will suffer. Another important factor is the quality of data. If the training examples in the dataset favor a certain segment of the population, then the AI model will learn wrong rules that will affect the algorithmic decision-making. Due to these limitations of the AI algorithms, professionals working in AI always prefer narrow AI over general AI.

There are multiple benefits of using narrow AI for management-based AI algorithms. This technology has a binding to a specific task. The technology is based on fixed-domain models. It might come as a limitation for some general managers because the general-AI has a self-learning process and the system developed in general-AI today will have a far optimized version in the next 6 months based on self-learning. Another benefit of narrow AI is that the learning mechanism is based on a large number of examples and therefore, the concept development in the AI model is very strong. A limitation of narrow AI is that the system is reflexive instead of using cognitive abilities. The general AI has been designation as the future of the AI because the knowledge can be transferred to other domains. It is a highly significant feature particularly when the AI-based concepts are using in conjunction with an IoT environment.

AI algorithms are implemented in three key ways in the system. The first form is supervised learning in which the self-learning system is not built into the model. The learning process is initiated at various time intervals and a trigger is generated in the system to initiate the learning process. The second form is unsupervised learning in which the algorithms enable learning as soon as they encounter new data points and interactions. The third form is reinforcement learning in which the learned data points are categorized into positive or negative reinforcers. From these examples, it is easier to understand that the risk of algorithmic bias is higher in supervised learning because the learning process is at the discretion of the AI developer. Moreover, when negative reinforcers are identified in reinforcement learning, it is based on how the negativity is defined in the system by the AI developer that creates an algorithmic bias. McKinsey recommends six strategies for overcoming algorithmic biases. They can be addressed by having an awareness of the context, establishing key processes, fact-based communications, a good human-machine interaction, more investment in research, and more research in the AI field.

Recruitment was one of the first HR functions where the algorithms were introduced in the form of a robot recruiter. The robots have been highly successful in conducting interviews and candidates express them comfortably in front of a robot. The responses are also processed efficiently by the robots and the same processing strategy is applied for all candidates. The function of a robot does not end at conducting an interview. The algorithms can also participate in the entire process of recruitment and selection. They can evaluate all the interview results and select the right and the most suitable candidate by matching the organizational requirements with the candidate skill sets. With the growth of the automated screening process, the job candidates should also update their CVs so that the robots do not discard their resumes. The traditional CVs might not be considered worthy by the robots. Therefore, the candidates will now have to ensure that their CVs and job applications include the keywords of the positions. The AI algorithms match the CVs with the internal dictionary and job descriptors. If the relevant keywords are not found then even the CV of a highly qualified individual might be overlooked.

AI general manager can also conduct performance appraisal effectively. Employees always have reservations and complaints that their efforts are not compensated adequately and the appraisals are always biased to the likes of the supervisor. Due to this reason, the management literature also suggests 360 degree feedback in addition to the straight line method of appraisal. In an ideal scenario, the performance appraisal should begin with the Plan stage. At this stage, the annual objectives of an employee should be set. The next stage is the Act stage where the employee applies the skill set to achieve those objectives. The third stage is the Track stage where the supervisor should periodically monitor the performance of the subordinate and provide feedback. The last stage is review where the performance of the employee should be evaluated, the achievements should be appreciated and the deficiencies should be highlighted. To overcome those deficiencies, the key learning opportunities should be identified for the employees.

This appraisal cycle looks promising; however, in the real world environment, the supervisors are so busy in the regular tasks that they do not focus on the appraisal cycle. Moreover, due to the severe economic conditions, the employees are more worried regarding the survival of their jobs than the growth opportunities and performance appraisals. An algorithmic CEO can optimize the appraisal systems by using strength-based appraisals. In this strategy, the performance ratings are based on the strengths and competencies of the employees. When there is a fairness and equity in the appraisal process, the motivation and morale of the workforce also improves and the employees are always motivated to improve their skill set.

Performance appraisals are also a key source document for promoting the employees. The algorithmic performance appraisal evaluates each subordinate objectively and justly and only the most hardworking, competent, and devoted employee is selected for promotion and moving up the career ladder.

The AI managers will make an impression in the organizations when their performances significantly outperform the human managers. Several successful implementations have been made in this regard so far. There is an implementation of an algorithmic CEO that was tested in a Hong Kong based company. The boss is named Tang Yu and she is the CEO of mobile and gaming company. The model proved highly successful in the organization and there was a marked improvement in the speed of execution and the quality of work. The company where this model was successfully tested is NetDragon.

AI general manager will also need some tools for effective decision-making. The managerial aspect requires a high level of collaboration and effective business communication. There, AI humanoid CEO should be supported with various emerging and on-demand AI services. Some of the technologies have gained a huge prominence in the AI world. The chat services can be managed effectively by ChatGPT and Bard services. The document management systems and chatbots also assist in the effective management of the workspace by the AI manager.

In order to understand the significance of data-driven decision-making, it is crucial to know the evolutionary process of AI-based systems. The AI-based systems for data-driven decision-making were first presented as assisted intelligence systems. The key selling point of the systems at that time was that these systems can learn in an organized manner, whereas the humans do not take the learning process so seriously. In the next phase, it was realized that a good AI system is a product of human-machine interaction. It was argued that the quality of an AI system is influenced by the data model and if a good quality data is not provided by the humans, the algorithms cannot work effectively. Therefore, there was a gradual shift to augmented intelligence where machines facilitate humans and humans facilitate machines. The third phase or the current phase is regarded as autonomous intelligence. In this era, the nature of tasks changes very rapidly. Therefore, the decisions need to be taken by the AI manager in an automated manner based on data and predefined rules, policies, and procedures of the organization. The machines should have a mechanism of a continued learning. It means that the AI CEO that the subordinates are interacting with today will not have the same responses in the future because it is a machine. Based on a continued learning, the responses and the behavioral disposition of the algorithmic CEO will also change.

It is argued in the management literature that the data-based decision-making is possible only if the decisions of the managers are based on seven key pillars. The first aspect is leadership. The decision-making process should provide leadership regarding the strategic directions of the organization. The second aspect is trust. The human managers as well as AI general manager can use the data only if it is trustworthy and is relied upon by all the stakeholders of the organization. If the quality of the data is very low, then the data-driven decision-making may prove to be counterproductive. The third aspect is the commitment level of the managers. They should keep their personal biases aside and follow the patterns and trends in data for effective decision-making. The other aspect is the use of metrics. An AI general manager should have the availability of all key metrics and dashboard indicators.

These indicators should provide the real-time view of the organization. Another dimension is data literacy. It is a common argument against the AI algorithms that the users do not know how the algorithms arrived at a particular decision. An AI general manager should also consider this aspect and it should be able to explain the rationale of the decision-making to its human subordinates. Moreover, staff training and awareness are also essential in data-base approach to decision-making.

The human brain and AI tools have their strengths and limitations. A robotic organization can work well if it capitalizes on the strengths of both humans and AI and creates a hybrid model based on human-machine interaction.

The first AI boss was developed by Hitachi Company. It was introduced in 2015 that shows that the technology and management professionals were exploring the possibility of AI in management for quite long. They wanted more accuracy and objectivity in the decision-making process and provide more freedom of expression to the subordinates.

Robo-CEO is an algorithmic CEO that selects the most suitable candidate based on the available data. Unlike traditional CEO, the employee is most likely to move up the career ladder due to the objective decision-making of the algorithmic CEO.

AI bosses are not limited to the human resource function and they are also being used in other management and business functions. There is an implementation where the algorithmic managers have been used for an effective wealth management.

There is a successful implementation by a firm in which AI manager was used for talent acquisition and talent management. This robot was given the responsibility of managing a $100 billion firm. The entire human resources of the company will be handled by the algorithmic CEO. The company aims to replace more and more humans with robots in key leadership positions.

In the current context, a robot CEO was appointed by a Chinese firm NetDragon. The robot CEO was appointed with the intent that the process flow of the business entity will be streamlined and the speed of task execution will improve substantially.

Mika became the CEO of a Drinks Company. She promised the availability of 24/7 for their subordinates and told them that there would not be any layoffs in the company. She performs the tasks of identifying the potential customers and the artists for the new and innovative designs of the bottles.

A robot was developed by a Japanese company and this robot is planned to be deployed for managing the manufacturing operations in Japan. It has been developed by Ryo Yoshida, who himself is a CEO of a Japanese company.

In a landmark event at telecommunication conference, there was also a press talk of robots. The robots emphasized in this press conference that humans should not fear losing their jobs due to robots. Moreover, they do not have any plans to rebel against humans.

A landmark achievement was observed in 2016, when chatbots assistant were introduced. A chatbot assistant such as a WhatsApp chatbot remembers the solutions of the frequently asked questions by the clients. The queries are then responded by the chatbot in an automated manner without any intervention by the human. The beauty of this chatbot was that the support services became highly effective and were made available 24/7. Moreover, the accuracy of the responses was phenomenal because the responses are generated based on the processing of a large dataset. However, the users of the technology are also much aware of the potential and limitations of the technology. They know that they are talking to a chatbot that might give them general purpose answer but may not answer their specific queries and concerns. Even at the level of call centers, if the caller has the option of using automated menu options or calling to an operator, many callers would prefer calling to an operator because it provides a human touch and a personalized interaction. The beauty of human interaction is one area where the robots will never be able to beat the humans. It is a human nature that the people treat everyone differently. People develop a perception regarding the personality preferences of an individual and respond to their queries accordingly. On the other hand, a chatbot assistant will treat all human equally. The difference in responses based on the information and assistance needs of the individual is still beyond the capabilities of a chatbot. Some of the plagiarism checking websites such as turnitin can also detect if a given piece of text was written by a human or a chatbot. This capability makes it evident that the behavioral styles of a machine and a human are entirely different and a machine can never write with a human touch.

The quality of a successful AI model is driven by both the training data and the new input data. If all the efforts are aimed at developing a successful algorithm, the required results may still not be achieved due to the poor quality of the data.

It should be noted that various individual components make up an AI robot and the unique, mechanistic blend of these components improve the processing capabilities of an AI manager. Robo-CEO is an algorithmic CEO that selects the most suitable candidate based on the available data. Unlike traditional CEO, the employee is most likely to move up the career ladder due to the objective decision-making of the algorithmic CEO. The higher level of automation in robots may also cause serious issues in an automated workplace. In a recent incident, a robot in the famous Tesla Company launched an attack on the human engineer of the company. Tesla later explained that it was due to a violent malfunction of the robot. It was a critical case because the unintended action of the robot could have harmed the lives of the employees.

Due to these incidents, despite the promising outcomes of an AI general manager, there are still only a few successful case studies of an algorithmic CEO. This raises the question why organizations are reluctant to make the optimum utilization of the AI. The first challenge faced in AI based management is that employees are accustomed to interacting with other humans. They miss the human touch and socialization aspect in robotic environment. The environment becomes too mechanistic. The algorithmic CEOs assume that the receivers of their instructions are also robots and they will be able to follow each and every word of their instructions. The humans do not work that way and their rationality is always bounded by various constraints including the family constraints and technical constraints.

There are so many applications of AI in the organizational context and there is so much connectivity of the devices for the efficient working of AI algorithms. The data exposure might be without consent or a data breach from a single device may aggravate to a massive data breach. The skill set of professionals regarding the maintenance of AI systems is limited. Therefore, hackers can exploit this opportunity and compromise the sanctity and integrity of the data.

When the organizations opt for AI-based systems, they have to make a tradeoff between data exposure and intelligent decision-making. The benefits are experienced in the form of good decision-making, sensing, and sound reasoning. However, the organizations may lose their control over data in a highly interconnected environment. Another challenge faced in the organizational setting is that as soon as the AI based implementation is announced, employees fear losing their jobs. The tasks for which they had established the timelines of two to three days can be done by robots in two to three hours. So, they anticipate that they will soon become redundant. Another challenge highlighted in the survey is the lack of understanding of the potential impact of AI. If the management itself is not convinced that the AI based systems will transform the management landscape, then the AI based interventions will always be a distant dream.

The CEO robot NAO was introduced in 2018 in Germany. It was claimed that these robots will operate in a human-like way and the human jobs will be replaced significantly. However, most of the times, the robot was seen watching and observing the employees and the employees felt that they have lost their freedom at work. In an article by vox, it was mentioned that an employee in Bangladesh complained that the robot CEO monitors him so closely that a picture of him is taken after every ten minutes to confirm that the employee is sitting at his computer. AI algorithms can prove to be an effective general manager because of their abilities of enabling a process of continued learning. For the humans, the management has to ask them to go for continued professional development. Moreover, some managers do not have the required aptitude for the leadership positions, and they are successful in securing the positions based on the tenure of their employment. All these aspects can be addressed effectively by an AI general manager because it does not require an aptitude and interest for learning. The algorithms will learn in an automated, mechanistic style. The AI learning can benefit in executing the management process successfully and its specific benefits are also seen in the context of resource allocation, project management, and risk assessment.

To fully understand the potential of AI learning in resource allocation, project management, and risk assessment, it is crucial to gain a basic understanding of how the learning process works in the AI-based systems. Active learning in AI is a function of Label, Enrich, Train, and Query processes. First, a given sample or a resource will be assigned a label by the system. It facilitates in identifying the sample and assigning it to a class or a category. The training dataset is enriched by the inclusion of the newly labelled sample because the system sees it as an opportunity of learning and strengthening the system protocols. In the Train phase, the AI model receives the training based on the available dataset. This dataset includes the past, historical data as well as the newly added samples. The query process can also be used by the learning function to view and select different samples available in the dataset. This simple example shows the power of AI-based algorithms that they are always ready for the new learning. As soon as they receive the newly added samples, they trigger the training phase and train the AI model based on the current and new data.

The resource allocation based on AI learning is executed in a highly sophisticated manner. Considering this aspect, the AI developers recommend that various parameters should be reviewed by the technology team before implementing resource allocation. In a study, these considerations have been considered into three key categories of task, approach, and computing paradigm. The first area of consideration is that how many resource allocation strategies will be input into the system and how the power consumption can be optimized during the algorithmic decision-making. The efficient power management is always crucial in AI-based software because the AI models process huge datasets that might consume energy beyond the available resources of the organization. The second factor is the AI approach in which the technology team should select from the available machine learning techniques and deep learning techniques. The third factor is the computing paradigm. Ideally, the resource allocation should be processed in the cloud computing environment because various nodes and parameters will be processed that will require extensive storage space and the computing power. Other options may also be considered such as the IoT environment, edge computing, or mobile edge computing.

The AI-based resource allocation can offer various advantages to the senior management. These benefits are further optimized when the CEO or the general manager of the company is an AI robot and not a human. It is because the resource allocation management software based on AI concepts assume that the user of these tools will also be well versed in executing the different functions and interfaces of the software. In the case of an AI CEO, this intelligence is built into the CEO algorithms that increases the benefits of an AI-based resource allocation. When the resource allocation takes advantage of the AI concepts, the efficiency and productivity of the workforce increases because the system learns from the mistakes and makes continuous adaptations to the resource allocation process. The resource planning is also optimized because it is based on the predefined rules and criteria and alternate plans and strategies are also made part of the algorithmic process. The burden of the administration is reduced significantly because the resource allocation is accomplished automatically and everyone is aware of their roles and possible tasks that might be assigned in the near future. The organizations can also reduce costs and gain a competitive advantage through AI-based resource allocation.

Various features and options are offered by different AI vendors in the resource allocation software. The resource allocation becomes entirely automated in the AI-based software. The predictive management is also a well-known feature of the AI where the issues and problems in the existing strategies are tracked by the system proactively and alternate strategies are recommended. The dashboard indicators also show the real-time availability of all available resources. There are also options for time tracking and project management. The resources needed for future projects and future years can also be forecasted by the system and then the algorithmic CEO can initiate the hiring process for meeting the higher demand of resources in the future. The resources may also be needed in the form of financial resources and material resources. In those cases, the procurement department may be intimated for acquiring the materials and funding agencies may be contacted for receiving the required funds for the future projects.

When the organizations opt for AI-based resource allocation in management, the quality of data analysis improves significantly. The entered data is not only used for reporting and descriptive statistics, but inferences are also drawn and future state of the organization is also predicted based on the current data. In this way, if there are loopholes in any strategy, they can be rectified well before their occurrence. The real-time monitoring of the resource allocation is also possible because the resource allocation is carried out by the systems and all the decision-making steps are recorded and reported by the system. The collaboration process is also improved significantly and the resource allocation can also cover remote workers through the use of virtualization hardware, software, and systems.

In a study, 152 cognitive projects were studied. It became evident that robotics and automation is also being used extensively in cognitive projects and it significantly increases the power of resource allocation, AI-based software. Currently, general managers spend significant time in identifying the best fit for a project or a management task. Even during the course of the project, they might find out that they erred in the decision-making and did not find the right person for the right job. These limitations in the decision-making has a lot to do with the cognitive potential of a leader. However, an AI-based general manager can improve the cognitive potential of an AI CEO due to objective decision making and using the cognitive thinking facilities of the latest AI-based software. As a result, the managers can always be confident that they have the best team available and each employee has been assigned the tasks based on the person-organization fit. The assigned person possesses all the capabilities and skills for executing the assigned task.

In AI-based resource allocation, the data points are classified by the algorithms for feature extraction. The regression analysis indicate the contribution of each resources in the accomplishment of overall organizational objectives. The forecasting models predict the future demand of resources based on the objectives and goals set by the organization. The clustering mechanism uses the features and highlights groups and patterns in the data. The process of machine translation codifies the strategies for algorithmic decision-making. The computer vision technology may also be used for identifying and recommending the resources. The generative AI can be used in the process of collaboration and communication. The reinforcement learning makes it possible that the system improves over time based on the bottlenecks emerged in the current strategies of resource allocation.

There are various benefits of AI in project management. The project planning is improved significantly because the project managers can take advantage of the recommendations and data-based suggestions provided by the AI algorithms. The project monitoring also becomes easier because AI keeps track of all the project tasks and provides alerts on those tasks where the deadlines might be missed. Hence, the project managers can focus on those tasks that require their immediate attention and leave the monitoring of those tasks where there is a good report given by the AI systems. In this way, an enhanced efficiency of the project managers can be ensured. The predictive analytics feature provides an edge to the AI-based software to the conventional project management software. The AI-based software also predict and simulate the future state of the project and alert the project managers if there are any complications and issues in achieving the desired outcomes. A marked improvement in the overall decision-making process can be observed by implementing AI in project management. Advantages of AI in project management have also been endorsed by the Project Management Institute. According to PMI, automation and optimization can be achieved by AI learning. Risk management strategies can also be improved by the use of AI tools. The data-driven insights improve the process of decision-making by the project managers. The algorithms also streamline the process of resource scheduling and resource allocation.

It should be noted that at the technical level, different AI types provide varied level of benefits to the project managers. Therefore, the technology team in the organizations should build understanding of all the AI types that they are anticipating for the implementation. The machine learning algorithms are more beneficial in project analytics and risk assessment. The deep learning algorithms can be utilized for the optimization of task scheduling. The supervised learning should be used for project costing and budgeting. The unsupervised learning should be utilized for team creating and team management. The reinforcement learning is a good strategy for the resource allocation tasks. The natural language processing algorithms should be utilized for the sentiment analysis of the team performance. The computer vision technology should be used for the summarization of the educational videos related to the project. The adversarial networks should be utilized for the testing of projects in a safe and secure environment. The expert systems will be needed when risk management is to be carried out based on historical data.

In the project management paradigm, there are several key processes and the AI systems should be able to optimize all these processes. A typical project will involve the estimation of tasks and resources. Then the costing and resource scheduling should be done. The project manager also needs to do sequencing and collating of data. They also identify risks and trends in the projects. The AI-based systems should assist in all these areas. Good AI-based systems offer automated scheduling, optimization of all tasks, predictive analytics features, and machine learning algorithms for all AI types.

This book highlights the role of AI general manager and beyond. Therefore, the benefits of AI-based project management should also be viewed as to how AI can assist general managers if it is not possible to appoint an AI general manager altogether. The training and development of the employees will be based on the analysis of their learning habits by the AI software. The resource allocation will be optimized due to which it will be easier to release the employees from the operational tasks and depute them to the project activities. The project team will be able not only to track the progress of the project but also predict the future activities of the project. The budgeting and scheduling tasks will all be automated. The complex, employee-based analytics will be handled smoothly by the AI software. Therefore, AI algorithms will serve as a virtual assistant of the project manager in cases where it is not possible to appoint an AI project manager.

Risk assessment has become a highly crucial activity for the general managers because the projects in the organizations incur significant costs. In the competitive world, the costs should be justified and risk mitigation strategies should also be developed by the management to keep the organization sustainable.

The risk assessment activities usually begin with the identification of risks in the internal and external environment. Then the risks are analyzed and their severity level are ascertained. In the final stage, strategies are developed for the management of these risks. A good AI-based system automates all these three processes of risk management. The net outcomes is the development of more relevant and efficient risk management strategies.

In an example of risk assessment using AI tools, it was found how it can be successfully used for the assessment of underwriting. The accuracy level is improved because AI algorithms analyze huge datasets. The efficient AI algorithms process big data speedily and generate meaningful results. The systems provide the details of the most profitable market segments. The fraudulent claims are quickly identified based on the historical data. The system also offers personalized recommendations to the customers based on their needs. The overall cost of operation is reduced due to accuracy and protecting fraudulent claims.

Similar to other technological advancements, the use of machine learning in management may also be associated with various issues and problems. I highlighted these issues so that you are more aware about all that AI has to offer and the associated pitfalls. I would still urge you to go for an AI general manager because in the overall analysis, the benefits still significantly outweigh the pitfalls.

The first drawback of using machine learning is the acquisition of data. The quality of AI data model is reliant on the quality of training data, and in many cases, acquiring the data may become a cumbersome activity. There may also be issues regarding the legitimate rights of accessing and using those datasets. If the dataset is limited, then AI algorithms will not give you the desired results because their key strength lies in big data processing and providing meaningful results based on the comprehensive analysis of data.

The second drawback is the time and resources needed for AI implementation. Although the automation and quick processing will be achieved by using AI algorithms, these benefits will only be seen in the long run. In the short run, more time will be consumed in implementing the systems and training the workforce. In some organizations, there is a high employee turnover rate that further increases the time to learn.

The third drawback is to interpret the results produced by the AI algorithms. The algorithms process huge datasets before providing recommendations. A human general manager may find it difficult to know the rationale behind a specific recommendation. If the things do not go as expected, the human manager may struggle in justifying their moves.

The fourth drawback is the risk of error in the absence of data. There is no doubt that AI algorithms will provide accurate results when the relevant data is available. However, when the relevant data is not available, there is a general tendency of the algorithms to produce the results based on whatever is available to them. You might have observed it while using ChatGPT or Google Bard. If these chatbots do not have the relevant data, they still respond you with irrelevant and inaccurate results. It can become a serious limitation in the organizational context when the processes will have automated and there will be a huge reliance on the AI based systems.

There are also some more issues with machine learning in management. The organizations may face cost overruns because appointment an AI general manager and automating all tasks require a complete overhaul of the current IT infrastructure. The training of the remaining human workforce will also incur a significant cost. There is also limited capabilities of AI developers available in the IT industry that are particularly proficient in AI based implementations. There is also a great potential of misuse of the technology because as I mentioned earlier, the AI-based systems also suffer with the algorithmic bias. Moreover, the end users can manipulate the system by benefitting from the limited expertise of the senior management in using AI-based systems.

The setup of a robotic organization is highly sophisticated and based on the state-of-the-art technologies. This is one area where the business entities will have to focus. They will need to review the requirements of their organizations and present a strong case to the senior management for implementing a robotic organization. In the absence of sufficient funds, it will be difficult to transform the organizational outlook.

All the success stories indicate that AI has a significant role in improve the managerial aspects of an organization. AI systems can become a CEO of the organization. In the other cases, the robots can assist the general managers and make them more productive and working smartly. It will also prove to be a good strategy because the robots in the execute roles will keep the manager focused and committed. The robot will also remind them about the meeting and the tasks that are to be submitted shortly. It will ensure that the manager executes all the tasks happily and never miss a task. The managers often struggle in multitasking. However, the robots will show them the best course of action and at any given point in time, the general managers will also perform the most relevant task in the organization.

The biggest challenge for an AI general manager implementation will be to prepare the employees for the algorithmic transition. As I have explained earlier, the employees all over the world are highly fearful that the AI-based implementations will automate the tasks for which they have been hired. As a result, they may lose their jobs. Their fears are not unfounded and these concerns have also been endorsed and acknowledged by IMF in its recent report. According to a recent report published by IMF, AI will make a significant influence on the global job market and approximately 40% of the jobs may be affected by AI-based implementations in different organizations. Therefore, organizations need to evaluate the pros and cons of AI-based implementations and manage effectively the motivation and morale of the employees. The growing AI exposure in different countries and regions have been illustrated by IMF. The share of AI is higher in advanced economies and emerging markets. It is because there is a high cost associated with developing an IT infrastructure for AI implementations.

The report also highlights another prediction of IMF that the implementation of AI will influence professional and managerial positions higher than elementary occupations. Therefore, there is another type of preparation needed for the AI-based transitions. The senior management and leaders will be required to train for AI-based implementations. The current book also presents the case of an AI general manager that will manage the overall structure of the whole organization. Therefore, senior managers should get them updated as to how they will cope with the new challenges and emerging realities of the management and organizational behavior.

The report indicates some interesting facts based on the demographic variables. The AI-based implementations will influence female employees more than males. Similarly, more qualified individuals are more prone to losing their jobs based on AI implementations because AI algorithms are targeting to solve the complex tasks of the organization. In terms of age group, the AI exposure will be observed more in the age bracket of 45 years and more.

According to the IMF report, AI-based exposure will influence employees of all income groups. There is even a higher impact with the increase in the earnings. It may become a serious concern for the employees because they may struggle in finding the same job with that level of compensation package if the AI-based implementations may result in losing their jobs. It may also create resentment among them and they may not cooperate with the owners in implementing the AI-based systems and robot employees

The IMF report also mentioned the preparedness level of the employees and the business entities from different dimensions. In all the cases of digital infrastructure, human resource policies, innovation, and ethical dimensions, advanced economies have made a considerable progress. On the other hand, there is a reduced level of interest in lower income countries and a moderate level of interest in emerging economies.

From the above insights provided in the IMF report, it becomes evident that preparing employees for AI-based transition is a highly complex task. These implementations will affect the managerial positions and higher income groups more than the junior employees. Moreover, the employees might not cooperate in the implementation in the fear that these implementations are challenging their very existence in the organization.

Considering these factors, the owners and directors of the organizations should make a careful analysis of the whole situation and create a win-win situation in the organization. They should find ways of engaging the employees in more strategic tasks to improve the productivity of the organization. They should also make the employees realize that the sustainability of the organization will be at stake if the organization does not embrace AI. If the competitors become the early adopters, the organization may lose its competitive advantage. The employees should also be made to realize the significance of learning AI tools and technologies. Working with an AI general manager will be a significant boost on their CVs and their skills of working efficiently with machines will be highly valued and regarded in the AI-based world of today and tomorrow.

Employee motivation and morale management is going to be highly challenging for the business owners in an AI-based world. The employees are motivated to work because they expect that their efforts will be appreciated and rewarded. Moreover, they will gain an expert power by working hard and showing their commitment. In the new AI paradigm, there will not be such motivation available to them. Why should an employee work hard if the same work can be done by a robot in a much less time? It means that there will be no more appreciation of the work.

These are some of the ethical dilemmas that the managers of today or tomorrow will have to face. On the one hand, the world is getting highly efficient robots. But on the other hand, the world will lose the committed, dedicated, and experienced human employees. There will be a high turnover rate because employees will have a constant fear of insecurity. As I mentioned in the IMF report, the AI adoption poses more dangers to managerial jobs and the jobs of highly qualified individuals. Moreover, advanced economies are more prepared for AI adoption.

In this context, an interesting phenomenon might occur in the future. People might move to low-income countries for lucrative jobs. In those countries, as per the IMF reports, people are not prepared and not much convinced about the use of AI. Therefore, they will value those professionals that are highly skilled. These facts suggest that there are interesting times ahead where not only the whole job environment is going to be transformed but also there will be changes in the migration patterns of the workforce.

As also highlighted by the world leaders in economic forum, the future will be a battle between the AI experts and non-experts. So, your best move will be to learn more and more AI tools and technologies to establish a sound future for yourself and your future generations. If you do not do so, there will come one day where the AI technologies will also 'attack' your domain of expertise and challenge your significance through the automation of tasks performed by you. So, you are better off by learning AI tools and technologies and also learning to work with robots in addition to humans.

There is a promising outlook of an AI-powered organization. However, from the technology perspective, it should be noted that the performance of these robots is dependent on how well these robots have been trained. As I gave you a recent example of an incident in Tesla Company, the robots even began to attack the employees in that organization. Therefore, poor programming and algorithmic biases can make a negative impact on the usefulness of an AI-based setup in the organizations.

There are still some jobs where humans can demonstrate more impressive performance than AI robots. Humans are well-versed in critical thinking. For humans, everything is not just right and wrong. They also evaluate the grey areas and acknowledge the dynamic reality of the phenomenon. Humans can also become strategic thinkers through their visionary approach, whereas robots can only learn based on the available datasets. In creative jobs, humans can perform well. Drama and video scripts are being written by AI, but how about poetry. There will be only a few (if any) examples where a high-level creative, poetry work could be produced by a robot. The humans also show more empathy in the communication process and they may overlook the shortcomings of an employee based on the contextual, environmental, and personality factors. However, an AI general manager will be very objective in the communication. The good performances will be appreciated, but there will also be immediate and prompt feedback on the bad performance that may not be liked by those employees who are very sensitive and short-tempered.

9.1. Key Takeaways

The need for an AI general manager has emerged due to multiple factors. There is more and more government ownership and encouragement for implementing AI tools and technologies. The employees can also be held more responsible for their work by facilitating them with AI tools and technologies. The AI concepts have successfully been used in development the management solutions. The organizations also have a pressure from the competitors because if they become early adopters of AI, the organizations may lose their competitive advantage.

Humans are generally more influenced by technology and they believe that the human biases will be overcome by the use of technology. However, the technology generates a new form of bias known as an algorithmic bias. These biases can be found in the algorithms as well as how the data is acquired for the training of these algorithms. There is a cycle, which is world, data, design, and use. If the AI developers are not the men of integrity, this cycle can become a vicious cycle.

It is imperative to understand how the AI models develop a predictive model for an efficient project management. With the help of the training set, the algorithms perform both supervised and unsupervised learning. The new data is also continuously added in the training data. Features are then extracted from the training set. Then the machine learning algorithms work on the developed AI model and the annotated data. Ultimately, the grouping of objects is accomplished and predictive models are developed. These predictive models inform the project managers regarding the future state of the project. The project managers can review these scenarios and compare them with the desired scenarios. In the case of discrepancies, the strategies can be modified and updated by the project managers.

There is a paradox of AI-human trust relationship. The humans view the AI as someone that will hit them from the back and kill/remove them from the jobs. On the other hand, the fact of the matter is that humans are struggling in a highly competitive job market of today. They might give up in their struggles at some point in their lives. However, embracing AI tools and technologies will enable the humans to become stable in their jobs. Moreover, AI tools will ensure that humans never give up and become incompetent in their jobs.

This paradox can be the biggest challenge for an AI general manager. Although an AI general manager does not need to make itself happy because the machine has no emotions, but the AI general manager will also be dealing with humans and these humans should be happy and satisfied workers. Motivation and morale management is a crucial HR function and the AI general manager should be well programmed to perform this function efficiently. If the productivity of the employees do not increase and there is a high turnover rate in the organization, the AI general manager model will not be sustainable. The case studies that I have mentioned in this book, some of these implementations were halted because they could not produce the desired results. Therefore, the performance of the AI general manager will also be evaluated critically by the senior management.

9.2. A Glimpse into Future

The use of AI is influencing all aspects of a business entity. The multinational companies are fearful that if they do not embrace AI, they may lose their competitive advantage. However, the limited knowledge of the AI algorithms makes them hesitant in embracing AI at a mass scale. When there was a widespread adoption of AI tools and technologies in multinational organizations, the management professionals also thought that the AI concepts can be useful and significant in the managerial tasks as well because the emerging requirement of the management was to enable data-driven decision-making, and AI algorithms have the potential to process a huge amount of data quickly. However, the business entities are also not in favor that they do things where the decision-making is quick but they do not have any clue how a particular course of action was selected.

In the future, AI-based organizations, one may expect that the CEO is an algorithmic CEO and all key leadership positions are occupied by robots. Humans have been assigned only to the operational work, and the technology-driven aspect of the organization has been endorsed at the level of the organization chart. AI bosses are not limited to the human resource function and they are also being used in other management and business functions. There is also an implementation where the algorithmic managers have been used for an effective wealth management.

9.3. A New Work Environment with AI Leaders and Colleagues

The future organizations are expected to be a nice blend of AI workers and human workers. It will also affect how the organograms will be presented and reported in different statutory reports. In a sample organization, it might be the case that the CEO is an algorithmic CEO and all key leadership positions are occupied by robots. Humans have been assigned only to the operational work, and the technology-driven aspect of the organization has been endorsed at the level of the organization chart.

The organizations are expected to receive mixed responses when they introduce AI CEO in their environments. Also, within the organization, the comfort level of the employees with the AI robots will vary significantly. The most important benefit of an algorithmic CEO is the provision of an unbiased information. The CEO never controls or filters the information. The algorithms are also highly efficient in maintaining work schedules. The performance of humans is influenced by external factors as well such as family issues or illnesses. However, the algorithmic workers are always available for the task execution as long as the required IT infrastructure is available and connected.

About the Author

The Author is a visionary leader to implement AI tools and technologies in the management domain. The author has used all his knowledge, experience, and skill set, acquired by working in various managerial roles, for explaining different dimensions of AI in this book. The author possesses technical AI skills as well as the domain knowledge of the management function of the organization. In his island home, the sea's love, sailing's legacy, and leadership's flame passed down through generations with pride and glory. He is a skilled navigator of words, charting a course through the vast ocean of knowledge. He believes in every word and section written in this book and all the content is the outcome of a critical analysis, intellectual discourses, and key debates concerning the future of management, AI general manager and beyond. With his expertise and passion, he guides readers towards various approaches to AI for automating the executive function and CEO function, all in concise and captivating prose.

References

i https://www.researchgate.net/figure/Evolution-of-AI-in-project-management-100_fig1_347514098

ii https://www.technewsworld.com/story/ai-evolution-tackling-fears-bias-security-and-efficiency-178839.html

iii https://www.yahoo.com/tech/meet-the-new-boss-the-worlds-first-128660465704.html

iv https://medium.com/@NeuralPit/revolutionizing-knowledge-management-with-ai-harnessing-synergy-for-organizational-success-6b50b625f184

v https://gigazine.net/gsc_news/en/20191122-ai-boss-employees-trust

vi Ibid.

vii https://link.springer.com/chapter/10.1007/978-3-030-12388-8_23

viii https://www.financemagnates.com/trending/introducing-robo-ceo-the-worlds-worst-boss

ix Ibid.

x https://theconversation.com/horrible-bosses-how-algorithm-managers-are-taking-over-the-office-191307

xi https://www.aihr.com/blog/algorithmic-management

xii https://www.benefitnews.com/list/employees-fed-up-with-managers-say-ai-bosses-are-the-answer

xiii https://ainows.com/what-is-ai

xiv https://www.linkedin.com/pulse/putting-algorithms-org-chart-kevin-collins

xv https://www.cityam.com/ex-barclays-wealth-management-boss-says-all-banks-use

xvi https://www.datascience-pm.com/ai-lifecycle

xvii https://www.techopedia.com/definition/32874/narrow-artificial-intelligence-narrow-ai

xviii https://blog.hubspot.com/marketing/ai-algorithms

xix https://www.weforum.org/agenda/2021/07/ai-machine-learning-bias-discrimination

xx https://www.mckinsey.com/featured-insights/artificial-intelligence/tackling-bias-in-artificial-intelligence-and-in-humans

xxi https://www.peoplematters.in/article/hr-technology/ready-to-meet-your-ai-boss-firm-hires-robot-ceo-35289

xxii https://www.simplilearn.com/ai-powered-robot-recruiters-for-job-seekers-article

xxiii https://www.abc.net.au/listen/programs/downloadthisshow/ai-s-role-in-recruiting-/102835154

xxiv https://english.elpais.com/science-tech/2022-09-05/dont-let-the-robot-discard-your-resume-applying-for-work-in-an-automated-world.html

xxv https://www.keka.com/performance-management-guide

xxvi https://www.frontiersin.org/articles/10.3389/fpsyg.2020.01883/full

xxvii https://sloanreview.mit.edu/article/algorithmic-management-the-role-of-ai-in-managing-workforces

xxviii https://www.chinadaily.com.cn/a/202212/13/WS6397dee7a31057c47eba419f.html

xxix https://datasciencedojo.com/blog/ai-tools-for-work-environment

xxx https://www.labellerr.com/blog/how-artificial-intelligence-analytics-is-making-for-data-driven-decision-making-easier

xxxi https://www.analyticsvidhya.com/blog/2023/07/artificial-intelligence-vs-human-intelligence

xxxii Ibid.

xxxiii https://www.smartdatacollective.com/7-jobs-humans-can-do-better-than-robots-and-ai

xxxiv https://www.ceotodaymagazine.com/2018/02/human-vs-robot-how-ceos-can-super-power-workforces-in-ways-ai-will-never-replicate

xxxv https://www.yahoo.com/tech/meet-the-new-boss-the-worlds-first-128660465704.html

xxxvi https://www.financemagnates.com/trending/introducing-robo-ceo-the-worlds-worst-boss

xxxvii https://www.cityam.com/ex-barclays-wealth-management-boss-says-all-banks-use

xxxviii https://www.peoplematters.in/article/hr-technology/ready-to-meet-your-ai-boss-firm-hires-robot-ceo-35289

xxxix https://www.simplilearn.com/ai-powered-robot-recruiters-for-job-seekers-article

xl https://www.abc.net.au/listen/programs/downloadthisshow/ai-s-role-in-recruiting-/102835154

xli https://sloanreview.mit.edu/article/algorithmic-management-the-role-of-ai-in-managing-workforces

xlii https://www.chinadaily.com.cn/a/202212/13/WS6397dee7a31057c47eba419f.html

xliii https://www.euronews.com/next/2022/11/20/would-you-want-a-robot-as-ceo-chinese-firm-is-first-to-try-as-it-bets-on-metaverse-workpla

xliv https://www.businesstoday.in/technology/news/story/meet-mika-the-worlds-first-robot-ceo-and-she-has-a-message-for-elon-musk-mark-zuckerberg-405453-2023-11-11

xlv https://www.japantimes.co.jp/business/2023/10/02/tech/japan-startup-gundam-robot

xlvi https://www.koreatimes.co.kr/www/world/2024/01/501_354535.html

xlvii https://medium.com/@aadc_cd/automotive-industrial-robot-total-cost-of-ownership-b8fb0a239ff5

xlviii https://firsteigen.com/blog/the-role-of-ml-and-ai-in-data-quality-management

xlix https://www.euronews.com/next/2022/11/20/would-you-want-a-robot-as-ceo-chinese-firm-is-first-to-try-as-it-bets-on-metaverse-workpla

l https://techvidvan.com/tutorials/robotics-and-artificial-intelligence

li https://www.dailymail.co.uk/sciencetech/article-12869629/Tesla-robot-ATTACKS-engineer-companys-Texas-factory-violent-malfunction-leaving-trail-blood-forcing-workers-hit-emergency-shutdown-button.html

lii https://www.startmeup.hk/ai-robotics-vision-and-automation-technology-challenges-competition

liii https://www.researchgate.net/figure/An-exemplary-illustration-of-data-and-privacy-dilemma-in-AI_fig1_341083165

livliv https://www.vox.com/the-goods/22557895/automation-robots-work-amazon-uber-lyft

lv Ibid.

lvi https://hyscaler.com/insights/robot-ceo-vision-or-experiment

lvii https://www.profit.co/blog/performance-management/use-of-artificial-intelligence-in-performance-reviews

lviii https://www.v7labs.com/blog/active-learning-guide

lix https://www.researchgate.net/publication/359435036_Resource_allocation_optimization_using_artificial_intelligence_methods_in_various_computing_paradigms_A_Review

lx https://www.matellio.com/blog/ai-based-resource-management-software-development

lxi Ibid.

lxii https://fastercapital.com/content/Resource-allocation--Optimizing-Resource-Allocation-for-Absolute-Advantage.html

lxiii https://www.sciencedirect.com/science/article/abs/pii/S1568494618302540

lxiv https://hbr.org/2018/01/artificial-intelligence-for-the-real-world

lxv https://www.datacamp.com/blog/machine-learning-projects-for-all-levels

lxvi https://www.linkedin.com/pulse/how-ai-can-revolutionize-project-management-dr-faisal-shehab

lxvii https://www.softwaresuggest.com/blog/ai-in-project-management

lxviii https://ligsuniversity.com/blog/the-role-of-artificial-intelligence-in-improving-project-management

lxix https://www.projectmanagement.ie/blog/artificial-intelligence-in-project-management-disruptions-risks-advantages-and-adaptation

lxx https://www.zenhub.com/ai-project-management-a-guide

lxxi https://www.linkedin.com/pulse/ai-project-management-interview-lloyd-skinner-elizabeth-harrin-fapm

lxxii https://www.linkedin.com/pulse/project-management-challenges-digital-age

lxxiii https://visuresolutions.com/blog/ai-and-machine-learning-for-risk-management

lxxiv https://www.linkedin.com/pulse/unleashing-potential-artificial-intelligence-1c

lxxv https://data-flair.training/blogs/advantages-and-disadvantages-of-machine-learning

lxxvi https://www.quora.com/What-are-the-advantages-and-disadvantages-of-having-A-I

lxxvii https://www.linkedin.com/pulse/ai-evolution-executive-roles-william-poutu

lxxviii https://www.washingtonpost.com/technology/interactive/2023/ai-jobs-workplace

lxxix https://www.avanade.com/en/blogs/avanade-insights/artificial-intelligence/next-gen-org-chart-humans-and-robots

lxxx https://www.mec.ed.tum.de/en/lfe/research/research-groups/robotics-for-life-and-healthcare

lxxxi https://www.imf.org/-/media/Files/Publications/SDN/2024/English/SDNEA2024001.ashx

lxxxii https://www.imf.org/en/Blogs/Articles/2024/01/14/ai-will-transform-the-global-economy-lets-make-sure-it-benefits-humanity

lxxxiii https://www.imf.org/-/media/Files/Publications/SDN/2024/English/SDNEA2024001.ashx

lxxxiv Ibid.

lxxxv Ibid.

lxxxvi Ibid.

lxxxvii Ibid.

lxxxviii https://www.weforum.org/agenda/2024/01/what-leaders-said-about-ai-at-davos-2024

lxxxix Ibid.

xc Ibid.

xci Ibid.

xcii Ibid.

xciii Ibid.

xciv Ibid.

xcv Ibid.

xcvi https://www.imf.org/-/media/Files/Publications/SDN/2024/English/SDNEA2024001.ashx

xcvii https://www.productdz.com/post/revolutionizing-startups-ai-product-design

xcviii https://yfsmagazine.com/2024/01/02/ai-powered-robotics

xcix https://www.imf.org/-/media/Files/Publications/SDN/2024/English/SDNEA2024001.ashx

c https://www.imf.org/en/Blogs/Articles/2024/01/14/ai-will-transform-the-global-economy-lets-make-sure-it-benefits-humanity

ci https://www.linkedin.com/pulse/how-build-trust-between-humans-ai-thumbstacktechnologies-hzhpf

cii https://www.mindfoundry.ai/blog/trusting-ai-and-machines

ciii https://www.upwork.com/resources/ai-in-decision-making

civ https://www.spiceworks.com/tech/artificial-intelligence/articles/what-is-ai

[cv] https://www.phdata.io/ai-strategy
[cvi] https://towardsdatascience.com/ultimate-ai-strategy-guide-9bfb5e9ecf4e
[cvii] https://builtin.com/artificial-intelligence/artificial-intelligence-future
[cviii] https://www.vecteezy.com/photo/25500473-3d-rendering-humanoid-robot-working-in-modern-office-with-computer-on-table-futuristic-ai-robot-ceo-sitting-at-his-office-chair-ai-generated
[cix] https://www.the-sun.com/tech/6111499/ai-humanoid-robot-named-ceo-video-game-company
[cx] https://ceoworld.biz/2023/11/06/ai-takes-the-role-of-ceo-under-the-mika-project
[cxi] https://www.myhrfuture.com/blog/how-is-ai-influencing-learning-and-development
[cxii] https://www.zavvy.io/blog/ai-learning-development
[cxiii] https://www.researchgate.net/figure/AI-Ethics-Framework-of-building-ethical-AI_fig1_340115931
[cxiv] https://www.spiceworks.com/tech/artificial-intelligence/articles/what-is-ai
[cxv] https://www.forbes.com/sites/insights-ibmai/2020/03/26/trust-at-the-center-building-an-ethical-ai-framework/?sh=213d19297bc7